DETENTION & TORTURE
in South Africa

Psychological, legal & historical studies

DON FOSTER
with contributions by Dennis Davis &
research assistance from Diane Sandler

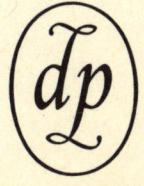

David Philip: Cape Town & Johannesburg

First published 1987 in paperback in Southern Africa by David Philip, Publisher (Pty) Ltd, 217 Werdmuller Centre, Claremont 7700, South Africa

ISBN 0-86486-078-1

Copyright © 1987 Donald Hugh Foster; and Dennis Davis (chapters 2 & 3)

All rights reserved. No part of this publication may be reproduced, stored in a retrieval system, or transmitted in any form or by any means, electronic, mechanical, photocopying, recording or otherwise, without prior permission in writing from the publisher.

Printed by Litho Process

Contents

    Preface iv
1 Detention and torture in South Africa 1
2 Historical considerations 11
3 Legal considerations 30
4 Psychological investigations 57
5 The empirical study 86
6 The process of detention: detainees' descriptions 119
7 Conclusions, interpretations and recommendations 153
    Postscript 181
    Appendices 195
    References 219
    Bibliography 238
    Index 247

Preface

Nothing could have been better calculated to draw attention once again to the iniquitous South African detention provisions than the tragically momentous and bitter events of the past year or so. For once the repressive forces of an exploitative and oppressive state became rather more visible and exposed. However, much of the workings of repression still remain hidden and veiled. It is the purpose of the work presented in this volume to bring some light to bear upon the dark and grim practice of detention, one of the central weapons in the repressive armoury of the South African state.

The infamous system of detention, regarded as almost synonymous with National Party rule, has been castigated, criticised and challenged for more than a quarter of a century – but to no avail. If anything, the use and abuse of these laws has become more extensive, the legislation itself more draconian with the passage of time. At a conservative estimate, about 70 000 people had suffered by the end of 1986 at the hands of the shadowy figures empowered by this legislation.

This interdisciplinary study of detention in South Africa covers legal, historical and psychological aspects. In detention, the might of the political system, the public realm, penetrates the very core of the personal. Under the god-like justification of state security (which state? whose security?), cold and stark laws, fashioned in the cauldron of historical struggle, are designed to probe, strip and expose the inner stories of personal lives. Therefore in this study of detention we attempt to examine both the public and the personal, the historical as well as the situational and the momentary.

Events in relation to detention – if not the laws themselves – change thick and fast in South Africa, never so much as during the past year. In this respect it is to be noted that a good deal of the present work, in particular the empirical study of security detainees, was completed before the recent (1986) declaration of a state of emergency, so the primary focus of attention in this book is on security legislation detention. However, a summary of the state of emergency period and other recent events relating to detention – updated more or less to March 1986 – has been included in a postscript. Elsewhere in the main text, material on detention events, legal aspects, and discussion of significant cases, have been updated to at least the end of 1985.

Since a study of this scope and topic requires a great deal of hard and dedicated work, the support, courage and effort of a number of people are acknowledged here with considerable gratitude.

The primary debt of gratitude is to the many former detainees who gave so freely of their time and who demonstrated great courage and trust in describing their frequently appalling experiences in detention. Their fortitude in agreeing to relive experiences that some may have preferred to forget, is greatly respected. Gratitude in equal measure is expressed to the interviewers who overcame difficult hurdles in completing their heavy tasks. If all of these people remain unnamed, it is due to research ethics of confidentiality as well as to current political circumstances. Great respect is accorded them all.

The work reported here was conducted under the auspices of the Institute of Criminology at the University of Cape Town. Professor Dirk van Zyl Smit was involved with the project from the ground level, and provided much needed support, encouragement and criticism throughout. Both the Director and staff members of the Institute of Criminology are thanked for resources, facilities and emotional support.

For financial assistance, both the research and the final product in the form of this book have been entirely dependent on a grant from the Ford Foundation. Appreciation is due to the Foundation and to Dr Bill Carmichael and David Bonbright in particular.

Venetia Lorenzo has shouldered a great deal of work associated with this study. Throughout the project she dealt with administrative burdens and various crises with efficiency, considerable tact, warmth and humour. In addition she took on most of the task of typing and correcting the manuscript for this book. She is rather inadequately thanked here for her splendid and dedicated efforts. Ann Wollaston is also thanked for her contribution in assisting the word processing of this manuscript.

The substantial task of transcribing interview material was excellently handled by a willing team and we extend thanks to Ingrid Awerbach (who also typed some draft material), K. Belchers, M. Cornell, S. Creed, P. Fahrenfort, S. Roussouw, D. Schmidt and other helpers. Assistance with computation of a large amount of material was provided by Patrick Hurley and Alan McCrindle. The librarians of Jagger Library and of the Archives division always provided excellent and friendly service. Digby Sales took on the task of indexing this book, and also assisted with some proofreading.

Thanks are due to David Philip for his readiness to publish this book and to Russell Martin for his careful editing.

Without the support of the community-based organisations the study would not have got off the ground, and credit and thanks are due in this regard to members of the Detention Action Committee, as well as the Detainee Support Committees and Detainees' Parents Support

Committees at various centres.

Despite all these considerable efforts responsibility for the work as a whole in this book remains that of the researchers and of the present writer in particular. Writing of this book was done in the main by Don Foster, who therefore bears responsibility for analyses and interpretations, with contributions by Dennis Davis (most of Chapter 2, Chapter 3, and parts of the final chapter and postscript). I express thanks to my co-workers for their dedicated efforts. On a personal level I am deeply grateful to Pari for her emotional support and encouragement through some rather turbulent times.

Gratitude is expressed to Diane Sandler for her committed involvement in this work.

This work reflects the law as at 31 May 1986.

D. H. FOSTER

1 Detention and torture in South Africa

It is approximately 25 years since detention without trial outside of war-time was introduced in South Africa and 20 years since it became a permanent feature of the South African legal system. However, the contemporary principle of peace-time detention without trial was introduced even earlier, in 1953, by way of the Public Safety Act, which provided for the summary arrest and detention of persons under emergency regulations.[1] Since then, despite persistent and widespread protests against detention and a considerable degree of critical attention directed at this system, very little change in a positive direction has been forthcoming. It could be argued that provisions for detention have become broader in scope and more draconian in effect over passing years. It has also been claimed that it is precisely the system of security legislation, possibly to a greater extent than laws discriminating on grounds of race, that has led to international criticism of South African policy.

After all it was not South Africa's race laws, but its security laws, that prompted the Security Council of the United Nations to order mandatory sanctions for the first time ever against a member state, when it directed states to impose an arms embargo on South Africa in the wake of the death in detention of Steve Biko and the security crackdown of 19 October 1977, in which eighteen organisations and three newspapers were outlawed, 47 Black leaders detained and seven prominent Whites subjected to restriction orders.[2]

While the relative weighting of security or race legislation as a source of antagonism may be open to academic debate, there can be no doubting the fact that South African security laws per se have come under sustained and strenuous attack.

Criticism of the security system as a whole has taken a number of forms, chiefly concerned with the following two points:[3]

(i) critics argue that security legislation is an unjustifiable violation of the 'rule of law', subordinating individual rights to those of the state;

(ii) critics question the role of security legislation in the maintenance of a fundamentally unjust social order.

Additional criticism directed against detention without trial covers many technical points which will be dealt with elsewhere in the volume, but involves mainly the following:

(i) there are inadequate safeguards to prevent physical torture of detainees;

(ii) there are inadequate laws and regulations to prevent psychological torture and abuse of detainees;

(iii) there are inadequate regulations to ensure appropriate medical care of detainees;[4]

(iv) the validity of legal evidence obtained under security legislation is questioned;[5]

(v) limitations are placed upon the ability of detainees to effect civil actions for alleged abuse while held under security legislation.[6]

A characteristic feature of security legislation since its inception during the early 1960s has been the widespread allegations of physical and mental abuse of people held under security detention in both South Africa and the 'independent states'.[7] Although the precise number of deaths in detention may be debated, the fact that a substantial number of deaths (at least 64) has occurred[8] under security legislation is not contested — even by state officials.[9] Yet no full-scale inquiry has ever been ordered to examine the high frequency of deaths or the frequent allegations of mental and physical torture. The present empirical study is intended to provide an investigation of such allegations. More specifically however, it is designed to examine a series of questions left unanswered — not even adequately posed — by the Rabie Commission of Inquiry into Matters Related to the Operation of South African Security Laws.[10]

According to the list of persons and organisations who testified before the Rabie Commission it appears that no former detainee gave evidence. The major purpose of this study is to present testimony from this unheard group. It is also not clear that expert evidence of the possible effects of solitary confinement was heard by the Commission.[11] The oversight will be rectified here by providing a comprehensive review of psychological and psychiatric literature argued to be of relevance for a full understanding of the processes and possible outcomes of detention. Along with the ubiquitous sensory deprivation evidence, we also examine other literature such as data on torture sequelae, on the concentration camp syndromes, and on psychological processes such as learned helplessness and reactance. The psychiatric post-traumatic stress syndrome is critically examined as a possible global description of sequelae.

The Rabie Commission in its report gave focus of attention to an analysis of security laws as they exist on paper, without adequately investigating the practice of detention. Criticism has been made[12] of this failure to examine actual cases and empirical data of actions under the security laws, particularly under those sections allowing for indeterminate periods of incommunicado detention and interrogation.[13] The present study provides empirical data from a fairly substantial number of cases as well as illustrative statements describing various aspects of experience under these conditions.

The Commission failed to consider, let alone answer, basic questions regarding actual methods of interrogation employed and the lawfulness of such methods.[14] In our study we hope to throw some light upon this dark matter. Despite frequent claims and allegations of physical and psychological ill-treatment given under oath in legal proceedings, the authorities have resisted any calls for inquiries into such assaults. Although important evidence of interrogation practices has emerged in inquests such as those of Aggett and Biko, a more general empirical picture of events under interrogation as claimed by a wide number of detainees is still required.

The Rabie Commission assumed that visits by magistrates and inspectors of detainees offer real and sufficient protection against police abuse.[15] Evidence from former detainees on this matter was however apparently not heard. The present study examines this aspect, and also provides in passing evidence on detainees' perceptions of available medical treatment and purported safeguards offered by district surgeons' visits. Data on detainees' claims of contact with such support persons as lawyers, families, and friends are also presented in this study.

According to the summary view of the *Report on the Rabie Report*[16] it seems that 'undue reliance was placed on the evidence of the security police without examining the other side of the case'. The study presented here may be seen in general as the view from this 'other side'.

This study may also be regarded as a somewhat belated response to an earlier paper by Roux,[17] which took a critical look at the well-known and oft-cited article on psychological aspects of detention by Mathews and Albino.[18] Roux, critical of the argument that detention in South Africa is analogous to laboratory conditions of experimental sensory deprivation, and clearly defensive about the system of detention, asked 'what evidence'[19] was available in South Africa with respect to possible deleterious effects of detention. In certain respects the answer to Roux's question has already been given in a theoretical form by the findings of the MASA Report,[20] but the MASA Report failed to provide any clear evidence of an empirical nature. Our concern here is therefore to develop further an answer to the question as posed by Roux, and to do so by way of clear empirical evidence.

The process of detention

A few further prefatory remarks are warranted. In recent years there has been a good deal of discussion in the press and among academics of the possible harmful psychological *effects* of detention. While in no sense wishing to minimise or detract from such evidence – indeed, explanation of such effects or outcomes remains of central concern to this study – it is perhaps more valid to refer instead to the physical and psychological *process* of detention. This is advantageous for a number of reasons. It has frequently been stated in relation to methods of psychological pressure in interrogation, that one of its dangers is that it leaves no physical traces, and also in certain cases only limited psychological traces. It is far more problematic in such cases to substantiate evidence of ill-treatment than in cases of physical abuse.[21] Effects may well be present, but either latent or difficult to detect. An apparently negative report regarding sequelae does not necessarily mean that the process of detention was non-coercive. Psychological torture and communicative entrapments during the course of detention may constitute highly coercive and influential processes, irrespective of the degree of subsequently verifiable sequelae. Furthermore, courts of law are likely to find themselves centrally concerned with actions and conduct during the process of detention in order to decide whether they are to admit statements as being made 'freely and voluntarily'. While verifiable effects may be said to be of critical import in such cases if courts are to be able to infer the presence of coercive instances, it may also be argued that a knowledge of conditions of detention and the likely occurrence of certain psychological processes under those conditions should constitute sufficient grounds for excluding the admissibility of detainees' evidence gained under such conditions, without recourse to evidence of effects.

A further reason for shifting attention to process rather than merely effects is primarily a theoretical one. Detention is more correctly viewed as a series of events, rather than a single event. The series unfolded through time could in itself constitute the coercive nature of the procedure. Events range from those preceding detention itself, through procedures of arrest, to the concrete conditions of confinement and interrogation, and include also the effects of such conditions. If it is considered in this more adequate sequential perspective, concern ought to be directed to signs and symptoms during the process of detention in equal measure to those that may appear as sequelae. This sequential perspective of the process of detention informs the present empirical study.

The wider context of repression

Before proceeding to detailed considerations of detention it is important to attempt to situate the conditions and behaviours of the microsetting within a larger socio-political context. Detention is just one area, although a highly significant one, in the wider picture of state repression in general in South Africa. Detention emerged in the 1950s and 1960s as part of a steadily growing package of laws and non-legal devices to maintain white, Afrikaner Nationalist rule in the face of the growing organisation and militancy of black (and white) opposition. The range of repressive devices is now very considerable indeed, and detention should be seen in relation to the apparatus as a whole.[22]

Given the range of different forms of detention (see Chapter 3 for details) it is clear that more than one aim is served by its use. The central purpose is the gathering of information, partly for particular purposes in political trials and partly for general purposes of policing all political opposition. Detention laws are also used for removing people from political organisations and for isolating groups in order to split the political opposition. Thirdly, the package of laws is used as a form of political and psychological violence, although this aim will always be denied and is not claimed to constitute one of the formal intentions of legislation. As a mode of psychological violence, the substantial number of deaths in detention and the widespread rumours of vicious treatment and torture at the hands of the security police both work to generate a climate of fear that operates in favour of the state, at least over the short term. The same processes in the longer run are likely of course to undermine the legitimacy of the state in serious ways.

Although the use of detention for obtaining prosecutions per se may be a subsidiary aim – the low percentage of persons charged after being detained suggests this – it is worth noting that the Rabie Commission claimed that it was policy to combat opposition through the courts as far as possible.[23]

The political trial in South Africa covers a very wide range of activities, ranging from major 'show trials' of political leaders, through charges under common law offences such as public violence and arson, to minor technical offences such as trespassing or entering townships without permits.[24] It has been noted by leading observers that the political trial has become a 'regular and, from the Government's point of view, necessary feature of the political process'.[25] The definition of offences under the former Terrorism Act and General Law Amendment Act (see Chapter 3) was very wide, enabling charges for relatively minor offences such as damage to property to be laid under the Sabotage Act.[26] Although the recent Internal Security Act of 1982 has sought to define major offences more precisely, definitions remain unacceptably wide and loose. Political trials additionally are characterised by substantial departures from the usual established rules of criminal procedure and evidence, and follow different procedures, over preceding years having allowed for the following: solitary confinement for interrogation, denial of access to legal counsel while in detention, exclusion of the jurisdiction of courts in the process of detention, minimum sentences on conviction, the passage of legislation to be applied retrospectively, a shifting of the burden of proof (for example in alleged duress), trials held at any place subject to the discretion of the Minister of Justice, and possible denial of access to a statement made in detention.[27]

Statutory offences now also include such bread-and-butter political organisational activities as strikes, boycotts and political campaigning.[28] Distribution of information in respect of a wide range of activities also has become a statutory offence covered by a number of Acts including the Protection of Information Act of 1982.[29] Charges laid under common law offences (not defined by statute) may be viewed as an attempt to depoliticise trials that otherwise would manifestly take on a political character. Prosecution under treason charges for non-violent activities may be seen as one example of this process.[30]

State repression also involves a wide range of administrative acts, which include bannings in a number of forms (of persons, organisations, meetings and publications); listing of persons, which precludes their being quoted;[31] deportation;[32] the use of prison regulations to punish convicted prisoners by limiting, for example, the number of visits they may receive; relocations; and emergency regulations, particularly in the Bantustans or so-called 'independent states', as well as the state of emergency declared in 1960 and again during 1985 and 1986 in South Africa itself.

It is possible to make a distinction between strictly legal and non-legal forms of repression. The demarcation lines between the two are frequently of academic interest only, however, and in practice the two work together. While it is likely that the state would wish to resort to legal procedures as far as possible, where this fails or where human passions exceed the bounds of legality, other measures will also be employed. Non-legal forms of repression include harassment and intimidation,[33] for example police raids, visits and threats of violence; attacks on people, such as the alleged systematic assaults by vigilante groups in the Ciskei[34] and recent sporadic attacks on supporters of the United Democratic Front; attacks on property, for instance the burning of offices of the National Union of South African Students (NUSAS) and the South African Institute of Race Relations; and widespread police brutality not necessarily directed only at political opposition[35] (as indicated by numerous actions brought against the Ministers of Justice and of Law and Order over the years). Attacks on squatter communities and sporadic bursts of right-wing violence against political opponents of the government[36] could also be included as part of the on-going forms of non-legal repression.

It is our contention that the process of detention cannot be fully understood outside this wider context of repression, of which detention is only one form. The number of people detained constitutes only a small proportion of the numbers experiencing forms of repression in their full extent. Indeed, since detention is such a 'visible' and unacceptable form in terms of international relations, it is highly conceivable that the government would wish to minimise its use and resort to other less visible or less reprehensible forms.

It may nevertheless be noted that detention has been retained and substantially increased as a central weapon of repression through recent years of state restructuring and constitutional alteration. During 1984, detention figures soared as a result of the state's effort to combat resistance to the new constitution.[37] During the course of 1985 detentions again increased massively. According to figures provided by the

Detainees' Parents Support Committee (DPSC), under formal security legislation 1 684 persons were held within South Africa and an additional 1 953 in the 'independent states'; a total of 3 637. Between 21 July and 31 December 1985 a further 7 361 people were detained under emergency regulations in South Africa, bringing the total figure of persons held under all detention provisions within South Africa and 'independent states' to an enormous 10 998.[38] There is thus no doubt that detention as a major form of state repression has gone hand-in-hand with the process of constitutional 'reform' and should be viewed as an integral part of the attempt to maintain white dominance and political control, albeit in slightly altered terms.

Resistance to detention

Detention has on the other hand become an important site of organised resistance. In the wake of the wave of detentions directed against trade unions during late 1981 and early 1982, and the death in detention of Neil Aggett, the Detainees' Parents Support Committee was formed on a national basis to provide information about detention and support for the families of those detained. The DPSC represents an organisational means of challenging the success detention hitherto had in individualising and isolating victims of detention.[39] A wide range of other organisations and persons, including church groups, trade unions, student and community organisations, newspapers and academics, has attacked the system of detention and criticised recent legislation as a continuation of previous draconian laws.[40] In 1984 the system of detention was again brought to international attention as a result of the detention of political leaders on the eve of elections for the new tricameral parliament, and subsequent events at the British consulate in Durban.[41] Even such traditionally august and conventional bodies as the Association of Law Societies[42] and the Association of South African Chambers of Commerce[43] became strongly critical of the detention system. National Detainees' Day has been observed on 12 March in recent years and has been the occasion of national protests. During 1984 there were also widespread protests, on 29 November, when 35 people were arrested in Johannesburg, and again on 10 December, Human Rights Day.[44] Again during 1985, there were countless protest meetings against all forms of detention, calling for the release of detainees and other political prisoners. Thus although detention remains a powerful weapon of state security, its increasing importance as a focus of challenge and resistance indicates that as regards the legitimacy of the South African state, it is a double-edged weapon. The continued use of detention during the 'reform' era has already seriously undermined the local and international legitimacy of the new constitutional dispensation, and will undoubtedly continue to damage its flimsy image.

The international context

Detention without trial and the frequently accompanying allegations of torture clearly are not confined to South Africa alone. According to the recent Amnesty International report,[45] incidents of torture were reported in 98 countries, and it is doubtful whether this figure fully represents the reality of torture worldwide. The case of detention in South Africa should be viewed within the perspective of action against detention and torture on an international scale.

Article 5 of the Universal Declaration of Human Rights, adopted by the United Nations General Assembly on 10 December 1948 (with South Africa abstaining in the final plenary vote), states that 'no one shall be subjected to torture or to cruel, inhuman or degrading treatment or punishment'. Article 9 of the same Declaration states that 'no one shall be subjected to arbitrary arrest, detention or exile'. Since then a considerable list of declarations, rules and guidelines has been adopted by a range of international organisations. Some of the most important of these are the following:[46]

(i) The Standard Minimum Rules for the Treatment of Prisoners, approved by the United Nations Economic and Social Council on 31 July 1957. These rules prohibited corporal punishment, placing prisoners in a dark cell, and all cruel, inhuman or degrading treatment as punishment for disciplinary offences. In 1977 the rules were extended to cover persons arrested without charge.[47]

(ii) The United Nations Declaration on the Protection of All Persons from Torture and Other Cruel, Inhuman or Degrading Treatment or Punishment ('Declaration Against Torture'), adopted by the General Assembly of the United Nations on 9 December 1975. Under its terms, no state may permit or tolerate torture or other inhuman or degrading treatment. This declaration also provided a definition of torture which included psychological aspects (see Chapter 4).

(iii) Guidelines for Medical Doctors Concerning Torture and Other Cruel, Inhuman or Degrading Treatment or Punishment in Relation to Detention and Imprisonment ('The Tokyo Declaration'), issued by the World Medical Association at Tokyo in 1975. The Medical Association of South Africa officially subscribes to this Declaration, which prohibits doctors from condoning or participating in any acts related to torture or to other cruel, inhuman or degrading punishments.

(iv) Code of Conduct for Law Enforcement Officials, adopted by the United Nations General Assembly on 17 December 1979. This states that no law-enforcement official may inflict, instigate or tolerate any act of torture or other cruel, inhuman or degrading treatment or punishment. Nor may exceptional circumstances such as war, or threat of war, a threat to national security, internal political instability or any other public emergency be invoked as a justification of torture (Article 5).

(v) Principles of Medical Ethics, adopted by the United Nations

General Assembly on 18 December 1982. Principle 2 states that it is a gross contravention of medical ethics, as well as an offence under applicable international instruments, for health personnel (particularly physicians) to engage, actively or passively, in acts that constitute participation in, complicity in, incitement to or attempts to commit torture or other cruel, inhuman or degrading treatment or punishment. It further claims that there may be no departure from this principle on any grounds whatsoever, including public emergency.

(vi) Unilateral Declarations Against Torture and Other Cruel, Inhuman or Degrading Treatment or Punishment. The General Assembly of the United Nations on 8 December 1977 called on member states to reinforce the UN Declaration Against Torture by making unilateral declarations against torture and other cruel punishments. According to Amnesty International, 34 countries had made such unilateral declarations as of mid-1983.

In addition to the above declarations, which though substantial and highly important symbolic devices tend to lack administrative effectiveness, a considerable amount of work against torture has been conducted by countless other bodies. One of the leading organisations in the worldwide struggle against torture and injustice is Amnesty International. Amnesty's Campaign for the Abolition of Torture was initiated in December 1972.[48] This programme has helped launch and coordinate many activities among organisations concerned with the international problem of torture. It is partly the work of Amnesty that has been responsible for the various international declarations against torture. It is also the work of Amnesty that has led to the formation of medical groups, and the recent concern with the collection and dissemination of medical research on the phenomenon of torture, and the even more recent concern with treatment of torture victims. In this respect the efforts of the Rehabilitation Centre for Torture Victims in Copenhagen, Denmark, and similar centres in Canada should be singled out for meritorious mention.[49]

Organisations of lawyers, church bodies (for example the organisation Christians Against Torture[50]), local communities, certain political bodies, and groups of oppressed people themselves, have all contributed considerably to the struggle against unjust detention and torture. There can be little doubt that greater knowledge about the international practice of torture is most important in attempting to challenge and eradicate what appears to be a resilient and unhappily spreading scourge. The purpose of this brief look at wider concerns has not been to provide a definitive view, but rather to draw attention to the fact that the struggle against torture has been taken up by many people.

Further preliminary remarks

A final preliminary caveat is required in order to situate the present study appropriately. It has been said before that efforts to conduct serious social research in South Africa are likely to be fraught with difficulties.[51] This effort is no exception. It should be stressed that the empirical study reported here was conducted under circumstances considerably less favourable than those available, for example, to judicial commissions of inquiry. The very presence of the battery of internal security legislative devices would deter some former detainees from speaking openly of their experiences. Distrust and suspicion, so rife in a deeply divided society such as South Africa, provided additional limitations upon optimal research conditions. Against this, however, it must be clearly stated that every effort was expended by the researchers to gain information in a thoroughly objective and open manner, and to conduct the inquiry in an extensive and detailed fashion.

The empirical evidence reported in this study is exclusively concerned with detainees within the confines of South African security legislation. It makes no effort to report on treatment of detainees in the 'independent states', neighbouring states or Namibia. This does not suggest by any means that abuse of detainees does not take place in these territories. On the contrary, a considerable amount of evidence has been produced to suggest that abuse is common, particularly in Ciskei, Venda, Transkei and Namibia. However, because there were sufficient difficulties regarding research procedures as indicated above, it was decided for practical reasons to limit this investigation to South African detention procedures.

This study includes both a full review of relevant literature and a presentation of empirical data. Chapters 2 and 3 provide an overview of recent historical and legal aspects of detention in South Africa, while Chapter 4 surveys material of possible psychological processes germane to conditions as outlined in Chapter 3. Chapter 5 describes research procedures and a summary of the main empirical findings. Remaining data of a more detailed nature are included in appendices. Chapter 6 gives examples of verbatim statements provided by former detainees of their experience, illustrative particularly of psychological processes hypothesised in Chapter 4 and of general trends presented in Chapter 5. A concluding chapter draws together the findings and offers some recommendations, while a postscript summarises responses to the publication of the preliminary version of this same study on detention and torture in South Africa.

2 Historical considerations

While it would be possible to provide a catalogue of the various statutes providing for detention without trial in South Africa, such a procedure would render little in the way of understanding the social and historical processes within which legal devices are embedded. This chapter therefore is intended to provide a picture of the recent historical context within which an increasingly draconian set of security laws was developed for the purpose of maintaining white hegemony in South Africa.

In most legal systems there are provisions whereby the freedom of action of both the individual and the group may be restricted. Such restriction is generally justified by the contention that a society may act beyond the limits of the rule of law when the exercise of freedom breaks into dangerous or unlawful action or threatens to erupt into activity which could undermine the very fabric of society. A justification of this sort, however, emerges usually when the society is under attack from a foreign force or alternatively a minority within that society.

During periods of political and social crisis the authority of the state is questioned and possibly denied by broad sections within society who articulate demands which go to the very basis of the existing social structure;[1] and it is preferable to analyse such a social formation in terms of the concept of a crisis of hegemony. As Stuart Hall has expressed it:[2]

> When the temporary balance of the relations of class forces is upset and new forces emerge, old forces run through their repertoires of domination. Such moments signal, not necessarily a revolutionary conjuncture nor the collapse of the state, but rather the coming of 'iron times'. It does not follow either that the 'normal' mechanisms of the state are abrogated. But class domination will be exercised, in such moments, through a modification in the modes of hegemony; and one of the principal ways in which this is registered is in terms of a tilt in the operation of the state away from consent towards the pole of coercion.

An understanding of the effects of a crisis of hegemony on the development of law can help to clarify our analysis of the historical and social context of security law in South Africa, and South Africa's security legislation will be examined here within this conceptual framework.

Provisions before 1948

Although this work is primarily concerned with security practices it is important to mention that the seeds of the modern system of security law were sown well before the National Party acceded to power. The Governor-General, as the Supreme Chief of all Africans in Natal, the Transvaal and the Orange Free State, was vested with wide powers to detain without trial. In terms of the Native Administration Act of 1927[3] the Governor-General was permitted to detain for 3 months any African who in his opinion might 'be dangerous to the public peace, if left at large'.[4] The same Act empowered the Governor-General, 'whenever he deemed it expedient in the general public interest, without prior notice to any person concerned, to order any African to withdraw from any place to any other place' within South Africa.[5] It is small wonder that Brookes and Macaulay concluded that 'theoretically all Africans not specifically exempted, practically all Africans in the Reserves, are placed under a system of legalised despotism without the right of appeal to the courts'.[6]

In 1930, the Riotous Assemblies Act[7] was amended to introduce a section which provided that:

> Whenever the Governor-General is of the opinion that the publication or other dissemination of any documentary information . . . is calculated to engender feelings of hostility between the European inhabitants of the Union on the one hand and any other section of the inhabitants of the Union on the other hand, he may by a notice published in the Gazette and in any newspaper circulating in the area . . . prohibit any publication or other dissemination thereof.[8]

Furthermore the Act empowered the Minister of Justice to prohibit any person from being in a particular area when he was satisfied that such person was promoting feelings of hostility between whites and blacks.[9]

Thus when the Nationalist government took office in 1948 the South African legal system was not free from either discriminatory or repressive features.[10] Indeed the National Party inherited a legal system which R. F. A. Hoernlé had criticised by suggesting that 'White domination . . . is firmly entrenched in South African law'.[11]

Post 1948

Despite the imperfection of the South African legal system in 1948, civil liberties and the rule of law were still vibrant concepts in the political life of the country.[12] The right to meet, to organise politically, to protest, and to express dissent was part of the fabric of the legal system. Within a few years 'by the introduction of a series of legislative measures which [were] fully expressive of the Nationalist ideology . . . this freedom [had] suffered almost total extinction'.[13]

The standard explanation for these developments has been that the implementation of the National Party's programme of apartheid inevitably led to an intensification of discrimination: this caused increased black resistance which in turn led to new legislation curbing individual liberty.[14] The fact that this is a superficially accurate description of events cannot elevate it to the level of analysis or explanation. A comprehensive explanation can only be developed on the basis of a detailed examination of the history of the period.[15]

The liberal explanation of the victory of the National Party in 1948 holds that it represented the victory of rigid, chauvinistic racial attitudes over a progressive, rational ideology created by the forces of capitalist economic development.

Capitalist development prior to 1948 did not prove notably conducive to deracialisation.[16] In fact, it brought, along with wage labour, factories and mines, the intensification of race discrimination. Virtually all the major groups in the dominant (white) racial section required it. The primary industries (such as mining) used the racial framework to help organise and control the labour force, to keep the labour force divided and, at least in the areas of subordinate (black) employment, unorganised. The artisan unions associated race with skill scarcity and effectively excluded black workers from the upper reaches of the working class. Industrial unions used race lines in the workplace and society to protect areas of white employment. Landowners responded to pervading commercialisation and increasing mobility of farm labour by circumventing markets in labour and elaborating the labour-repressive framework. It was during this early period of capitalist development that racial domination was given a 'modern' form, whereby repressive features were elaborated and institutionalised.

It has been shown by a number of contemporary commentators[17] that this period represented in effect the hegemony of commercial farmers during the transition to capitalist agriculture. The other sections of the economy responded and adapted to the racially biased environment. However it was essentially in the rural areas that notions of white domination and *baasskap* were legitimated. It was here that political parties which argued in favour of racial domination and repression found their main support.

The period of intensifying racial discrimination saw the development of a sophisticated state racial apparatus. At one level, the state expanded as a simple instrument of group needs: employing white workers and maintaining vigilance over the areas of protected employment; intervening in the labour market, and helping organise the black labour force for agriculture and industry. However, the state racial apparatus evolved beyond mere labour repression. It also began to represent and manage the increasing formalisation of race lines. Primary industry such as mining became relatively less important in the economy as a whole, with the manufacturing industries achieving greater prominence. The changing composition of capital demanded that South Africa move beyond the rigid labour control which was essential during the earlier period.[18] The pressures for change to the social system brought about by development of the capitalist economy in South Africa were reinforced by other factors. Conditions in the overcrowded reserves had declined rapidly with the result that they could no longer play the same role in subsidising wages. Consequently the proletarianisation of Africans continued at an ever increasing pace.[19]

Given the growing urban black population, there was a considerable escalation of trade-union organisation and general working class militancy, culminating in the 1946 African mineworkers' strike.[20] Some form of solution was needed and the Fagan Commission,[21] appointed by the United Party government, proposed a modest liberalisation of the social structure. It rejected the idea of total segregation and accepted the fact that policy in respect of blacks must accept the existence of a permanent urban black population.

In contrast National Party policy offered a 'hard' solution to the crisis of the 1940s, in terms of apartheid. This solution appealed to the Afrikaner working class who wished to resist competition from a proletarianised African workforce. It also appealed to the agricultural sector, which was concerned that the United Party would not intervene to control the drift of blacks to the towns or control developments that would benefit industrial capital, and fail to take account of whether this labour force came from capitalist agricultural areas or the reserves. Such a development would have resulted in a major shift in the black labour force from the farms to the towns, hence exacerbating an already serious farm-labour shortage.[22]

Development of this nature did in fact take place in the 1940s. As a result of the election victory of the National Party in 1948, policies were implemented to curb the feared changes in labour patterns. The migrant labour system was strengthened with the introduction of stringent labour controls in order to reconcile the flow of black labour with the demands for that labour.

Simultaneously the government began to clamp down fiercely on all political movements that challenged its supremacy. If the cooptive strategy of Fagan was to be rejected, the only other alternative to the crisis was to respond with the full might of the state's repressive apparatus and bear down upon those movements that had begun to grow dramatically during the last years of United Party rule. In keeping with its fundamental policies, the new Nationalist government refused any recognition of African trade unions as this would have implied a recognition of African urban rights. Social control was to be centred within the reserves and to be extended from there to the towns. This was the way in which the National Party sought both to provide a solution to escalating conflict within the country and to promote those interests which it ultimately represented.[23] More stringent political control constituted an important part of the new government programmes. One of the first pieces of legislation passed to repress opposition political activity was the Suppression of Communism Act of 1950.[24]

The Suppression of Communism Act

The introduction of this Act was justified on the basis of the need to outlaw communism. While not stated explicitly in the Act, the major objective appeared to be the desire to curb the activities of trade unions and black political movements which opposed government policy. An examination of the debate in parliament reveals the extent to which the government was concerned with union activity. Referring to the increased level of strike action in South Africa during the immediate postwar period, the Minister of Labour told parliament that the

> Australian economy was almost paralysed by Communist-incited strikes. The British economy was almost paralysed as a result of the Communist-incited dockworkers' strike. France had a general strike a few years ago which almost resulted in chaos. Czecho-slovakia, immediately before the Communist coup, had as a prelude to the coup a general strike. That is the method which the Communists use when they want to paralyse the economy of a country by organising strikes.[25]

Events in other countries also played a role in shaping the form of the Act as well as the discourse in which it was justified by the government. The post-1945 period was characterised by a cold war between the two major superpowers and their allies and satellites. There were fears in the West of the 'Russian bear' capturing by stealth what Hitler could not gain by force. Governments were susceptible to those who orchestrated and manipulated divergent views amongst the population. In the USA the Subversive Activities Control Act was passed in 1950, introducing a system of registration for certain organisations, and in 1954 the Communist Control Act, purporting to outlaw the Communist Party.[26] In 1950 Joseph McCarthy began his rise to prominence. On 9 February of that year he told the Women's Republican Club in West Virginia

> to remember in discussing the Communists in our government [that] . . . we are not dealing with spies who get 30 pieces of silver to steal the blueprint of a new weapon. We are dealing with a far more sinister type of activity because it permits the enemy to guide and shape our policy.[27]

For almost five years McCarthy's agitation helped strangle civil liberties within America and although he brought about his own downfall in 1954, it has been argued that McCarthyism was not just an anachronism:

> McCarthyism has been dismissed by some as a passing aberration, a chimera of mid-century politics. It was not. It was a natural expression of America's political culture and a logical though extreme product of its political machinery. What came to be called 'McCarthyism' was grounded in a set of attitudes, assumptions, and judgments with deep roots in American history.[28]

In similar fashion the Australian government introduced the Communist Party Dissolution Bill which allegedly sought to curb communism in Australia. The bill provided for the dissolution of the Communist Party while individual communists could be dismissed from the military forces, the public service and from any position in a union operating in a 'vital' industry. The definition of communist was wide in scope, the reason being expressed by premier Menzies:

> Nothing nauseates me more than to discover the skill with which these Communists can put into their vanguard some deluded minister of the Christian religion. I should like to say to all of them that I have no hostility to minority movements. Christianity itself is the greatest minority in history, but they should remember the words of its founder. Christianity from the beginning was never the enemy of law or order. 'Render unto Caesar the things that are Caesar's, and unto God the things that are God's.'[29]

Although the ideological forms used by the Nationalist government were similar to those adopted elsewhere at this time,[30] the scope of the definition of communism in the 1950 Act was evidence enough that this was not a legislative aberration, not a means simply to control a few communists, but rather a means of suppressing all those movements endangering white rule. The premises underlying the Act were well stated in parliament, namely that communism

> causes trouble among the Natives, that it incites the Natives and that it preaches equality. Now when one preaches equality it means that all the Natives will eventually have to get the franchise on the same basis as the European, then this will not be a white republic or a white dominion but it will be a black republic. That is the danger. That is why we come here and state in the definition of Communism that a person is not allowed to cause trouble between Europeans and non-Europeans.[31]

The Act empowered the Minister to suppress organisations and newspapers, to impose severe restrictions on individuals by means of 'a banning order' which drastically curbed the freedom of movement, speech and association of any person whose activities he deemed to be furthering the objects of communism. There was to be no right of appeal to the courts against such orders.

The key concept of communism was widely defined to include doctrines or schemes 'which aim at bringing about any political, industrial, social, or economic change within the Union [of South Africa] by the promotion of disturbance or disorder, by unlawful acts or omissions, or by means which include the promotion of disturbance or disorder. . . .' It also included doctrines or schemes 'which aim at the encouragement of feelings of hostility between the European and Non-European races of the Union, the consequences of which are calculated to further the achievement of any object referred to earlier in the definition.'

The definition of a 'communist' made provision for the inclusion of 'any person who at any time had professed to be a communist; anyone who, either inside or outside of the Union, had encouraged in any way the achievements of any of the objects of communism; anyone who had at any time been a member or active supporter of any organization which in any way furthered any of the objects of communism.'

Within the first five years of the passage of the Act, 76 trade unionists had been listed as communists and 57 had been ordered to sever all ties with their respective unions.[32] Amongst the first to be banned were Solly Sachs of the Transvaal Garment Workers' Union, who had been expelled from the Communist Party in 1931, and J. B. Marks, one-time president of the African Mine Workers' Union, which had organised the 1946 strike.[33] As Grey Coetzee[34] points out, the effects of the Act were quickly felt so that during the ten years after the passing of the Act there were no major industrial disputes, a development 'which was most certainly also due to the fear of the powers of the Act'.[35]

The Defiance Campaign and security legislation

The early 1950s saw two important enactments introduced, namely the Public Safety Act[36] and the Criminal Law Amendment Act,[37] both passed in the wake of the Defiance Campaign of 1952. Although a detailed discussion of this important campaign falls outside the scope of this analysis, some mention of important aspects must be made as the legislative response to it directly influenced the development of security legislation.

Upon its accession to power the Nationalist government moved to cast the existing pattern of customary segregation into a rigid legal form. Racially mixed marriages were prohibited in 1949, and in 1950 the Population Registration Act and the Group Areas Act were passed. In 1951 the government made its most controversial political move to date. It produced a bill aimed at the removal of Coloured people from the common voters' roll. It was met with vigorous protest from both black and white citizens. In May 1951 an ad hoc and co-ordinating body formed to oppose the bill, the Franchise Action Council, called for united action by national organisations in a nationwide struggle against the entire apartheid system.[38] The call was echoed by members of the African National Congress and the South African Indian Congress, and by July 1951 a joint conference was held between these two bodies at which a five-man Joint Planning Council was constituted in order to plan a defiance campaign.

The campaign commenced in earnest on 6 April 1952 with a series of mass rallies in Johannesburg, Pretoria, Port Elizabeth, Durban, East London and Cape Town. At a mass rally on 31 May Dr Moroka of the ANC called for 10 000 volunteers to come forward and participate in the campaign. The government responded to the announcement of the Defiance Campaign by ordering five leaders to resign from their organisations in terms of the Suppression of Communism Act.[39]

Despite such government action the campaign continued to broaden its support, and on 22 June 1952 large meetings were held in Port Elizabeth and Durban.

The government responded with police raids on 30 July, during which papers were confiscated from ANC and SAIC offices in sixteen centres. The hitherto unprecedented raids were followed two weeks later by the arrest of twenty leaders of the campaign, including Nelson Mandela, J. B. Marks, Walter Sisulu and Dr Moroka. The accused were found guilty of 'statutory communism' and sentenced to nine months' imprisonment with hard labour, suspended for two years.

By 1953 the government moved to increase its ability to deal with mass campaigns. The Criminal Law Amendment Act of 1953 was justified on the ground that no existing law provided the means to deal with mass disobedience. Up until 1953 those charged for offences committed during the Defiance Campaign received short jail sentences, often suspended or with the option of a fine. The new law provided that any person who committed any offence by way of protest or in support of any campaign against any law could be sentenced to a whipping of 10 lashes, a £300 fine, three years in jail or a combination of any two of these penalties. Upon a second conviction, whipping or imprisonment as well as a fine was obligatory. For persons whose words or actions were calculated to cause another person to commit an offence as a means of protest, the maximum penalties were increased by an additional £200 or two years.

The Public Safety Act, also passed in 1953, empowered the Governor-General to declare a state of emergency if he was of the opinion that public order was being seriously threatened. The object of such legislation was expressed by the Minister of Justice, as follows:

> We cannot allow, no government can allow, that people who cannot have their way at an election and who do not get the government they want and are dissatisfied with the laws passed by the elected government, that they say that they will paralyse the country and bring it to a standstill. . . . This state of affairs, of course, caused tremendous panic among the public. . . . Unfortunately . . . there was no legislation authorising me to proclaim an emergency in a limited area. Then I used existing legislation like the Riotous Assemblies Act to prohibit certain meetings but in doing so I had to cause inconvenience and difficulties to all peace-loving citizens of the country for I could not prohibit meetings of Natives only, I had to prohibit all meetings.[40]

The Treason Trial

During the two years following the Defiance Campaign, the security police intensified its surveillance of and its raids upon the ANC and associated organisations. Such police activity increased in response to the intensified organisation associated with the Freedom Charter, and culminating in the largest nationwide raid undertaken in South African history to date. On 29 September 1955 policemen searched almost 500 persons in their homes and offices and investigated 48 political and social organisations.[41]

As a result of its investigations the police arrested 160 persons in December 1956 on charges of high treason and ancillary offences. Later arrests brought the total to 156.

The court proceedings lasted for more than four years and ended in an acquittal. The court found that on the evidence presented and on the findings of fact, it was impossible to conclude that the ANC had acquired or adopted a policy of overthrowing the state by violence in the sense that the masses had to be prepared or conditioned to commit direct acts of violence against the state.[42]

In one sense the Treason Trial constituted a defeat for the state. However, Oswald Pirow, who led the prosecution team during the early part of the Treason Trial, claimed the trial was largely responsible for the relatively quiet period during 1957 and 1958: this bought the government valuable time, he said, during which the police could become more efficient in dealing with a small number of agitators who were 'playing upon an hysterical Native population'. The government was able to utilise such time to pursue its plans for separate development.[43]

Rural concerns

When Dr Verwoerd became prime minister in 1958 the pace of change increased. It had become more difficult to reconcile the demands for the control of urban blacks as well as the attainment of a reliable labour supply. The government began to develop its decentralisation policies at great speed. The purpose was to encourage labour-intensive industry in the homelands and support the development towards capital-intensive industry in the towns.

The Bantustan policy had begun in 1951 with the passing of the Bantu Authorities Act,[44] which radically altered the structure of local government in the reserves. In 1959 the implementation of the policy was taken a significant stage further when parliament enacted the Promotion of Bantu Self- Government Act,[45] which, according to its long title, was to provide for the gradual development of self-governing 'Bantu' national units and for direct consultation between the government of the Union and these national units in regard to matters affecting their common interests.

The policy was implemented in the teeth of a sustained struggle, particularly in the Transkei where deep-seated antagonisms to government institutions and administrative measures as well as to the 'Bantu authorities' which implemented them, fuelled widespread rural unrest. A full account of the rural struggles of the late 1950s and early 1960s has not yet been written[46] and obviously falls beyond the objectives of this work. However, reference must be made to the Mpondo revolt,[47] as a result of which a stringent security dispensation was introduced into the

Transkei.

The unrest among the Mpondo was directly connected to the introduction of Proclamation 180 of 1956, which altered the Transkeian Central Council (or Bunga) system in two notable ways, namely, (i) the decrease in electoral participation in local government, and the consequently increased reliance on government-appointed chiefs and leaders, and (ii) the transfer of a number of functions of local government from the magistrates to the chiefs. Such unilateral changes caused deep resentment among the Mpondo.

By 1960 the unrest was so widespread that a state of emergency was proclaimed in terms of a proclamation in the Government Gazette.[48] According to the proclamation entry into the area of East Pondoland, where the greatest unrest existed, was tightly controlled; furthermore, it became illegal to organise or to take part in any organised boycott. The paramount chief was empowered to remove any African without prior notice from one district to another. The proclamation further provided that 'no civil action whatsoever in respect of any cause of action in connection with the operation of these regulations shall be capable of being instituted against the State'.[49]

Special police squads trained to counter unrest had operated in Zeerust and Pondoland since 1958. With the revolt against the Bantustan policy showing no sign of abating by 1960, the police were reinforced by a Mobile Unit, the most intensively trained fighting unit in the South African Defence Force, which was sent to Pondoland in December 1960.[50] Charles Hooper described the activities of the Mobile Police Unit as follows:[51]

> Between 10 o'clock in the evening and three o'clock in the morning the Mobile Column was at its most active; it was, according to testimony by a member of the Column, between these hours that police chose to visit villagers for the maintenance or reassertion of law and order.

In the same month Proclamation R400 was amended to allow for the detention and interrogation of Mpondo suspected of having committed or intending to commit any offence.[52] This measure was applied immediately and its effect was soon felt. Two days later it was reported that as local jails were all 'crammed with prisoners', army vehicles were being used to take some of the detainees to Matatiele, Kokstad and even Pietermaritzburg.[53] In January 1961 the Minister of Justice reported that 4 769 Africans, 2 whites and 2 others had been arrested under the new provisions.[54]

By February 1961 the revolt was on the wane, and by May 1961 most of the troops were withdrawn from the Pondoland area.[55]

Sharpeville and detention laws

Tom Lodge[56] has pointed out that during the late 1950s and early 1960s there were two related black political struggles in South Africa. In the reserves and, in particular, in the Transkei, there was an intense struggle over the implementation of the Bantustan policy. To a large extent the ANC did not play an important role in the rural arena, as it did not see the necessity of linking the peasant struggles with those of the workers and broad-based urban political campaigns. Hence the latter proceeded in a parallel course to the rural unrest, the culmination of which was the events surrounding Sharpeville in March and April 1960.

Within ten days of the shootings at Sharpeville on 20 March 1960 the government declared a state of emergency in terms of the Public Safety Act of 1953, and assumed broad powers to act against all forms of alleged subversion, including the power to arrest and detain indefinitely any person suspected of anti-government activity.

Detention was authorised by two provisions of the emergency regulations:[57]

(i) Regulation 4 authorised arrest and indefinite detention if, in the opinion of the Minister of Justice or a magistrate or a commissioned police officer, such arrest or detention was desirable in the interests of public order or of the person concerned. The conditions of the detention were to be determined by rules laid down by the Minister. These ministerial rules prohibited visits to the detainee, including visits by a legal adviser, unless permission was granted by the Minister or someone acting under the Minister's authority. On 11 April further rules were gazetted 'for the administration and good government and the maintenance of order at any place where persons are being detained pursuant to the Public Safety Act or the Emergency Regulations'.[58] These rules provided that a detainee could not receive newspapers or any other literature containing general news. No magazine or book, toilet requisites, smoking requisites, or food sent by friends or relatives of the detainee to the place where the detainee was being held, would be received by the officer in command of the place of detention.

(ii) In terms of Regulation 19 of the emergency regulations the Minister of Justice, the Commissioner of the South African Police, a magistrate or a commissioned police officer was empowered to cause the arrest and detention of any person suspected of having taken part (or intending to take part) in the commission of any offence with the 'intent to hamper the maintenance of public order or to endanger the safety of the public', or suspected on reasonable grounds of having information in regard to such an offence. Once in detention, the detainee might be held until the officer concerned was satisfied that he or she had truthfully and fully answered all the questions that had been put to him or her. Access to a legal adviser without the permission of the Minister was, once again, prohibited. The conditions of the detainee's detention were the same as those for a detainee held under Regulation 4; that is, the 11 April rules were applicable.

Initially the state of emergency affected 82 magisterial districts but within two weeks another 39 magisterial districts were added to the list.

Armed with these wide powers the police began to arrest leaders from a vast range of political organisations. In total, 11 274 Africans, 90 Asians and 18 whites were detained under the emergency regulations.[59]

On 8 April 1960, the government announced the banning of the African National Congress and the Pan-Africanist Congress under the newly enacted Unlawful Organizations Act. In support of such action the Minister of Justice claimed that the aim of the ANC and PAC was 'to bring to its knees any White government in South Africa which stands for White supremacy and for White leadership. . . . [They] do not want peace and order; what they want is our country.'[60]

The repression of political activity continued until 31 August 1960 when the state of emergency was lifted. By 1961 the ANC, now unbanned, was organising once more. At the 'All-In Conference' held in Pietermaritzburg on 25-6 March 1961, Nelson Mandela called for the government to prepare a national convention of elected representatives of all adult men and women on an equal basis, irrespective of race, colour or creed. If such a step, he warned, were not taken by 31 May of that year (the day upon which South Africa was to become a Republic), 'massive demonstrations' would be organised from 29-31 May, after which the ANC and associated organisations would pursue a policy of non-collaboration with the government.[61]

The proposed demonstration took the form of a stay-at-home, which was intended to last for three days. After one day Mandela called it off, claiming that it was not the success that had been hoped for. For the ANC this failure meant the end of the course of non-violence which had been pursued for almost 50 years. In his statement at the Rivonia trial Mandela explained the change of thinking: the ANC 'could not escape the conclusion that fifty years of non-violence had brought the African people nothing but more and more repressive legislation. . . . Africans had either to accept inferiority or fight against it by violence.'[62] The government responded vigorously to this change of tactics. In October 1961 the Minister of Justice warned of drastic legislative enactments.

Less than a year later the so-called Sabotage Act was passed.[63] The Act provided that any person who committed any wrongful and wilful act whereby he injured, obstructed, tampered with or destroyed the health or safety of the public; the maintenance of law and order; the supply of water, light, power, fuel or foodstuffs; sanitary, medical or fire-extinguishing services; postal, telephone, telegraph or radio services; or the free movement of traffic; any property; or if he attempted to commit such offence, or conspired with or encouraged any other person to do so; or, if in contravention of any law, he possessed any explosives, firearm or weapon, or entered or was upon any land or building, should be guilty of sabotage. No trial for the offence of sabotage would be instituted without the personal written authority of the Attorney General or acting Attorney General of the area concerned.

Anyone convicted of sabotage would be liable to the penalties for the offence of treason, which would include the death penalty. If a sentence of imprisonment was imposed this must be for a minimum of five years, whether or not any other penalty (except death) was also imposed.

The Act also extended the Minister's power of banning. It gave him wider power in relation to the banning of individuals under the Suppression of Communism Act and it deleted the restriction (under the Unlawful Organizations Act) that organisations could only be banned for 12 months unless this period was extended by proclamation. Shortly after the enactment of these provisions the government banned 102 persons from attending gatherings, and by the end of 1962 another 50 persons had been added to the list.[64]

The violent campaign continued, notwithstanding such new legislative power and the subsequent trial and conviction of Nelson Mandela on a charge related to organising the 1961 stay-at-home and leaving South Africa without a permit. After the killing of two whites and the near fatal attacks on three others on the Rand by PAC activists in November 1962, as well as the death of five whites in the Transkei in early 1963, the government passed the 90-day detention clause[65] in order to 'break the back' of the armed wings of the ANC and PAC (Umkonto and Poqo).[66] The government again adopted the strategy of attempting to resort to the widest possible powers without having to call a general state of emergency, a strategy first employed in 1953 when the Public Safety Act was passed. As the Minister of Justice told parliament when introducing the clause:

> The hon. leader [of the opposition] asked me whether the emergency regulations do not provide me with all these powers I am asking for. My reply is yes. . . . [However] this is not the kind of emergency that warrants the application of the Emergency Act. There is no spontaneous rebellion in South Africa. It is an organised rebellion by a group of people inside and outside South Africa, a group who know all the tricks to stay out of the hands of the law and which has at its disposal the best possible advice. . . . Must I now for the sake of these people plunge the whole of South Africa into a state of emergency? . . . It would not be fair to the public, but what is more, it would do our economy tremendous harm, if I were to do so.[67]

The '90-day' provision empowered a commissioned police officer to arrest without warrant and detain any person whom he suspected upon reasonable grounds of having committed or having intended to commit an offence under the Suppression of Communism Act, the Unlawful Organizations Act, or the crime of sabotage, or of having any information in regard to such offences or crimes. A detainee could be held in custody for interrogation until he had in the opinion of the Commissioner of Police replied satisfactorily to all questions, or for ninety days on any particular occasion. This provision was interpreted by the Appellate division in *Loza* v *Police Station Commander Durbanville*[68] in a manner that allowed for the redetention of any person for an additional period of 90 days. Provision was made for visits each week by a magistrate, but detainees were not permitted visits by legal advisers or any other visitors.

From the time of its enactment until its withdrawal on 11 January 1965, 857 Africans, 102 whites, 58 Coloureds and 78 Indians were detained under the '90-day' provisions. Of these persons 575 were subsequently charged and 241 gave evidence for the state.[69] The detention provisions had an important effect upon the struggle waged by Umkonto and Poqo for, as Feit[70] points out, by isolating members of the ANC and PAC the police were able to put enormous pressure upon detainees. Thereby the police gained information which was used to destroy the internal cell networks of these military wings of the ANC and PAC.

Permanent measures

Detention under solitary confinement first became a permanent feature of South African law during 1965. Soon after the withdrawal of the 90-day law, parliament enacted the '180-day detention law' by inserting a new provision, 215 *bis*, into the Criminal Procedure Act of 1955.[71] This authorised an Attorney General to order the detention of persons likely to give material evidence for the state in any criminal proceedings relating to certain political or common law offences. Detainees could be held for 6 months in solitary confinement, and only state officials were permitted to have access. No court had jurisdiction to order the release of persons so held. This provision became a permanent part of the legal system as unlike the '90-day' provision it required no subsequent renewal. In 1976 it was re-enacted with minor modifications as Section 12B of the Internal Security Act.

The '180-day law' differed from the '90-day law' in that it did not formally authorise police interrogation. Ostensibly its purpose was the detention of potential witnesses, but, in practice, detainees could be questioned, and in fact some ended up as accused rather than as witnesses. The 180-day law was widely used between 1965 and 1967, and nearly 400 persons were detained in terms of its provisions. Fewer than half of these were called as state witnesses.[72] In certain respects the 180-day law was more drastic than the 90-day law in that the period of possible unbroken solitary confinement was doubled, it broadened the net to include potential witnesses, and it was a permanent measure.[73]

In 1966 the first of the 'anti-terrorist' legislative devices was introduced. Section 22 of the General Law Amendment Act[74] provided for arrest by a police officer of or above the rank of Lieutenant Colonel and detention of a person suspected of terrorist activities for a period of 14 days. The period of detention could be extended only on application to a judge of the Supreme Court but detainees could be held while application was under review. Apart from this, jurisdiction of the courts was excluded.

Although it remained on the statute book, in practice the 14-day detention law was replaced by the Terrorism Act of 1967,[75] which became the central piece of security legislation until the Internal Security Act was passed in July 1982. In the parliamentary debate the provisions of the Terrorism Act were justified by the Minister of Justice on the grounds that extensive legislative powers were needed by the police in South West Africa. To some extent existing legislation did meet the needs of the situation, argued the Minister, but there was some doubt as to whether certain amendments to the Suppression of Communism Act covered persons who received training for sabotage in South West Africa before 4 November 1966. Furthermore the government preferred not to use the Suppression of Communism Act as the stage of an ideological struggle against communism had passed, the authorities no longer being confronted with 'Red ideology but with Red arms'.[76]

The Terrorism Act introduced the concept of indefinite detention without trial in the statutes of South Africa. The Minister of Justice claimed that the measure was necessary because only after thorough questioning of suspects and intensive checking of details obtained from various sources could the police gain an adequate 'picture of the general situation'. Documents found in the possession of suspects were often in foreign languages and in code and had to be translated before being examined. Information obtained from detainees had to be followed up to help trace escaped terrorists, potential terrorists and their contacts among the local population. Furthermore the difficult terrain in northern South West Africa was almost impossible to patrol adequately and investigations took a long time to complete. The Minister suggested that if a definite period of detention was stipulated, terrorists would be indoctrinated and prepared in advance to withstand questioning for that stipulated period.[77]

Section 6 of the Terrorism Act authorised a police officer of or above the rank of Lieutenant Colonel to detain persons with a view to obtaining information or on suspicion of offences under the Terrorism Act. The definition of 'terrorism' under this Act was very broad indeed, and brought 'virtually every criminal act within the statutory scope of terrorism'.[78] No time limit was prescribed for detention; it could be continued until detainees had satisfactorily replied to all questions or no useful purpose would be served by continued detention. Even weekly visits by magistrates – an absolutely minimal safeguard – were not included in this Act. Instead, visits by magistrates, 'if circumstances so permit',[79] would be allowed once a fortnight. Jurisdiction of courts to intervene was almost non-existent and the public was not entitled to information regarding persons held under this section. Detainees held in terms of Section 6 were virtually at the mercy of their captors.[80] Section 6 detention became a regular feature of political investigations, and most persons in such trials, either as accused or as state witnesses, experienced considerable periods of solitary confinement and incommunicado detention prior to court appearance.[81]

It is not possible to gain a full picture of the number of persons detained under Section 6. Scrutiny of the Annual Survey of Race Relations from the late 1960s until the mid-1970s shows that the Minister consistently refused to disclose any figures in this respect, usually on the grounds that it was 'not in the public interest to disclose the required information'.[82] It was left to non-official organisations to establish the extent of application of Section 6 legislation. As examples of such estimates, it was claimed that from the beginning of 1974 until 30 April 1976 some 217 persons were held under the Terrorism Act for a total of 22 566 days, a mean period per person of between three and four months.[83] In another estimate it was claimed that by December 1976 there had been 433 persons detained under various security provisions since mid-1976.[84] In September 1977 the Minister gave the following figures for the period between June 1976 and August 1977.[85] A total of 2 430 persons had been detained in terms of security legislation, of whom 817 had been tried and convicted, 118 were awaiting trial, 392 were undergoing investigation and 135 were held in preventive detention. Figures released in the Annual Report of the Director General of Justice for the period 1 July 1980 to 30 July 1981 claimed that 77 persons had been held under Section 6 while a total of 472 had been held under all security laws. In 1983 the Minister of Law and Order said that 4 104 persons had been detained under Section 6 of the Terrorism Act since its introduction in 1967 until 1 July 1982.[86]

In keeping with the proclaimed purpose of the Terrorism Act, the first case to be heard under the Act concerned 37 men who were charged with participation in terrorist activities in South West Africa.[87] However, by 1968 the Terrorism Act began to be used to charge persons who had committed acts in South Africa with the object of overthrowing the exisiting order.[88]

The overall effect of the series of security measures passed in the 1960s was a decreased level of overt resistance throughout the decade. In this period, the larger mining houses began their expansion into industry on a large scale, and within the mining industry itself, concentration and centralisation began to increase significantly.[89] Between 1960 and 1970, the gross national product of the Republic increased from about R5 200 million to R12 400 million, which meant that the South African economy together with Japan had the highest growth rate in the world at that time.[90] In his explanation of this astonishing economic performance Hobart Houghton emphasised the importance of the security measures taken by the government in restoring confidence, 'for they demonstrated that it [government] was not prepared lightly to capitulate to the pressures of African Nationalism'; thus many investors concerned with instability in Africa were reassured.[91]

After a period of relative political calm from the mid-1960s to the early 1970s, there was a recrudescence of political activity among blacks. In 1971 security police raided the homes of 115 people of all races in various parts of South Africa. At least 7 people were detained in terms of Section 6 of the Terrorism Act, one of whom, Ahmed Timol, died whilst in police custody. Another detainee, Mohammed Essop, successfully brought an action to the Supreme Court for an interim interdict restraining the police from interrogating him in any manner other than that prescribed or permitted by law or from applying any undue or unlawful pressure on him. In his judgment Mr Justice Margo suggested that a full investigation be made into Mr Essop's case and that private doctors of the parents' choice be permitted to examine him. Both these recommendations were rejected by the police.[92] The next year, Essop and three others were charged under the Terrorism Act as having unlawfully endangered the maintenance of law and order by conspiring with one another to promote the cause and policies of the ANC and the South African Communist Party.

In 1973 the government appointed a commission to inquire into the activities of the National Union of South African Students (NUSAS), the Christian Institute, the South African Institute of Race Relations, and the University Christian Movement. The Schlebusch Commission concluded that NUSAS, in particular, opposed not only the present government but also the entire existing order in South Africa including the 'capitalist system, existing moral norms and forms of authority'.[93] As a consequence eight student leaders named by the Commission were served with banning orders 'in the interest of the country and of students and of parents who sent their children to universities'.[94]

1973 witnessed the beginnings of organised worker struggle with the outbreak of strike action at textile plants in Natal. In the first quarter of 1973, there were 160 occasions when black workers withheld their labour in support of demands for higher wages and improved working conditions.[95] Industrial action which had been almost non-existent from the mid-1960s increased with considerable intensity from 1973.

By the time of the Soweto unrest of 1976 the problem of security legislation had once more become an important part of the political agenda. As B. J. Vorster said after a series of violent confrontations in the Cape Peninsula:

> There is no way of governing South Africa other than by the policy and principles of the National Party. . . . The police have contained the disorder under difficult circumstances and with a minimum of violence. . . . If it does not stop and stop immediately, other steps will have to be taken.[96]

Vorster's warning was matched by security police action and between 1 June and 30 November 1976, some 352 people were detained including black pupils, students and almost the entire leadership of the Black Consciousness movement.

Preventive detention and the 1970s

Thus in 1976, as a direct consequence of the Soweto unrest, a further measure of preventive detention or internment, not linked to emergency legislation, was introduced through the Internal Security Amendment Act.[97] Considerable changes were introduced to the Suppression of Communism Act, which was renamed the Internal Security Act. The draft bill was entitled the State Security Act and during the ensuing debate critics labelled it the 'S. S. Bill'. The name was dropped and the bill emerged as the Internal Security Amendment Act. The purpose of the Act, according to the Minister of Justice at the time, was to broaden the focus of security legislation, from subversion by communists to subversion in general.[98]

Section 10(2)(a) *bis* of this revised Internal Security Act allowed for arrest and detention of persons apparently engaged in activities which endangered or were calculated to endanger the security of the state or the maintenance of public order. A review committee of three persons (a sitting or retired judge or magistrate and two others) was established to investigate the Minister's actions not later than two months after the commencement of detention and thereafter at intervals of not more than six months. This committee could hear evidence or representations from any person; recommendations were to be made to the Minister but the Minister was not obliged to follow the recommendations. The review committee met in camera, and no court had jurisdiction to pronounce upon its functioning or recommendation. Preventive detention would be in force for twelve months at a time and in such parts of the country as determined by proclamation.

In introducing the bill in parliament, the Minister of Justice justified the proposed legislation on the grounds of the political conditions arising from activities of black political organisations. The intention of the government was to 'shift the emphasis of the Suppression of Communism Act so that it will be clear that the Act does not simply deal with subversion by Communists but with subversion in general'.[99] The Minister suggested that the bill was to be seen as a response to changed political conditions in which 'activist politics will be stepped up on the campuses and the campaign against military service under the guise of conscientious objection will be intensified. . . . In the labour area . . . there is in operation a centrally directed plan for the organisation and the mobilisation of the workers into a force to be used by underground politicians for the furthering of their own causes'.[100]

Following events of June 1976, Section 10 provisions of the Act were made operative throughout South Africa.[101] By 10 December 1976 a total of 144 persons had been held in terms of the Internal Security Act.[102] Conditions of preventive detention were generally better than those for interrogation purposes, and detainees were granted rights similar to those of awaiting trial prisoners, with certain exceptions; for example, no person could have access to detainees without approval of the officer commanding the place of detention. Similar restrictions pertained to written communication by detainees.

On 11 August 1980, Section 10 was again brought into operation for twelve months and renewed for a further period in August 1981 until its provisions were incorporated into the new Internal Security Act of 1982. In March 1982 the Minister of Law and Order said that 192 persons had been held under Section 10 in 1980 and Section 11 in 1981.[103]

Concluding comments

In this survey it has become apparent that detention without trial has increasingly assumed a central place within a vastly expanded system of state security. Faced with successive waves of organised black resistance, the state responded in terms of security legislation that paid scant respect to any conceptualisation of the rule of law.

If we view the past 35 years in terms of major event-crises which posed substantial threats to white domination, it is clear that the state increasingly armed itself with ever more repressive measures. In the space of a period of about 13 years between the early 1960s and the mid-1970s, the principle of peace-time detention without trial had become an accepted part of the apartheid regime. Over this period the range of detention provisions available to the state had also increased substantially – to the extent that the 1953 emergency provisions were not required to deal with nationwide crises in the months following Soweto 1976.

While the rhetorical justification for the security apparatus has consistently invoked some notion of a communist threat – and to an extent still does so in the mid-1980s – the pattern of historical events shows that the expanding security system was primarily a response to emerging organisation on the part of unenfranchised and oppressed people of South Africa. By the late 1970s this situation was partly conceded by the state, and the language of reform was initiated. A series of commissions was established to consider new responses in specific areas such as education, labour legislation and industrial relations. In addition, the system of security legislation appeared prominently on the political agenda during this period. The following chapter examines recent events in respect of South African security legislation.

3 Legal considerations

By the late 1970s, the South African criminal justice system included a formidable battery of permanent procedures for the detention of persons without reference to courts of law. Citizens could be detained as potential witnesses, or as a preventive measure, or for purposes of interrogation. In addition, the new 'independent states' not only retained detention provisions similar to those held prior to obtaining 'independence' but also used them extensively.

With the mounting number of deaths of security detainees and the persistent international and internal criticism of detention laws, it may have been hoped that the rhetoric of reform would bring some necessary change to the system of security legislation. Such optimism failed to appreciate the central role of detention in maintaining the political and economic status quo. For, as subsequent events have revealed, any hope of enlightened reform of the system of detention without trial in South Africa has proved to be ill-founded.

This chapter describes the recent history of detention with particular reference to the Rabie Report, and reviews current legislation as well as medical considerations. Finally the legal problem of the validity and admissibility of evidence presented by detainees is examined.

The Rabie Report[1]

Following the death of Steve Biko and the grim revelations about detention conditions at the subsequent inquest, opposition to security legislation mounted, and the government appointed a commission of inquiry, chaired by Mr Justice P. J. Rabie (currently chief justice). However, an explanation for the appointment of the Rabie Commission must be based on grounds that extend beyond the death of Biko. The accession to power of P. W. Botha heralded the commencement of a changed state strategy. Faced with a dramatic increase in industrial unrest after 1973, businessmen and industrialists began to call for reform with increasing vigour.

By the late 1970s P. W. Botha's government had realised the need for reform, for apart from the pressure exerted by capital in general and Afrikaner capital in particular, Botha's links with the military and his responsiveness to their demands were to prove extremely significant in this respect. The military had been propagating a 'total strategy' from the mid-1970s for as General Magnus Malan, then Chief of the South African Defence Force, stated:

> Bullets kill bodies, not beliefs. I would like to remind you that the Portuguese did not lose the military battle in Angola and Mozambique but they lost the faith and trust of the inhabitants of those countries. The insurgent forces have no hope of success without the aid of the local population.[2]

However, for P. W. Botha, reform needed to be introduced in a manner that would not divide Afrikanerdom too irreparably and at the same time would prove acceptable to a moderate black community.

Early evidence of this form of government thinking was provided in the Report of the (Steyn) Commission of Inquiry into the Mass Media.[3] The Commission found that South Africa was a dynamically developing and expanding democracy burdened by certain vexing perceptions requiring urgent rectification. At the same time it found that the Republic was being subjected to an onslaught, total in its ambit and escalating in its intensity, which was both external and internal.[4] To protect the process of democratic development any security measure could be justified on the basis of the belief that the security, preservation and welfare of the state were the 'highest law', which should be accorded precedence when weighed against other rights and interests. If the interests of the state required that the rights of the individual or of certain groups, for example the press, be curtailed, it should consequently be accepted in law that such curtailment must follow.[5] Thus reform was to be managed along strict authoritarian lines, and in this context security legislation was an important managerial tool.

Given the ever-increasing criticisms by a wide range of organisations of South African security legislation, particularly after the death of Steve Biko, there was a need for some mechanism by which to legitimate the security system. In appointing the Rabie Commission, the Minister of Justice reflected this approach.[6]

> Over the past almost thirty years, it was necessary, from time to time, to place statutory measures on the lawbook to counteract the constantly changing threats to the internal security of the Republic. For the following reasons the Government has decided to recommend the appointment of a commission to inquire into all these measures and to make recommendations thereon:
>
> (1) Threats against the internal security change constantly as to source and emphasis. It is therefore possible that some of the measures that were necessary at a particular moment in the past, may now no longer be necessary and that they can be removed from the statute book.
>
> (2) In the meantime the security situation has again changed and consideration must again be given to the question whether the existing statutory measures still satisfy the demands of today.
>
> (3) Over the years it has been alleged from different sources that some of the measures confer administrative powers that are unfair, especially in that there is an alleged insufficient provision for judicial supervision over the exercise of those powers. The commission will be able to give attention to such viewpoints

and to make recommendations in this regard.

(4) The measures are spread over a number of Acts with the result that they are not easily identifiable and manageable; they have therefore as a group possibly become an unwieldy instrument and on the other hand the mere number of security measures has become handy anti-South African propaganda material. Some of the measures resulted from emergency situations and were therefore drafted in haste with the result that they were perhaps not so elegantly formulated. The commission will thus also be able to consider the possibility and desirability of reformulation and consolidation. . . .

The Rabie Commission's Report adopted an approach similar to the Botha government's managerial strategy. Addressing itself to criticisms levelled against Section 6 of the Terrorism Act, the Commission accepted the police evidence that Section 6 was indispensable in combating activities endangering the state, for 'information on planned and purposed activities of this nature was their main weapon in the combating thereof'.[7] For this reason the Commission rejected the criticism that as far more people were detained in terms of the legislation than were charged, the police were using Section 6 for interrogation purposes to obtain information rather than for prosecuting the persons concerned in the courts. The Commission expressed the view that such criticism misunderstood the purpose of the section, for 'although it was aimed at combating treason as a crime, and therefore at being used with a view to prosecuting people in court, it does at the same time have an operational object, namely the prevention of terrorism and the preservation of internal security'.[8]

In a report on the Rabie Report,[9] the contents of which were formulated at a seminar of prominent legal experts chaired by Mr Sydney Kentridge S.C., criticism was lodged at the many shortcomings of the Commission. Particularly sharp criticism was directed at the proposals regarding the various forms of detention, and the Commission's failure to hear evidence from former detainees or to investigate methods of interrogation. The recommendations failed to provide any real safeguards for detainees held for interrogation. Furthermore, the Rabie Report did not deal in any depth with the question of reliability or admissibility of evidence obtained from persons held in solitary confinement.

When the Rabie Report was tabled in parliament the Minister of Law and Order said that 'every possible measure was taken to ensure that detainees could not injure themselves and commit suicide'.[10] Ironically, two days later, on 5 February 1982, Dr Neil Aggett died in detention at John Vorster Square. A careful analysis comparing the Rabie Report with details of detention conditions revealed by the Aggett inquest[11] showed that the Rabie Commission had failed to present an accurate account of the system of detention for interrogation purposes. In particular Rabie was overly dependent upon certain assumptions – that inspectors or magistrates may always gain access to detainees, that the police are really concerned and hold watch over the welfare of detainees, and that police know and adhere to safeguard regulations. The Aggett inquest demonstrated that these assumptions were false. Notwithstanding such criticisms, a new Internal Security Act based directly on the recommendations of the Rabie Commission was introduced in 1982.

The Internal Security Act[12]

During the 1982 parliamentary session the recommendations of the Rabie Commission were translated into law in four Acts,[13] the most important of which for purposes of detention was the Internal Security Act. Virtually all the existing provisions were re-enacted. The Act, which is the current law in this area, makes provision for four different types of detention:

(i) Detention of state witnesses.[14] Section 31 re-enacts the 180-day provision, described above. It empowers the Attorney General if he is of the opinion that there is any danger that any person likely to give material evidence for the state in any criminal proceedings relating to certain specified offences may be tampered with or intimidated or that such person may abscond, or whenever he deems it to be in the interests of such person or the administration of justice, to issue a warrant for the arrest and detention of that person. The period of detention is for the duration of the criminal proceedings or, if no charge sheet is brought, for a period of 6 months. Courts of law are precluded from intervening in respect of release, or of conditions of detention. In terms of Section 31, detainees are to be visited not less than once a fortnight in private by a magistrate and by a district surgeon. The detainee may be refused visits by family and access to a lawyer. Upon release a person may be redetained.

(ii) 'Short-term' detention.[15] Section 50 of the Act repeats the provisions of the former 14-day detention clause, namely Section 22 of the General Law Amendment Act.[16] It allows a policeman of the rank of warrant officer or above to detain anyone thought to be contributing to a state of public disturbance, disorder or riot. To detain for longer than 48 hours, the police must obtain signed permission from a magistrate. This detention is for a maximum period of 14 days, including the initial 48-hour period.

(iii) Detention for purpose of interrogation.[17] Section 29 replaces Section 6 of the Terrorism Act of 1967, and thus maintains the principle of indefinite detention. Section 29 allows any commissioned police officer of or above the rank of Lieutenant Colonel to arrest without warrant any person believed to be connected with the very broadly defined offences of 'terrorism' or 'subversion'.[18] A person may be held until the police are satisfied that 'the said person has satisfactorily replied to all questions at the interrogation or that no useful purpose will be served by his further detention'.[19] However, detention may not be for longer than 30 days without the written authority of the Minister of Law and Order to extend the period. Furthermore, after 6 months the Commissioner of Police is required to give reasons for non-release to a board of review. If the detainee is still not released, such reasons have to be given again at intervals of 3 months. The Minister is free to reject any recommendations of the review board, and as with earlier legislation, a court of law has no jurisdiction to pronounce upon the validity of any action taken under Section 29 or to order the release of any person detained under its terms.[20]

Section 29 detainees must be visited in private not less than once a fortnight by a magistrate and by a district surgeon. In addition, an inspector of detainees is required to visit as 'frequently as possible so as to satisfy himself as to the well-being of such a person'.[21] Apart from these visits a Section 29 detainee may not be visited by anyone, whether friends, family or legal advisers, without the consent of the Minister of Law and Order or the Police Commissioner. These conditions are far more severe than those applying to convicted prisoners.

Unfortunately none of these provisions supply even the beginnings of adequate safeguards. Detention is entirely a closed system with all authority in the hands of state officials. The Aggett inquest revealed that magistrates, inspectors and district surgeons do not always have ready access to detainees,[22] and furthermore it is unlikely that detainees would place full trust in state officials. An absolutely minimal safeguard would require independent access to detainees by doctors of detainees' choice as well as by legal advisers.

As with previous legislation it is apparent that considerable numbers of people have been detained for interrogation since the introduction of Section 29 in July 1982. According to the Minister of Law and Order, some 130 persons were held under Section 29 from July 1982 to February 1983.[23] During the course of 1983 a total of 453 persons were held under all security laws, including those of the homelands.[24] According to data collected by the Detainees' Parents Support Committee, a total of 1 149 persons were detained under all provisions, including those of the homelands, during 1984. Of these, 280 were detained under Section 29.[25] Between January and December 1985 a further 406 persons were held under Section 29.[26]

(iv) Preventive detention.[27] Section 28 replaces Section 10(1)(a) *bis* of the Internal Security Act and empowers the Minister of Law and Order to detain persons if, in his opinion (a) there is reason to apprehend that the person in question will commit the offence[28] of terrorism, subversion or sabotage; (b) if he is satisfied that such person will endanger the security of the state or the maintenance of law and order; or (c) if he has reason to suspect that a person who has been convicted of a scheduled offence[29] is likely to endanger the security of the state or the maintenance of law and order.

A Section 28 detainee may be held for whatever period is specified on the detention order. No court of law may intervene in the regulation of detention. Only state officials and judges of the Supreme Court have access to persons in preventive detention. In addition legal assistance is available to Section 28 detainees for the limited purpose of making written representations to the Minister regarding their detention or release. Such representations must be made within 14 days of the issue of the detention order. After this 14-day period the Minister must give reasons for the detention to the review board. The review board is required to investigate and consider all representations, but the Minister is not obliged to act on its recommendations. After a period of 6 months and at subsequent intervals of 6 months, the detainee may again request the Minister to resubmit his case to the review board.

The board of review is empowered to investigate and consider the detention, and may hear oral evidence or representations from any person.[30] The detainee may himself apply in writing to give oral evidence to the review board, and that board is required to accede to this request unless the chairman is of the opinion that it would not be in the public interest to do so.

When a board of review has considered and investigated a detention referred to it by the Minister of Law and Order, it is required to furnish him with a written report on its findings. This report is required to state whether grounds exist for the amendment or withdrawal of a detention notice, and to make recommendations accordingly. The Minister must, as soon as possible after receiving the report, notify the detainee of the recommendations and findings of the board.

A detainee may have his case referred to a review board at intervals of not less than 6 months after being notified of the outcome of the original investigation. The Minister of Law and Order is not obliged to give effect to any recommendation made to him by a board of review. However, if the effect of the Minister's refusal to accept a recommendation of a review board is that stricter measures in respect of the detainee will remain in force, the Minister is obliged within 14 days after such refusal to submit to the chief justice, for purposes of review, the papers submitted to the review board, a copy of the board's report and any further report as he deems necessary.

The chief justice or another judge of the Appellate division designated by him is required to consider all these documents and, if he is satisfied that the Minister exceeded the powers conferred upon him by the Act, acted in bad faith or based his decision on considerations other than those specified by the Act, he may set aside the detention. If the chief justice or judge of the Appellate division is not so satisfied, he is obliged to endorse the Minister's statement of the reasons for the detention to the effect that no grounds exist for setting aside the notice. Courts of law are specifically precluded from pronouncing on a finding of the chief justice or judge of the Appellate division. Where the chief justice or judge of appeal does set aside the decision of the Minister to detain, he is required to furnish the Minister with reasons. He is not obliged by the Act to furnish the detainee with reasons for a refusal to set aside the detention.

Owing to the lack of access to detainees by independent persons such as lawyers and medical practitioners, as well as the lack of any binding power granted to the review board, Section 28 detainees are, like those under Sections 29 and 31, without any meaningful forms of protection against abuse.

The detention provisions of the 1982 Internal Security Act constitute a slight improvement on previous legislation.[31] However, the powers of the executive are very extensive indeed, and safeguards against possible physical and psychological torture of detainees are minimal. Conditions of detention do not depart in any substantial manner from those that have led to the death of nearly 60 persons held under earlier security legislation.

Regulations for the treatment of detainees

Following Biko's death in detention and the subsequent worldwide condemnation of South African detention laws, some state response was made in terms of regulations providing for the appointment, from June 1978, of two inspectors of detainees. The appointees were two retired officials of the Department of Justice, a former chief magistrate and a former Attorney General.

Inspectors were required to visit Section 6 detainees in private and to report confidentially to the Minister of Justice on conditions of detention and treatment of detainees.[32] According to the Rabie Commission, one of the inspectors stated that from June 1978 to March 1980 he had seen 213 detainees and received 32 complaints about health.[33]

During 1978, some instructions were issued by the Commissioner of Police about the treatment of detainees held in terms of Section 6, including directions regarding medical treatment, nutrition, sleeping and exercise facilities.[34] These guidelines do not, however, have the status of any law and thus appear impossible to enforce.

Evidence in the Aggett inquest showed that, in practice, many security policemen were unaware of the 1978 regulations; that exercise regulations were entirely ignored; that inspectors of detainees were not always granted immediate access to detainees; and that cells were not regularly visited by ordinary police responsible for such tasks.

Thus during the Aggett inquest, for example, it emerged that one inspector had experienced cases where detainees were reluctant to report maltreatment to him for fear that such information would be given back to the security police. The inspector claimed that under such circumstances he did not feel able to extract the information from the detainees.[35]

Subsequent to the enactment of the Internal Security Act of 1982, a new set of directions regarding treatment of detainees for interrogation was issued by the Minister of Law and Order on 24 November 1982.[36] Paragraph 15 of these directions states: 'A detainee shall at all times be treated in a humane manner with proper regard to the rules of decency and shall not in any way be assaulted or otherwise ill-treated or subjected to any form of torture or inhuman or degrading treatment.'

In outline these Directions Regarding the Detention of Persons in Terms of Section 29(1) of the Internal Security Act attempted to ensure that detainees were informed of their limited rights; detainees' families were informed of their detention; the health of detainees was protected; police were to be responsible for the general well-being of detainees; complaints by detainees were to be speedily investigated by another branch of the police force; certain rules were to be observed during interrogation; detainees were to be visited by magistrates, inspectors and district surgeons under specified circumstances; and records of such visits were to be kept and reports submitted by officials on observations during visits.

As with previous regulations, the central problem remains the lack of independent access (by lawyers, doctors, family or detainee support groups) to detainees, and the prohibition of any judicial intervention in the process. In addition, the 'Directions' were couched in extremely equivocal language: for example, detainees should 'where practicable' only be held in cells that have an exercise area, washing facilities and a flush toilet in the cell or exercise area; two police members 'shall normally be present' during interrogation; in the case of women a policewoman should be present 'if available'; senior police officials should 'as far as their duties permit' make periodic unannounced visits to the place of interrogation; the right of access to detainees by magistrates, district surgeons or inspectors is not absolute and they simply have to report 'instances where a detainee is not available', together with the reasons therefor. It became apparent during the Aggett inquest that it is precisely during the critical periods of lengthy interrogation that a detainee is likely to be 'unavailable' to guardian officials.

Another argument concerning the Directions was that they lacked the status of law, as they were not issued in terms of an enabling statute. Consequently, it was suggested, they could not be enforced by the courts or by any independent body. If the Directions do not have the status of law, no charges can be brought against captors who failed to adhere to these guidelines. However, Mathews provides a cogent argument in favour of regarding the Directions as legally binding upon the police. He notes that the Directions were issued in terms of the Internal Security Act. Moreover, to describe the guidelines as Directions rather than regulations should not be sufficient to deprive them of legal enforceability.[37] A final problem is that no detailed specifications are given to limit interrogation practices. The present guidelines are broad, vague and filled with provisos. The length of detention and interrogation is covered only by the statement that 'the investigation . . . shall be concluded as rapidly as possible so as to limit the period of detention to the minimum'. Firearms are prohibited in the interrogation room, 'unless there are compelling security reasons for doing so'. In this regard it should be recalled that Mr Paris Malatji died at the hands of the security police on 5 July 1983. Sergeant J. H. van As was subsequently convicted of culpable homicide for shooting Malatji through the head at point-blank range during interrogation. Van As was sentenced to ten years' imprisonment. Later the Malatji family sued the Minister of Law and Order for R51 600.[38]

The directions fail to define any limits to interrogation behaviour and fail to explain operationally what is meant by such vague terms as 'humane manner', 'rules of decency' and 'inhuman or degrading treatment'. Regrettable is the lack of any reference to the Code of Conduct for interrogations as provided by the Bennett Committee[39] in the United Kingdom. The Bennett Report recommended the prohibition of the following acts on the grounds that they constituted degrading treatment: orders to strip naked or to expose; unnatural or humiliating postures; physically exhausting actions or stances; obscenities, insults or insulting language; threats of physical force; threats of sexual assault or misbehaviour. The Bennett Report also specified limitations on the duration of interrogation.

Considered overall, the directions in theory provide a more generous approach to the treatment of detainees than was previously the case. In practice, however, the substantial limitations mentioned above indicate that Section 29 detainees are not likely to enjoy any real protection beyond that provided by earlier legislation.

In a further move to provide so-called safeguards for detainees, the Minister of Law and Order announced on 2 May 1983 that 24-hour closed-circuit television was to be installed in the cells of detainees at John Vorster Square police headquarters.[40] This measure was planned to minimise instances in which detainees could come to harm. Such monitoring, however, required that lights would be kept on continuously in cells. This proposal was heavily criticised,[41] the main thrust being that it was the interrogators who required monitoring, not the detainees, and furthermore that 24-hour cell monitoring would add to the stress of detention and provide an invasion of existing limited privacy that could be abused. The Minister immediately shelved the monitoring plan 'pending expert advice'.[42] But in 1984 news was received from former detainees that closed-circuit television had been installed at John Vorster Square[43] without further public announcements in this regard.

If considered in general, it may not be too harsh to describe provisions for detainees' protection and welfare as characterised by attempts to shield and protect the system of interrogation from exposure rather than to grant real protection to its victims.

The MASA Report

The important Report on Medical Care of Prisoners and Detainees (the MASA Report) was formally adopted by the Federal Council of the Medical Association of South Africa on 10 May 1983.[44] The findings of the MASA Report were generally critical of security legislation and held that the Internal Security Act failed to provide sufficient safeguards for the protection of detainees. It also found that detention presented potential hazards to the mental and physical health of detainees, beyond that of convicted prisoners; detainees' defence against mental breakdown is removed as a result of the imposition of a state of helplessness; the alleged interrogation process could, along with general conditions of detention, lead to serious mental breakdown; information gained under such conditions is likely to be unreliable and therefore of limited legal use; current conditions of detention could lead to suicide, psychiatric disorders or serious mental breakdown; and moreover there have been cases of dereliction of duty on the part of district surgeons.

These findings expressed a belated seriousness of purpose and ethical responsibility on the part of the South African medical authorities,[45] but the same cannot be said for the recommendations of the Report,[46] which included the following:

(i) district surgeons should have free access to detainees at all times, and obstruction of their duties should be a criminal offence;

(ii) the adequacy of health care of detainees by district surgeons should be monitored by a 'peer review' system, by a committee appointed by MASA and the Department of Health;

(iii) isolation should not exceed 7 days in the absence of regular physical and psychiatric assessments;

(iv) during interrogation at least two persons should be present, it should be television-monitored, and no physical torture should be permitted;

(v) if requested, examination by an independent medical practitioner (of detainee's choice and at detainee's expense) should be provided; examination should be in the presence of a district surgeon if a security risk is suspected; and

(vi) all detainees should be examined within 24 hours of release, and if psychiatric assessment is required, it should be conducted as soon as possible.

Although the MASA Report was heralded as 'an impressive document',[47] there are a number of grounds for considering it to be inadequate:

(i) There is a lack of clarity with respect to what is meant by isolation, and how the isolation period of 7 days is to be broken. The Report does not specify whether the independent doctor is to have unrestricted access. It is also not made clear who is to be responsible for the 'close observation of psychological reactions in the detainee which may indicate suicidal tendencies'.[48] It seems doubtful whether either the security police or district surgeons are the appropriate personnel for such a task. It is not clear who is to monitor the closed-circuit television of interrogation, nor is it clear why no call was made for the abolition of psychological torture during interrogation. Finally the Report stresses the need for personnel who are 'adequately trained',[49] that is, persons with a knowledge of psychology, but it is unclear what could be meant by 'adequately trained'.

(ii) By condoning the retention of isolation and in fact the whole process of detention as recognised in its own findings, the Report may be interpreted as being in contradiction to the Tokyo Declaration,[50] which holds that 'the doctor shall not countenance, condone, or participate in the practice of torture or other forms of cruel or degrading procedures, whatever the offence'.

(iii) Recommendations of the MASA Report do not provide measures in keeping with its own findings. Detention is retained insofar as it is regarded as necessary by the authorities. Medical safeguards are introduced only 'so as to prevent abuse of the system as far as is possible'.[51] This retention of the detention system despite findings that it forms a health hazard is simply untenable. The recommendations propose little to alter the general state of helplessness which reduces defence against breakdown. The present arrangements regarding isolation from lawyers, family and friends is retained, as are solitary confinement, albeit limited, and intensive interrogation. In the recommendations, the district surgeon still retains the central role despite the recognition in the findings that there have been 'serious instances of dereliction of duty on the part of district surgeons'.[52]

In many respects the MASA recommendations go no further than providing minor modifications to the existing situation. While one can agree with the Report's conclusion that 'it is of the utmost importance to ensure that the rights of detainees and prisoners and the concomitant duties of police and prison personnel be set forth statutorily, in a comprehensive form, by way of parliamentary legislation',[53] it is not possible to conclude that the MASA Committee's recommendations constitute an adequate basis for such regulation.

On 26 May 1983 the Minister of Health and Welfare in conjunction with the Minister of Law and Order announced the government's acceptance of all but two of the MASA recommendations,[54] namely the right of a detainee to treatment by his or her own doctor (which was refused for security reasons) and the peer review system of treatment adequacy (which proved unacceptable to the Minister of Health). To date, however, the government has failed to respond to the concluding recommendation, for no statutory changes in the conditions of detainees have been forthcoming. Furthermore, given the serious limitations as outlined above, it is doubtful whether legal embodiment of the MASA recommendations would lead to any substantial further safeguards for detainees.

In 1985[55] MASA announced that detainees would have access to doctors other than district surgeons. Such doctors would be chosen by a detainee from a panel selected by MASA and would be available to the detainee if additional medical care (other than that offered by a district surgeon) was requested. At the time of writing it is unclear as to how the scheme will operate although, if the panel allows doctors other than those who are district surgeons to have access to a detainee, it may contribute towards some improvement of the current system.

Admissibility and validity of detainee evidence

It is trite law that admissions and confessions must be freely and voluntarily made without undue influence.[56] This principle of the free and voluntary character of statements as a prerequisite for admissibility as court evidence was given statutory force in Sections 217(1) and 219(A) of the Criminal Procedure Act of 1977[57] as far as confessions and admissions respectively are concerned.

The difficulty confronting the courts has been to reconcile this basic principle of South African law with the fact that evidence of detainees has been gained by the police whilst persons were held in solitary confinement. As Didcott J. explained in *Nxasana* v *Minister of Justice*:[58]

> In providing for the detention for indefinite periods of those who have not been convicted of crimes, for their isolation from legal advice and from their families, and for their interrogation at the risk of self-incrimination, the legislature has pursued its object by the enactment of measures which are undoubtedly foreign to the ordinary principles of our law.

Despite the fact that the concept of statutory detention for the purposes of interrogation was 'something entirely alien to our legal system'[59] when it was introduced, the courts will only disregard an admission or confession made by a detainee to a magistrate if the accused can prove on a balance of probabilities that such a statement was not made freely or voluntarily and was indeed made as a result of undue influence on the part of the police.[60]

It is quite clear that the requirement of voluntariness is absent where admissions or confessions have been obtained through the exercise of physical force. However, within the context of detention the two crucial questions to be answered are: what factors short of physical assault would deprive a statement of its free and voluntary character, and whether evidence elicited under security provisions for detention and interrogation or under conditions of solitary confinement fulfils the prerequisite for admissibility.[61] In other words the question is whether detention itself, under conditions allowed for in terms of security legislation, is a sufficient condition to render a statement inadmissible.

As far as physical duress is concerned the Appellate division in *S.* v *L. M. Mogale*[62] held that the accused had successfully discharged the onus of proving the involuntariness of his confession, having shown that the security police had seriously assaulted him in order to compel him to confess. What has remained in dispute, however, is the validity of evidence gained by means of interrogation methods not involving physical assault.

As mentioned earlier this issue was ignored by the Rabie Commission and by subsequent legislation. The Rabie Commission did not consider this issue to be a problem, given the fact that 'the evidence of such witnesses [detainees] is . . . also treated by the courts with the utmost caution'.[63] The Commission then quoted from the *Gwala* case where the court held that 'no court of law in this country would in any circumstances condone the employment by the police of any set pattern of interrogation which is either intended or calculated to result in a witness giving false testimony on oath'.[64] On the basis of such a cautious approach by the court the Commission concluded that 'evidence before the Commission shows that the Police are well aware of this and we are of the opinion that this contributes to a realisation that the improper treatment of a detainee serves no useful purpose, but can indeed serve to defeat the object which the Police are trying to achieve by interrogating a detainee'.[65]

Despite the confidence of the *Gwala* court there have been extremely few cases in which a court has found that conditions of solitary confinement or the interrogation procedure adopted by the security police constitute sufficient grounds to render evidence inadmissible. By contrast the American Supreme Court in *Miranda* v *Arizona*[66] held that confessions elicited as a result of solitary confinement could not be regarded as admissible evidence. The court stated:

> It is obvious that such an interrogation environment is created for no purpose other than to subjugate the individual to the will of his examiner. This atmosphere carries its own badge of intimidation. To be sure, this is not physical intimidation, but it is equally destructive of human dignity. The current practice of incommunicado interrogation is at odds with one of our Nation's most cherished principles – that the individual may not be compelled to incriminate himself. Unless adequate protective devices are employed to dispel the compulsion inherent in custodial surroundings, no statement obtained from the defendant can truly be the product of his free choice.

English courts have been far more reluctant to exclude such evidence. Where a confession is not technically involuntary, exclusion rests upon a discretionary basis, and exercise of that discretion has generally been confined to cases where the accused's mental state has been clinically assessed as subnormal or abnormal.[67] In *R.* v *Isequilla*[68] the court rejected an argument that a confession made by an accused whilst in a hysterical state caused by fright upon being apprehended by police, should be automatically excluded on the basis of involuntariness. Lord Widgery C.J. held that a confession cannot be regarded as involuntary unless there has been an element of impropriety in the form of a threat, an inducement or oppressive conduct on the part of the police interrogators.

Since the introduction of the '90-day' clause in South Africa it has been argued repeatedly that the very nature of the conditions of detention, including solitary confinement and intensive interrogation, is likely to reduce the validity and reliability of detainees' evidence, thus rendering it of questionable legal value.[69] The central argument is that detention conditions are likely to disrupt or impair a number of psychological functions, casting the detainee into a state of heightened vulnerability to threats or promises, and increased susceptibility to suggestions. Under appropriate conditions of stress, anxiety or psychological manipulation most persons may be made to confess to crimes of which they are innocent. In some cases arrest, custody or interrogation may precipitate states of temporary abnormality such as hysteria in otherwise normal persons, or may induce a state of heightened susceptibility to persuasion and influence by the interrogators. As the Royal Commission on Criminal Procedure pointed out, given the very nature of the relationship between the police interrogator and the suspect being interrogated, 'powerful psychological forces are at play upon the suspect'.[70]

Such a conclusion is supported by the evidence of Professor Albino in 1973 in the *Hassim* trial, where he claimed:[71] (i) that the proceedings used are a form of duress in that they compel a person into a state where he is not in full possession of his faculties; (ii) the methods used are likely to compel the subject to comply with the interrogator's demands and this may occur without any conscious intent on the part of the subject; (iii) it is highly probable that under such pressures false statements may be made without either the interrogator or the author being aware of the falsity.

As shown earlier nothing much has changed in the conditions of detention since the early 1970s. Recent years have, however, seen an increase in the critical attention given to examining detention conditions, and a number of articles analysing admissibility of detainee evidence have appeared.[72] While the central thrust of the arguments remains similar to those of Albino[73] a number of useful additional points have been raised.

The nature of the political trial. A central distinction must be drawn between the political trial and the ordinary criminal trial. A political trial can be identified by its being based upon legislation specifically designed to protect the government from activity directed against its existence or political interests. Alternatively a political trial can be characterised by the nature of the political motives and interests of the accused.[74] Thus in South Africa there exists an extensive body of legislation designed to protect the security of the state, providing for rules of procedure and evidence that are 'alien to our legal system'.[75]

In legal practice there are a number of clear differences between political and ordinary criminal trials. Political trials often involve witnesses who have been detained in solitary confinement for lengthy periods, and political trials have different procedural rules. Thus although the political trial may have the surface appearance of an ordinary trial, this is simply not the case in practice. As prominent South African advocate Sydney Kentridge has said:[76]

Now, a visitor walking into a court in which one of these trials is going on will see a trial being conducted with all the customary decorum of our courts. He will see a judge obviously exercising the utmost judicial care, and he will have the impression he is watching an ordinary trial at law. But of course he is not. He is watching a procedure in which all our cherished rules and maxims, or many of them, have gone by the board. There is an onus on the accused; there is a form of hearsay evidence which is admissible beyond anything that the reformers of the law of evidence have ever thought of. The state witnesses are all under pressure and, I think it must be said, the lawyers appearing are perhaps under some pressure themselves. . . .

The pre-trial stage. A second important distinction is that between the pre-trial stage and the trial itself. Kamisar likens the courtroom to a 'mansion' and the police-station to a 'gatehouse', the latter being a 'much less pretentious edifice . . . with bare rooms and locked doors'.[77]

In this 'gatehouse' of . . . criminal procedure – through which most defendants journey and beyond which many never get – the enemy of the state is a depersonalized 'subject' to be 'sized up' and subjected to 'interrogation tactics and techniques most appropriate for the occasion'; he is 'game' to be stalked and cornered. Here ideals are checked at the door, 'realities' faced, and the prestige of law enforcement vindicated. Once he leaves the 'gatehouse' and enters the 'mansion' – if he ever gets there – the enemy of the state is repersonalized, even dignified, the public invited, and a stirring ceremony in honour of individual freedom from law enforcement celebrated.

I suspect it is not so much that society knows and approves of the show in the gatehouse, but that society does not know or care.[78]

In recognising the same two-stage process, Fine nevertheless presents cogent reasons for seeing the two as continuous in the case of the political trial. This is largely because 'convictions in such political trials hinge to a large extent on evidence of statements extracted from detainees who stand accused or who have emerged as state witnesses, usually after a prolonged period in detention'.[79]

Although protective procedural measures in the courtroom 'mansion' of the political trial may be less than those of the ordinary trial, it is obvious that it is the 'gatehouse', the process of detention, that is primarily lacking in safeguards. It therefore follows from the above that the 'detainee evidence' under question concerns evidence extracted from detainees at the gatehouse stage. It includes confessions or admissions made by detainees who are subsequently charged and appear as accused, as well as statements made by detainees who later appear in court as state witnesses. It excludes *viva voce* evidence given by ex-detainees called as defence witnesses or state witnesses, when that evidence is unlinked to actual statements made during detention.[80]

In other words, the 'detainee evidence' being questioned is primarily that extracted *during the closed system* of detention. Nevertheless, considerable caution should be exercised in evaluating *viva voce* evidence of former detainees, because of possible long-term psychological sequelae of detention.

We have argued that detainee evidence should be excluded as a matter of course by courts on three legal grounds:[81]

(i) The reliability principle. According to this principle detainee evidence may not be true and would therefore be unreliable evidence. The psychological processes at play in a closed system of detention are likely to 'render the detainee susceptible to suggestion with no limit to the potential distortion of information obtained'.[82]

(ii) The disciplinary principle. This holds the need for discouraging bad police interrogation methods as a ground for excluding detainee evidence. It is not entirely divorced from the 'reliability principle' in that vicious interrogation methods are likely to reduce the truth value of detainees' statements.

(iii) The protective principle. This holds that it would be in accordance with justice to convict an accused on the basis of statements extracted by improper means. This principle has been argued to be the most pertinent exclusionary rule in that convictions in political trials frequently 'hinge on the outcome of trials-within-trials, and the subsequent weight, if any, put on detainee statements'.[83]

The three principles appear to be intertwined, in that the 'improper means' of the protective principle are operationalised as the 'bad police interrogation methods' of the disciplinary principle, and these in turn constitute the conditions, both physical and psychological, for doubting the validity and reliability of detainee evidence.

The record of the South African courts. The crucial thread connecting the three exclusionary principles apparently depends upon psychological evidence which shows that South African detention conditions, including solitary confinement and psychological techniques used during interrogation, constitute 'improper means'. However, the record of the courts in security cases reveals a pattern of considerable reluctance to accept such psychological argument and hence reject evidence gained from detainees.

The courts were first confronted with the question of the conditions of a detainee under interrogation in *Rossouw* v *Sachs*,[84] where a practising advocate had been detained in terms of the '90-day' clause. He had applied for a court order declaring that he was not entitled to be deprived by the police of his rights and liberties save to detain him for interrogation and to deprive him of access to other persons. He further asked for a declaration that he be entitled to the same rights as awaiting trial prisoners, particularly insofar as rights to exercise and to receive reading material were concerned.

The Cape Supreme Court having found for the detainee, the security police appealed to the Appellate division. Delivering the judgment of the court Ogilvie Thompson J.A. said that 'it may readily be postulated that Parliament can never have intended that any detainee should, in order to induce him to speak, be subjected to any form of assault or that his health or resistance be impaired by inadequate food, living conditions or the like'.[85] However, the purpose of detention was to 'induce the detainee to speak' and hence 'the purpose and express terms of Section 17 . . . do not appear to me to reveal any intention on the part of the legislature to alleviate the lot of a detainee during his detention'.[86]

In a revealing passage Thompson J.A. rejected the view of Van Winsen and Banks J.J. in the court *a quo* that a detainee can be equated with an awaiting trial prisoner and hence is entitled to all his pre-detention rights, save insofar as detention itself impairs those rights:

> Moreover where is the line to be drawn? In the present case we are concerned only with reading matter and writing materials; but is the detainee who in happier days habitually enjoyed champagne and cigars entitled, as of right, to continue to enjoy them during his detention? That example, is, no doubt, extreme but it serves to underline the difficulties attendant upon the view taken by the court below.[87]

A different approach to the matter was adopted by Milne J.P. in *S.* v *Ismail and Others* (1),[88] in which trial of a number of accused on the charge of having committed an act of sabotage, objection was taken to the admissibility of a confession made by one of the accused when he had been detained under the '90-day' clause. The accused contended that his statement had not been made freely and voluntarily as the only alternative open to the accused if he did not make a satisfactory statement was that he would be detained under the '90-day' clause. This factor, together with long and persistent interrogation, including four hours before 8 o'clock in the morning and four hours at least after 5 in the afternoon, 'was claimed to have . . . operated to impair the accused's freedom of volition'.[89] The judge agreed with this submission, concluding that 'the mere authorization of this machinery by Parliament for obtaining the desired information cannot be treated as rendering the making of a statement free and voluntary when it is made in order to avoid the 90-day detention'.[90]

However, Milne's approach has proved to be an exception and has not been followed by other courts. Thus in *S.* v *Hlekani*[91] the court followed the *Rossouw* v *Sachs* approach, holding that, as the purpose of detention laws was to induce the detainee to speak, evidence obtained from the detainee would be admissible, subject to certain safeguards: 'that a detainee is not to be subjected to any form of assault, or to any maltreatment in body or mind, nor that his health or his resistance should be impaired by inadequate food, living conditions and the like, nor that the interrogation sanctioned should amount to third degree methods'.[92] The premise upon which the court based its conclusions was that the '90-day' clause constituted a radical departure from the common law, and given its nature and the circumstances surrounding its enactment, the courts must interpret the clause to give full effect to its 'general policy'.[93]

The Appellate division was given the opportunity of adjudicating upon the precise problem of the admissibility of detainees' evidence in *S. v Alexander*[94] but it expressly refused to decide the matter, and in the judgment implicitly supported the *Hlekani* approach. In *Schermbrucker* v *Klindt*[95] the Appellate division reiterated its position expressed in the *Sachs* case, namely 'the purpose of the detention, though it temporarily deprives the detainee of his liberty, is intended to induce him to speak, and any interference with that detention which may negative the inducement to speak is likely to defeat the purpose of the legislature'.[96] Thus the court decided that it had no power to order a detainee to appear personally before it to be examined and cross-examined on allegations that the police were maltreating him. In a minority judgment Williamson J.A. argued that the purpose of the detention procedure could not be extended to include bringing pressure upon a detainee. The only purpose of Section 17 was to deny the detainee access to any outside person whilst he was being interrogated:

> I consider it would require different words and different circumstances to justify a necessary inference that Parliament intended to create a system of 'inducement to speak', subject only to a detainee not actually being assaulted, not having his health or resistance impaired by inadequate food or living conditions, and not being interrogated in a manner commonly described as third degree methods.

In what became the leading case concerning the admissibility of evidence by a detainee held in terms of Section 6 of the Terrorism Act, *S. v Hassim*,[97] the court held that although the object of the section was to acquire information, the court retained its normal power to pronounce upon the evidence placed before it, bearing in mind that the circumstances under which the evidence was obtained might affect its credibility.[98] For this reason 'no hard and fast rule can be laid down', each case turning 'on the totality of its own particular facts and the impressions which the various witnesses make on the Court'.[99]

Hassim's case adopts the so-called 'piecemeal' approach to detainees' evidence, in contrast to the assertive approach in terms of which detainees' evidence is excluded on the grounds of psychological factors.[100] The adoption of an approach similar to that employed in ordinary criminal trials illustrates how the court treats the political trial as little different from an ordinary criminal trial.[101] In other words the *Hassim* court was only prepared to determine the truthfulness and reliability of a witness or accused who has been detained, on the basis of the ordinary methods for judging such evidence – namely demeanour, consistency and general impression created by the witness. Notwithstanding that such findings are notoriously difficult to reach, even where witnesses have not been subjected to interrogation in isolation,[102] the court was not prepared to adopt a different approach to detainee evidence.

A clearer example of the courts' reluctance to consider the process of solitary confinement as a form of duress sufficient to render inadmissible evidence gained during such period of solitary is found in *S. v Moumbaris*.[103] In that case Boshoff J. held that as the purpose of Section 6 of the Terrorism Act was to facilitate police investigation of 'terroristic activities and offences', it was extremely unlikely that the intention of the legislature would have been to regard such evidence as inadmissible owing to its being given during a period of detention. Consequently there was nothing in Section 6 which 'either expressly or implicitly precludes the police or the State from using such information obtained from a detainee in the prosecution of offences under the Terrorism Act or any other offences for that matter'.[104]

The judgment in *S. v Hoffman*[105] is an exception to this approach. In this case the court stated that the invocation of Section 6 of the Terrorism Act was, in itself, probably sufficient to tarnish the witness's image and make it impossible for the court to proceed with confidence on the basis of such evidence.

However, a number of cases subsequent to *Hoffman* have continued to ignore the effects the detention process has upon the credibility of evidence gained thereby. In *S. v Gwala* the court was prepared to hear evidence from an American professor of psychiatry, Dr Louis West, about the psychological effects of detention, but rejected such evidence. The court held:

> There is a great deal of acceptable police evidence to refute the allegation that they fed false information to detainees or subjected them to assaults, degradation or any other form of ill-treatment. . . . Although there may have been isolated instances of assault or improper treatment of detainees . . . the evidence as a whole satisfies us that the police did not follow the set pattern or system suggested by the defence and did not employ any such means to induce potential witnesses to make false statements.[106]

The refusal by the courts to consider the psychological impact of detention upon the detainee and the evidence gained in detention stems, to a considerable extent, from a complete lack of perception of the closed nature of the detention system.[107] For example, in the Appellate division judgment in the *Gwala* case,[108] Wessels J.A. said of Dr West's testimony: 'that interrogation of a detainee could have the effect referred to by Dr West must, in my opinion, be accepted. However, it must be borne in mind that a detainee is not wholly within the power of his interrogators.'[109]

The factors which Wessels J.A. regarded as constituting safeguards against the arbitrary exercise of power by the police were the Commissioner of Police's power to order a detainee's release, the requirement that the Commissioner supply the Minister of Justice once a month with reasons why a detainee should not be released, the fact that a detainee may write to the Minister who may order his release, and the fortnightly private visit by a magistrate if circumstances so permit.[110]

If the *Gwala* case revealed a misconception of the effect of the detention process as it exists in South Africa, the judgment in *S. v Christie*[111] reveals an even greater inability to take into account 'the compulsion inherent in custodial surroundings'.[112] In this case the court was required to decide upon the admissibility of a confession made by the accused in Johannesburg whilst being held under Section 22 of the General Law Amendment Act.[113] The accused had been arrested in Cape Town and interrogated by the security police throughout the night. On the following morning he had written a statement which, after it had been read by a Colonel in the security police, was signed by Christie in the presence of a police officer who was a justice of the peace. The next day Christie was transferred to Johannesburg where he made another statement prefaced with the words that he would 'add details to the statement already made.'[114]

Although the Appellate division assumed that Christie had been unfairly treated in Cape Town, that he had been made to stand all night while he was being questioned, that his feet became swollen and that he became tired, and that these circumstances induced him to speak, the court nonetheless concluded that the evidence established that the harassment to which Christie was subjected in Cape Town had ceased to operate in Johannesburg. While the court observed that 'had the first statement been tendered in evidence the trial court may have looked on all-night interrogation with jaundiced eyes and may well have excluded the statement',[115] it nevertheless held that his Johannesburg confession had been freely made without undue influence and was not invalidated by the earlier inducement to speak. The court supported its conclusion by reference to the following considerations, which have been extracted from the judgment of Diemont J.A.:

(i) A new team of policemen took charge of Christie in Johannesburg. They treated him with punctilious correctness.

(ii) Christie was cooperative in Johannesburg and, indeed, volunteered assistance in order to clarify details of the statement made in Cape Town, which the police had found to be unsatisfactory.

(iii) In answer to questions before the peace officer as to whether any promises had been made, or whether he was encouraged to make the statement, Christie replied, 'I am making this statement so that interrogation will not be unnecessarily prolonged, and so that it will not be necessary to arrest and interrogate a number of innocent parties'.[116] On this point, Diemont J.A. remarked:[117] 'He did not say that he feared that he would be made to stand again or that he feared that he might be subjected to other molestation.'

(iv) The peace officer confirmed that when Christie made his statement he appeared to be completely at ease and in an elated mood, such that his conduct could not be described as that of a browbeaten or frightened person.[118]

(v) The content of the confession revealed glimpses of his confidence, self-assurance and pride in his achievements.

(vi) The court asked why, if he were not acting under compulsion or undue influence, would he make a statement implicating himself so deeply. The court found the answer in the fact that Christie had become aware that the police had intercepted his mail and that consequently they had far more information at their disposal than he had originally thought. He must then have realised that the police knew not only what he had done but had proof of his 'underground' activities.[119] He was anxious to protect people whose names and addresses the police had found in a notebook, and in particular a young woman in whose company he had been seen.

The court thus concluded that 'the evidence establishes that the confession was freely and voluntarily made and was not induced by events in Cape Town'.[120]

Remarkably, Diemont J.A. was able to compartmentalise Christie's Johannesburg experience and separate it from the all-night session of interrogation in Cape Town. This approach is all the more surprising when it is considered that Diemont J.A.[121] referred with approval to the dictum of Schreiner J.A. in *R. v Nhleko*[122] to the effect that the onus rests on the state to prove that any statement of the accused which it tenders before the court was freely and voluntarily made and that if there was any violence before the statement it did not induce the statement immediately or because the effect of the violence had continued to operate. Given the nature of Christie's interrogation in Cape Town, which the court itself conceded might have resulted in Christie's statement being excluded,[123] it is extremely surprising that the court could be sufficiently confident that Christie's behaviour in Johannesburg was not that of a psychologically disturbed person, albeit temporarily, a confidence which allowed it to find that the confession was admissible.[124]

The meaning of 'freely and voluntarily' in relation to confessions and admissions was discussed in some depth by Williamson J. in *S. v Mpetha and Others*.[125] Here the issue was raised as to whether or not a statement obtained as the result of a statutorily authorised interrogation conducted under the express or implied threat of further lawful detention can in law be said to be freely and voluntarily made without there being undue influence present. The judge concluded that the criterion as to whether a statement had been given freely and voluntarily within the context of South African law was whether or not there had been an 'improper bending, influencing or swaying of the will, not its total elimination as a freely operating entity'.[126]

In deciding what considerations a court should take into account in deciding whether a statement has been given freely and voluntarily without undue influence, Williamson J. said:

obviously threats or promises are important factors and usually result in the exclusion of the statement for it is, from the practical point of view, exceedingly difficult for the prosecution to prove beyond a reasonable doubt that they did not influence the making of the statement or that their influence had been dissipated by the time the statement was made. More difficult to evaluate are the more intangible factors such as lengthy interrogation, confrontation, fatigue, youthfulness, etc. In general any practice is 'undue' which, if introduced into a court of law, could be repugnant to the principles upon which the criminal law is based. The practical problem is how to weigh such influence in the scale and evaluate its effect upon the will of the accused. It seems to me that in the end it comes down to a fair-minded practical judgment of the situation.[127]

As far as concerned the validity of statements made whilst a person was detained under Section 22 of the General Law Amendment Act or Section 6 of the Terrorism Act, the state argued that as these sections provided that a person be detained until he or she answers questions to the satisfaction of the police, any pressure exerted upon such person by the process of detention was lawful and did not amount to undue or improper influence.[128] By contrast *Mpetha* contended that as a matter of law any statement made in detention was inadmissible by reason of the inherent element of compulsion.[129]

The court adopted the piecemeal approach developed in earlier judgments described above, holding that the fact of detention should be taken into account when judging the admissibility of a statement made by an accused, but that as a matter of law the process of detention does not have 'to play a role of such significance that it automatically excludes any statement made pursuant thereto'.[130]

Thus Williamson J. was not prepared to consider that the process of detention per se rendered inadmissible any statement made during such process. Significantly, however, he rejected the state argument that detention creates a statutory duty to give information.[131]

Once the person being interviewed is cautioned and then indicates that he does not want to say anything it is in my opinion improper to direct further questions to him. If he answers these further questions the irresistible inference is that his earlier expressed decision to say nothing has been made to crumble by the pressures of the situation in which he then finds himself. All the more is this the case where a youngster in detention is confronted by policemen who appear to pay no heed at all to his clearly expressed choice.[132]

A survey of the record of the South African courts in relation to detainees' evidence and the 'right' enjoyed by detainees whilst in detention must at least allude to the attitude which has recently been adopted in Namibia by the South West African Supreme Court in *Nestor and Others* v *Minister of Police and Others*.[133] Although the detainees were released prior to the matter being heard by the court, a decision in respect of costs made it necessary for the court to decide whether an application for an interdict, inter alia, restraining the security police from assaulting the detainees, exerting unlawful pressure on the detainees in an attempt to influence them to answer questions, and holding the detainees in solitary confinement, would have been successful. Although on the evidence, the first two grounds for an interdict were rejected, the contention in respect of holding detainees in solitary confinement was successful. As the jurisprudential foundation upon which the judgment was predicated, Becker J.P. adopted the approach of Corbett J.A. in his minority judgment in *Goldberg and Others* v *Minister of Police and Others*,[134] and held:

> A convenient starting point flows from the fundamental approach that every person is entitled to the natural rights relating to his personal or his 'civil liberties', unless such rights are limited or taken away by legislative enactments or regulations, or are necessarily inconsistent with the purpose of the enactment under which they are held or with the circumstances of their detention.[135]

Distinguishing *Nestor*'s case from that of *Rossouw* v *Sachs*, Becker J.P. held:

> The right to be detained in solitary confinement and the right to take daily exercise in the open air appear to fall within the category of such basic rights. The various cases dealing with what have been held not to be basic rights, or comforts, such as for instance *Rossouw* v *Sachs* 1964 (2) SA 551 (A), concerning the right to be supplied with reading matter and writing material to detainees held under the provisions of Act 37 of 1963, are therefore of little assistance.... I have no doubt that, taking into consideration the principles which can be extracted from the various cases dealing with the rights and privileges of detained persons, a detainee held in terms of the provisions of AG 9 is entitled as of right to be detained in a cell of reasonable size under hygienic conditions, and that he is entitled as of right not to be held in solitary confinement, that is being kept in isolation without being allowed to work or to take any exercise and, following from this, that he is entitled to adequate exercise in the open air.[136]

Recent developments

Two recent decisions of the Natal Supreme Court cannot be omitted from this survey.

In *Mkhize* v *Minister of Law and Order and Another*[137] the full bench of the Natal Supreme Court had to decide whether or not it was legally possible for a court to order a magistrate to interview a detainee about alleged assaults by security police and to report his findings to the court.

It was argued on behalf of the Minister that while a magistrate who visited a detainee, as provided for in Section 29(9) of the Internal Security Act, was acting by virtue of his office in the service of the state, when such visit was conducted as a result of a request by a court he would be acting by virtue of the court's request.

In rejecting this argument Wilson J. said: 'There is nothing contained in Section 29 which in any way prevents the magistrate or the district surgeon from complying with the court's request during a visit to the detainee empowered in terms of the section, and that the magistrate or district surgeon in complying with the court's request would be acting by virtue of his office in the service of the State.'[138] The second leg to the Minister's argument relied upon the case of *Cooper and Others* v *Minister of Police and Others*,[139] according to which information gained by a magistrate would not be official information in the sense provided for in Section 29(7), such that the court was not entitled to this information.

In analysing the meaning of 'official information' Wilson J. said: 'I have no difficulty in understanding the prohibition in Section 29(7)(b) if the concept of 'official information' is confined to matters, directly or indirectly, relating to the reasons for, or the purposes of, the detention. Information of this kind is clearly of an official nature and one can understand why it might be contended that its disclosure would run counter to the purposes of the Act. Information relating to a detainee's health and his treatment whilst in detention is clearly of a different nature. In the absence of very special circumstances such information could not, in any way, adversely affect the reason for, or the purposes of, the detention. The legislature could not have intended that the information sought in this application would fall under the description "official information" and so leave it to the Minister to decide how much of the reports made by the magistrate or district surgeon should be disclosed to the court hearing such an application.'[140]

As for the decision of Trengrove J. in *Cooper*'s case that the court was not entitled to such information, Wilson J. said:

the statement that, because information is acquired by an official of the State, it becomes 'official information' in terms of the section, is, in my respectful view, a non sequitur. I prefer the reasoning of Didcott J. in *Nxasana*'s case. Like Didcott J., I consider that the decision in *Cooper*'s case ought not to be followed. I also agree with his criticisms of the expression 'official information'. The expression is not one capable of precise definition; nor is it necessary to seek to define it exactly. Usually it will not be difficult to decide what does or does not amount to 'official information'. One can, however, imagine cases, depending upon the circumstances, where such a decision may give rise to problems.[141]

However, in this case it was quite clear that information covering the health and welfare of the detainee did not amount to 'official information' as contained in Section 29(7). Such a finding allows the court to acquire direct information concerning detainees once an application has been made for an interdict restraining the police from assaulting a detainee.

An even bolder approach to ouster clauses contained in the Internal Security Act was adopted by Leon A.D.J.P. in *Hurley and Another* v *Minister of Law and Order and Others*.[142] The applicants approached the court for an order that a Section 29(1) detainee should be released. The application was brought on the grounds that (i) the requisite jurisdictional fact required in terms of the section to justify the detention could not even on a balance of probabilities be said to exist; and therefore (ii) the court's common law jurisdiction to protect the subject from deprivation of liberty and freedom against his will had not been excluded in terms of Section 29(6) of the Act. Mr Justice Leon first analysed the 'requirement that before a person can be detained in terms of Section 29, the policeman of, or above, the rank of Lieutenant Colonel must "have reason to believe" that a person has committed or intends to commit an offence as specified in the Act or is withholding certain information from the police'. For Leon A.D.J.P., this phrase meant:

the police need only adduce evidence showing that they have reason to believe. That means that they need only produce such evidence which shows that their belief is reasonable. They do not need to go the distance of producing additional information to show that their belief is correct and it would still be possible, in furnishing the required information, for the police to protect the identity of their informants and conceal the sources of their information.[143]

The court then examined the ouster clause and considered if it prevented a court from adjudicating upon whether the policeman in question had 'reason to believe'. The court interpreted the ouster clause restrictively, holding that there was nothing to prevent the courts from deciding whether the action taken by the police fell within the ambit of the legislation. In other words, the police objectively had to have 'reason to believe' that a person had committed or intended to commit an offence as defined in the Act, or was withholding information relating to such an offence, before it could be said that the police were acting within the scope of the Act. Only after the court had satisfied itself that such jurisdictional facts existed, would the ouster clause come into effect.

The approach of the *Hurley* court has found favour in South West Africa in the case of *Katofa* v *Administrator-General for South West Africa and Another*.[144] In this case the court, inter alia, examined Section 2(1)(a) and (b) of Proclamation AG 26 of 1978, which empowered the Administrator-General to issue a warrant for the arrest or detention of any person, if he is satisfied that the person concerned has committed or attempted to commit or in any manner promotes or has promoted the commission of violence or intimidation.

Levy J. held that 'to be satisfied the Administrator-General must have reason to be satisfied. In other words objective reasonable grounds must exist to make him satisfied and he must apply his mind to the consideration thereof.'[145]

In terms of Section 4(2) of the Proclamation, a detainee can insist on being furnished with reasons for his detention. Given this provision, Levy J. could find no reason why the Administrator-General should not divulge such information to the court. The court would then be able to consider the decision to detain and unless the Administrator-General could show some legal cause for his detention the court would be obliged to order the release of the detainee.[146]

The approach adopted by the *Hurley* and *Katofa* courts was not entirely novel. A number of academic commentators had argued in favour of such an approach for many years.[147] However, what was refreshing was the court's willingness to accept such arguments in favour of greater judicial control over the detention process. Such willingness was motivated by a clearly articulated premise, that 'illegal deprivation of liberty is a threat to the very foundation of a society based on law and order. Through the centuries the courts in democratic countries have jealously guarded and protected the rights of the individual to his liberty and their own jurisdiction in respect of such matters.'[148]

The Appellate division has given its imprimatur to the *Hurley* approach. In *Minister of Law and Order* v *Hurley and Another*, Rabie C.J., although relying on a narrower basis than Leon A.D.J.P., held that the detaining officer's 'belief' must be based on reasonable grounds and that the court is entitled to inquire whether the belief was reasonably held. In addition the court held that the onus was on the detaining officer to justify the detention under Section 29.[149]

Conclusion

Notwithstanding the recent enlightened approach of the courts to security legislation, the approach of the courts to the admissibility of confessions and admissions made by detainees has been disappointing, with one important exception. The South African courts have not been prepared to hold that a confession or admission made by a detainee is inadmissible unless there is clear evidence that it was made as a result of coercion or physical assaults during interrogation. It has been argued before the courts that from a scientific point of view information derived from detainees under conditions of detention will be tainted, for, as West has explained, 'you'd never know what part was true, what part was false and you couldn't rely on the witness if he was assured of the protection of the court from that moment on to ascertain at the time he was giving testimony whether it was true or not'.[150] However, the courts have refused to follow such an approach, and hence have used similar techniques in security cases to those employed in evaluating evidence in ordinary criminal trials.

Nonetheless, as has been mentioned above, the Appellate division in *S.* v *Gwala* warned that 'no court of law in this country would in any circumstances condone the employment by the police of any set pattern of interrogation which is either intended or calculated to result in a witness giving false testimony on oath'.[151] In political cases where the courts have been confronted with arguments that seek to prove that the process itself is oppressive, the supporting evidence has been derived either from studies relating to prisoners of war[152] or from academic articles summarising some of the psychological literature on the subject,[153] with particular reference to sensory deprivation. To date there has been no scientific evidence available that suggests that the South African security police employ a set pattern of interrogation designed to extract information in an involuntary fashion.

The objective of this study is to investigate such a possibility in order to assist in the development of a more accurate approach to the admissibility of detainees' evidence by South African courts. As part of this quest the following chapter reviews the psychological literature relevant to this area.

4 Psychological investigations

What psychological and physical processes and sequelae may be involved in the process of detention under South African security laws? In seeking some answers to this question, the following chapter examines the literature of a fairly wide range of psychological and psychiatric investigations. Certainly the studies, or even the areas of study, may not all be directly relevant to the South African situation. What precisely constitutes the South African situation is a matter for empirical investigation and is the concern of Chapters 5 and 6. However, knowledge of a wide range of potentially relevant or related studies provides a general picture of hypotheses, conjectures, and patterns of findings, and so is of use in this study.

Viewed from an armchair perspective, what does the situation of detention involve?[1] Clearly it includes actions of arrest and incarceration, for unspecified periods, with the strong possibility of prolonged periods of solitary confinement – even if the place of detention is not technically that of a solitary confinement cell formally used for punishment of convicted prisoners. It also clearly includes interrogation by security police, which may embrace a range of possible coercive techniques, both physical and psychological. Finally, in terms of statutory provisions it clearly includes the condition of social isolation, since family, friends, legal advisers, and medical doctors of choice are not necessarily granted access. The process may also involve some measure of either sensory or perceptual deprivation or both.

What are the demands of the situation from the point of view of the detainee? The answer is obviously to talk, or more correctly to answer questions to the ultimate satisfaction of the security police. In practice this means, in general, a demand to produce a written statement which may subsequently be used in evidence either against the detainee himself or herself or against fellow detainees. The potential penalties in both cases are severe; lengthy prison sentences for conviction under security laws or possible social ostracism or worse in the case of state witnesses. There are further subtle but equally stressful social psychological demands, such as maintaining face and dignity vis-à-vis the interrogators, and not betraying friends or political ideals. Any objective account must necessarily hold the situation to be a highly stressful one.

The psychological literature most frequently employed to account for processes and effects of the detention situation is that of sensory deprivation,[2] but it may not be the most appropriate analogy and would be dependent upon the actual techniques used for interrogation and confinement. A Canadian researcher, Suedfeld, in particular has presented a strong and persuasive case against viewing solitary confinement and sensory or perceptual deprivation as analogous situations.[3] His grounds for criticism are that the two situations use very different subject populations, the situations themselves differ in a number of respects, and people come to these situations from differing conditions of daily life. He also argues that sensory deprivation research is not analogous to political detention as the latter situations typically involve a number of additional techniques in conjunction, such as physical and psychological abuse, fatigue, hunger and sleep deprivation, all of which are highly stressful and anxiety-provoking. Therefore, effects in the case of political detention confound the differential contributions of solitary confinement on the one hand and more stress-inducing conditions on the other. Suedfeld has maintained that solitary confinement per se is not really a stressor. This claim will be critically examined later in the chapter.

What emerges from this kind of argument is the need at the very least to make distinctions between various kinds of conditions and their differential effects. For this reason the present chapter examines in turn research on psychological processes involved in sensory and perceptual deprivation, social isolation and confinement, torture, concentration camp conditions, the post-traumatic stress syndrome, conditions of learned helplessness and reactance, and finally, distorted communication techniques. We argue that all of these conditions, to varying degrees, may be implicated in detention situations in South Africa, and that a full review of research is necessary for an understanding of possible psychological processes and sequelae.

Restricted environmental stimulation

Suedfeld has suggested that the label 'restricted environmental stimulation' is more appropriate than the widely used term of sensory deprivation, as (i) many studies do not alter the level of sensory input, but rather their patterning, and (ii) the term 'deprivation' is inappropriate if it means complete removal; it is not, for example, analogous to food deprivation.[4] He argues that the term Restricted Environmental Stimulation Techniques, for which the acronym REST is a useful shorthand, is a more accurate term describing the various conditions.

Three different techniques are identified under the REST label: (i) reduced stimulation, formerly the term sensory deprivation, in which attempts are made to reduce the overall level of sensory inputs; (ii) perceptual deprivation, which alters the patterning or variation of stimuli, sometimes producing an overstimulation effect; (iii) monotonous stimulation, which involves reducing the variation of sensory stimuli. REST may also involve variations and combinations of these techniques. Additional variables such as social isolation and physical confinement (i.e. restriction to a limited space), which may have effects of their own, are frequently confounded with the first three conditions. Effects of REST may also vary owing to exposure variables such as duration and repetition.

It is now almost 35 years since the first experiments were conducted at McGill University by Hebb and his colleagues. Viewed in historical perspective, the research can usefully be divided into three phases. The first phase during the 1950s produced the 'discovery' studies of dramatic and sometimes bizarre effects, including visual hallucinations, anxiety symptoms and psychotic-like symptoms.[5] A number of the more dramatic experiential and experimental findings of the discovery were not subsequently replicated, and in retrospect are seen to have been due to certain peripheral features of the experimental conditions, which in turn provided an anxiety set. For example the 'panic button' was a common feature of experimental settings, to allow anxious subjects to release themselves from the experiment. In 1964 an experiment produced sensory-deprivation-type effects in subjects who were not exposed to sensory deprivation at all, but who were given the 'panic button' option to withdraw.[6] Therefore, when these fear-expectation techniques were withdrawn from experimental procedures, the more bizarre effects disappeared.

However, a number of effects were reliably obtained in the second phase of research, roughly between the late 1950s and end of the 1960s. This phase saw a refinement of research programmes, theories and techniques. Experiments were more sophisticated and programmes of research at places such as the Universities of British Columbia, Maryland and McMaster gave greater clarity to results.[7] Awareness was gained of the complexity of variables involved and of the complexity of interactions among variables. Most of what we now know as the reliable effects were established in this second phase.

The third phase, roughly from 1970, has shown a considerable decrease in interest although certain specialised programmes have continued. One example is the work concerned with compensation of certain sensory modalities when others are subjected to reduced input – the notion that blind people may hear better. The most striking feature of the third phase, though, has been the programmatic work of Suedfeld to demonstrate that REST and social isolation may have substantial positive applications, notably in the areas of clinical treatment of phobias and eating disorders, and in treatment aimed to reduce smoking.[8] He has also been particularly concerned to show the merits of solitary confinement as a rehabilitative technique in prison settings.[9] Other research in the general area of REST has clarified and consolidated results established during the second phase.

What then are the findings from reduced environmental stimulation research?

(a) Subjective phenomena: Early findings reported gross disturbances in perceptual fields, but later research failed to replicate these effects, and the present view is that very few subjects experience real hallucinations. If stringent criteria are used to define hallucinations, notably that the percept has an 'out-there' quality, it is perceived as uncontrollable, and also as real, then approximately three-quarters of subjects experience visual percepts, but only about 2 per cent experience hallucinations.[10] To clarify the concepts, visual experiences are labelled as Reported Visual Sensations (RVS). Results have tended to show that RVS incidence is lower for sensory deprivation (SD) than perceptual deprivation (PD) conditions. The range of unusual experiences has been confirmed by later studies. For example, subjects following 7 days of PD reported a higher incidence, compared to ambulatory controls, of vivid dreams, RVS, changes in body image, vivid memories, temporal disorientation, restlessness, anxiety, hunger and speech impairments.[11] SD in general seems to produce a lower incidence of symptomatology than does PD. Finally the RVS are now held to be more similar to drug-induced images[12] than psychotic-like states, where auditory stimuli dominate. As with many results from this area, effects are also subject to wide individual variation. Time variables have also been noted, with a progression from simple to more complex percepts over longer REST duration.

(b) Cognitive measures: There is common agreement that REST reliably produces cognitive changes, with the greatest changes occurring in a critical period of from one to two days. The greatest changes seem to occur under monotonous stimulation and PD conditions. Impairment has been found in respect of tasks requiring abstract reasoning, space visualisation, verbal fluency, numerical reasoning, but not tasks involving rote learning, recall and verbal reasoning.[13] There is evidence that cognitive decrements are transitory in nature and specific to the isolation environment. In general the pattern is that the greatest impairment occurs for the most complex and least structured tasks, requiring active reflection and manipulation of ideas, whereas highly structured and well-learned cognitive operations are the least impaired and sometimes indeed are facilitated. Suedfeld claims that a compensatory mechanism may be operating whereby logical, analytic thought based on verbal symbols deteriorates, while there is an increase in more involuntary-type imagery in various sensory modalities. It is also possible that cognitive changes are confounded with motivational alterations.[14]

(c) Susceptibility to influence: There is little doubt now that REST increases susceptibility to influence. It is precisely this feature that has led researchers over the last decade to perceive the more positive clinical uses of REST. Data show that primary suggestibility – body sway, susceptibility to autokinetic effect – is increased along with levels of basic hypnotisability, and increases are retained after release. Results

also show a general heightening of susceptibility to attitude change, but this differs across individuals and is highest among less intelligent and conceptually less complex subjects. It seems difficult however to generalise to areas involving strong commitment on the part of subjects, as most experimental procedures have used peripheral attitudinal areas.[15]

(d) Motor functioning: There is clear recognition of deleterious effects on dexterity, hand–eye coordination and other kinds of motor performance following prolonged periods of reduced stimulation. Gross motor coordination is also severely disturbed.[16]

(e) Motivation effects: Strong and consistent results have been shown for increases in a range of stimulus-seeking actions during and following periods of REST. The central idea is that stimulus reduction disturbs input balance, and the organism, operating on homeostatic principles, seeks to reinstate an optimal level of arousal and stimulation. This leads to behavioural attempts to obtain an increased variation of sensory input. Solid findings of increasing stimulus-seeking behaviour over successive days of impaired stimulation provide firm evidence to suggest a drive process associated with REST.

Jones has postulated an 'information drive' on the basis of evidence showing that information, rather than simply sensory input, is the stimulus most sought.[17] But with more complex information, subjects may be responding on the basis of competence motivation rather than simply information drive. In addition it is important to take note of a frequently ignored factor. Stimulus reduction also involves response reduction and concomitant reduction of feedback from the response. Behaviour usually elicits feedback to test the appropriateness of output, and this component may be a crucial aspect of appropriately adaptive functioning.[18]

That the homeostatic process is centrally mediated is demonstrated by established findings that deprivation in one sensory modality may be compensated by adjustment of sensitivity in another modality. These data reflect a basic organisational principle of the central nervous system, characterised by functional connections of a compensatory nature between the various sensory modalities.[19] The degree of stimulus-hunger varies across individuals, but there is little clear evidence of what the predictor factors may be in this regard.

(f) Physiological effects: Probably the most reliable finding is that of change in the functioning of the central nervous system as a result of REST. Most studies report change in EEG activity, regardless of length of experimental period. The pattern is one of progressive slowing of mean occipital alpha frequency during REST, which persists after removal but progressively increases over a subsequent week.[20] Greater reduction is found in PD conditions rather than SD conditions, akin to the greater cognitive impairment due to PD rather than to SD. REST also seems to affect physiological phenomena during sleep, revealing

changes in rhythms of sleep phases and an increase in amount of REM sleep. Once again substantial individual variations in physiological effects have been found.

(g) Individual differences, endurance and counteracting effects: One of the intriguing aspects of research has been the considerable individual variation in reaction to REST. Some subjects terminate within hours while others last two weeks with ease. In North American research the quitting rate has remained relatively constant; about one-third of subjects fail to last the initial prescribed period, whether that be specified as two, four, seven or more days. However, quitting rates did decrease slightly with the removal of anxiety-provoking experimental cues such as the panic button, and cultural factors also seem to play a role, as Japanese studies have shown a far lower rate of quitting.[21]

Despite the consistent findings both in tolerance for and in reactions to REST, there has been an equally consistent failure to find systematic personality predictors of these differences. On both fronts – endurance and reaction – the data have been 'unexciting and inconsistent'.[22] Measures of introversion–extraversion, field-dependence, ego-strength, neuroticism and anxiety have been employed with surprisingly little success. The strongest indicators are that creative and cognitively complex subjects tend to show lower decrements after REST, and that those with higher scores on an index of 'positive contemplation' (which reveals a positive reaction to opportunities for thinking about life and the meaning of things) are stronger on isolation tolerance.[23] Additional pointers are that those with a low index of control on projective techniques and those with a high gross motor-restlessness score may be lower in tolerance.

As regards possible counteracting devices to effects of REST, Zubek has shown that exercising, vitamin-enriched diets, and prior exposure to isolation, or conversely some prior training, are all factors that tend to reduce impairments and anxiety.[24] Secondly, periods of exposure are far less stressful, indicating that expectancy plays some significant role.

(h) Theoretical formulations: Three broad types of explanations have been utilised to explain effects of REST. *Neurophysiological* theories emphasise the function of the Reticular Activating System (RAS), which plays an important role in governing attention, perception and motivation. The RAS is conceived of as a homeostat, adjusting input–output relations. Low or unpatterned sensory input disturbs RAS relation to the rest of the brain, thereby producing both behavioural and physiological effects. A basic drive of the organism is therefore to maintain an optimal level of stimulation.[25]

Psycho-analytic theories conceive of a change in the relationship between ego and id functioning, as a result of a reduction in ties with external reality.[26] The central concept is that of ego-autonomy, which is seen as a capacity for self-government in relation to demands of both id and external reality. Reduced external stimulation threatens a capacity for reality-testing, thus disturbing ego-autonomy from external sources, as well as from inner id sources, since there is an increase in primary process activity and concomitant regression. Increases in visual imagery, fantasy, distortion of body image and depersonalisation would be expected. Miller argues that activities, such as mental exercises, that aid the autonomy of the ego will allow the adaptive process of 'regression in the service of the ego'. This permits spontaneously reversible mental images and fantasy, which closes off threatening aspects of external reality. Autonomy and self-government are retained however. To the extent that ego-autonomy is impaired, ego-passivity occurs, and with it 'regression proper'. Here repressed material begins to emerge into consciousness, because of lack of ego-autonomy from the id, and it is this material which is anxiety-provoking. According to this perspective, therefore, impairment of ego-autonomy could lead to serious psychological disturbances.

This sort of theorising provides us with some clues about mental survival mechanisms in the face of serious external threats, including severe interrogation, torture, or prolonged social isolation. Efforts to maintain ego-autonomy by self-stimulation – by mental exercises, singing, humming, reminiscence, or controlled fantasy – will improve tolerance for situations of either excessive or diminished stimulation. The general prediction is that those who are able to draw on inner resources without threatening ego-autonomy from the id are likely to adapt and show greater tolerance for REST, as well as for other stress-inducing situations.

Cognitive theories lay stress on the notion that REST reduces the person's search for order, information and meaning or disrupts processes whereby cognitive schemata are monitored or corrected. As a result there are increases in stimulus-seeking behaviours and compensatory shifts to obtain information from other cognitive sources, including visual images and fantasy.

It is clear that these three theories operate at different levels and utilise different languages, making comparison extremely difficult. All have certain heuristic strengths, and as the phenomena under study are highly complex it is premature to exercise final judgments in terms of their relative merits. Definitive evaluation will have to await further research.

It is quite clear that REST does produce a wide range of reliable effects across all aspects of psychological functioning. Earlier research indicated that most of the effects were psychologically deleterious, but more recent perspectives suggest that many of the effects could be utilised in positive directions. Psychological research over the past decade or so has become far more aware of the social context as an important explanatory variable, and it is highly likely that the evaluation of REST as either positive or negative will depend to a large extent on such wider contextual issues. A fuller picture of this aspect will emerge in the following section, which deals with the closely related situations of isolation and confinement.

Social isolation and confinement

Do conditions of social isolation and physical confinement per se, whether considered separately or in combination, produce negative psychological effects? The problem is nicely situated by contrasting the views of Lucas and Suedfeld.[27] Lucas, along with others,[28] has claimed that solitary confinement (SC) is a form of torture. Because of variations in the intensity of the experience, individual differences in response, and absence of clearly observable sequelae, Lucas suggested that solitary confinement is not always recognised for what it is. He acknowledged that not all instances of solitary constituted torture, but noted that solitary was frequently used as a measure of coercion and control. Clearly the other extreme, used for political interrogation, would be perceived as torture.

Against this Suedfeld argued that it was false to regard SC itself as a form of torture. His main argument claims that false analogies have been drawn between brainwashing and solitary effects, that in political situations solitary is commonly used along with a variety of other treatments, and that Lucas failed to mention any beneficial effects of controlled isolation. Suedfeld suggested that SC could be used as a commendable rehabilitative technique: severity and duration could be 'strictly controlled to prevent harm to the individual'. At the same time he recognised that it could 'be misused by being applied to individuals who react badly to it, or by being administered to an excessive degree'.[29] Suedfeld does recognise at least the potentially harmful nature of SC under certain conditions.

How does the available evidence help us in forming an opinion about these opposed stances? In making distinctions between the three major dimensions of isolation, those of social isolation, confinement and sensory reduction, we are following categories recognised by earlier researchers.[30] In practice, of course, they seldom occur in such discrete categories, but usually in combinations.

Evidence in the form of anecdotal accounts and written personal experience of castaways, explorers, isolated small groups, and prisoners is fairly abundant,[31] and all report the experience to have been stressful. Yet the reports of survival tactics and adaptive and coping strategies are equally impressive, showing that people can and do cope with very prolonged and extreme conditions of social isolation. But these are the survivors; and highly verbal, intelligent and capable ones at that. The data, while important and impressive, are clearly drawn only from a limited and biased sample. The problem, however, with more controlled studies is that the period of social isolation is usually fairly brief, and subjects are volunteers who usually may choose to leave the situation. Thus there is not really much firm evidence about effects of social isolation.

In a recent study comparing conditions of REST and social isolation (24-hour period) with ambulatory controls, it was found that both REST and social isolation separately increased motivation for information, with social information preferred above non-social information.[32] An earlier study by Zubek and colleagues found effects for both social isolation and confinement separately, in comparison with ambulatory controls (one week periods for each). Significant decreases in alpha frequency were obtained for both social isolation and confinement. Similarly both conditions involved greater variety of visual experiences, greater subjective restlessness, worry, inefficient thoughts and body image changes than for control subjects. In addition, questionnaire data found that 'loss of contact with reality' was more frequently experienced in social isolation than in confinement or controls.[33] These studies indicate that part of the pattern of REST results may be due to social isolation per se. Haythorn, in reviewing a range of work, commented that although much of the evidence was indirect there was positive support for the notion that 'social isolation is by itself a significantly stressful condition for at least a substantial number of people, and that reactions to it are distinguishable from those of confinement and stimulus reduction'.[34]

Solitary confinement effects, usually in prison settings with voluntary subjects, have been studied and one recent review reported that no major adverse responses were observed in seven studies.[35] A closer examination of some of these studies suggests however that the reviewer's conclusions were oversimplified. Gendreau and colleagues studied twenty prison-inmate volunteers, randomly assigned to seven days' SC or a control condition (still in cells but not isolated). Among SC subjects they found progressive decrease in EEG alpha frequency similar to that of SC and PD experiments. Related to this they found that 'visual evoked potential' latency became shorter over time, indicating an increased readiness to respond to external stimulation as SC progressed.[36] Another study showed low levels of physiologically measured stress in prisoners subjected to ten days of SC. But it is notable that there was a high degree of early termination; and 7 of the first 16 subjects withdrew within the first two days, and were replaced in the study. Thus low stress results could have been the product of sampling bias.[37] Furthermore, caution should be exercised in interpreting these studies, which used other confined prisoners as controls, for confinement itself has been shown to be stressful and therefore may mask adverse effects of SC.

In a more extensive recent study by Suedfeld and others, 103 prisoners from three types of institutions were tested on a range of measures. Some 71 had experienced SC while 32 acted as controls. Very little difference was found between the two groups for separate institutions. When subjects from two of the institutions were pooled, however, data showed that longer time in SC was associated with distrust, suspicion and higher levels of hostility. Similar subjects with experience of solitary from the third institution also showed higher measures of hostility. As there were no pre-measures, it is of course not possible to argue that these resulted from SC. On subjective stress measures there were no differences between ratings of SC by subjects with experience of solitary and ordinary prisoners' ratings of general prison environment. From interview results the researchers concluded that there was 'no evidence to support the hypothesis that SC is universally or uniformly aversive or damaging to inmates'.[38] Apparently the first 72 hours were quite difficult but adjustment after that made SC quite tolerable. After SC, some complained of being unusually shy or 'spaced out', but there was pride in doing SC time and coping, which added to status among inmates. As regards overall attitudes toward SC, however, 59 per cent were negative, 25 per cent indifferent, and only 16 per cent were positive.[39] In conclusion the authors claim that SC is tolerable and sometimes beneficial. This they suggest contradicts the notion that prison SC is equivalent or even close in experience to either experimental SD or solitary confinement for interrogation purposes. The present interpretation of this study is that the data are very mixed; while there appear to be no serious retrospectively reported adverse effects of SC, the prisoners also did not seem to be overjoyed by the prospect of SC.

In considerable contrast, Grassian recently reported a study conducted through a court order mandating psychiatric evaluation of 15 inmates in Massachusetts, who had experienced a median period of two months of SC. Findings based on clinical interviews suggested that 'rigidly imposed SC may have substantial psychopathological effects' and that 'this study strongly suggests that the use of SC carries major psychiatric risks'.[40] In the interviews, prisoners seemed to minimise the quality of reactions to SC, yet went on to report serious symptoms. Of the 14 interviewed, 11 reported generalised hyperresponsivity to external stimuli, 10 reported affective disturbances (massive free-floating anxiety, dizziness, racing heart, panic), 8 reported difficulties with thinking, concentration and memory (4 of these reporting acute confusional states and subsequent partial amnesia) and 7 reported perceptual distortions and de-realisation experiences. Further psychiatric symptoms evidenced were disturbances of thought content (for the most part ideas linked with persecutory fears) and problems with impulse control. The set of problems was seen as strikingly consistent across the range of inmates. Finally, all reported very rapid diminution of problems on release. Symptom severity apparently did not correlate with speed of recovery.

Very different pictures of the effects of SC in prison settings emerge from these different studies, probably in part because of variations in methodology. Evaluation of this work will be held over until confinement effects have been examined, but at this stage it could be suggested that SC looks less and less like a single unified entity, but more as a situation varying along a continuum of severity.

Confinement as an independent variable has been clearly shown to produce adverse effects. In a study comparing SD, social isolation and confinement, Zuckerman and colleagues[41] concluded that stress effects of confinement were 'rather massive' without subjects being socially or sensorily isolated. Confinement produced negative affect, somatic complaints, tedium, and arousal stress and endocrine arousal. Similarly, in the study cited above, Zubek and colleagues[42] showed that both confinement and social isolation produced effects. Their interpretation claimed however that much of the effect may have resulted solely from confinement. In a further interpretation they suggested that at least half of EEG effects supposedly due to PD may in fact be the product of confinement.

Wider reviews have also concluded that confinement per se is stressful. Haythorn concluded in a review article that confinement was a stress-inducing entity.[43] Zubek reached the same conclusion, adding that the physical size of the confinement chamber may be important. He cited evidence showing that smaller cubicles were responsible for greater slowing of alpha rhythms than larger chambers.[44]

If we draw together the evidence presented above it is possible to make the following general statements. Confinement itself clearly seems to be aversive, and while the data on social isolation are less clear it also appears to have effects that contribute to overall REST outcomes. The data from prison SC studies are equivocal, but if one considers them overall in conjunction with results from confinement, it is possible to suggest that Suedfeld has presented an over-positive view of SC. If we return at last to an evaluation of the Suedfeld–Lucas debate in the light of evidence that both confinement and social isolation in themselves are stressors, it seems that the weight of evidence favours a cautionary view of SC. Suedfeld unquestionably has made important points, and it is certainly no longer possible to view outcomes of REST or isolation in only negative terms. He has also noted that SC may be used for four rather different purposes: indoctrination and interrogation by totalitarian regimes, quarantine, punishment, and rehabilitation.[45] As regards rehabilitation it must be recalled that a good deal of highly impressive evidence has been collected, showing that brief periods of voluntary and controlled isolation can be successful in facilitating smoking cessation as well as clinical treatment of phobias, eating disorders and other problems. But we should also recall that Lucas similarly claimed that not all forms of SC or isolation could be regarded as torture. The most solid finding, then, with which both Lucas and Suedfeld must agree, is that SC is not a single entity with a unitary set of effects. Rather, effects will depend on specific conditions of isolation and more importantly on the social context of the process.

With respect to this social context of SC we suggest that the argument tilts in favour of Lucas. Suedfeld, in his commendable efforts to promote the newer, positive view, has tended to underrate in tone rather than in terms of facts the possible negative effects of solitary for coercive purposes. By his own admission solitary for interrogation usually involves a cluster of procedures, which in combination produce a situation of overstimulation, high in intensity, low in predictability and controllability. In our view Suedfeld tends to slide over the centrality of SC within that noxious treatment package. The most correct view seems to be that SC heightens vulnerability. Indeed, it is exactly this state that enables it to be useful for therapeutic purposes. However, a state of induced psychological vulnerability in the context of coercive measures is unlikely by any stretch of the imagination to result in positive outcomes. As SC in prisons would largely be a method of behaviour change under fairly coercive conditions, this too should be questioned. Viewed in this social contextual perspective, there seems little doubt that solitary confinement for purposes of interrogation, indoctrination or information extraction does have aversive effects and should be regarded as a form of torture.

Research on sequelae of torture

The United Nations' Declaration Against Torture, adopted unanimously on 9 December 1975, provides the following definition of torture:

(1) For the purpose of this Declaration torture means any act by which severe pain or suffering, whether physical or mental, is intentionally inflicted by or at the instigation of a public official on a person for such purposes as obtaining from him or a third person information or confession, punishing him for an act he has committed, or intimidating him or other persons. It does not include pain or suffering arising only from, inherent in or incidental to, lawful sanctions to the extent consistent with the Standard Minimum Rules for the Treatment of Prisoners.

(2) Torture constitutes an aggravated and deliberate form of cruel, inhuman or degrading treatment or punishment.[46]

This is currently the most authoritative internationally recognised definition. The main points are the severity of suffering, the deliberateness and purposefulness of the act, and the involvement of state officials. For the first time the notion of severe mental suffering was explicitly included as part of the full definition of torture. This means that psychological methods involved in coercion of detainees have been declared as torture and are thus prohibited. There are limitations in the definition, in particular the exclusion section in Article 1 (even though it is covered by the earlier Rules for the Treatment of Prisoners[47]) and the precise definition of 'cruel, inhuman or degrading treatment or punishment', but it is more embracing than earlier efforts and is important in terms of its covering psychological techniques.

Research on physical, psychiatric, and psychological sequelae among torture victims has increased considerably in recent years, largely as a result of the efforts of medical groups in Amnesty International and the International Rehabilitation and Research Centre for Torture Victims in Copenhagen. At least two special issues of medical journals have been entirely devoted to torture research.[48] The review here will be primarily concerned with psychological and psychiatric aspects, but mention should be made of the important research attempting to trace skin sequelae to electrical torture.[49]

What are the usual forms of torture employed? A number of studies have revealed a sadly standardised list of procedures.[50] Beatings and physical assault always head the list, with more than 90 per cent of victims reporting such treatment. Other physical procedures include falanga (beating on the soles of the feet), trauma to the head, forced standing, electric torture, food and sleep deprivation, suspension, and sexual assaults. Less frequent, but also reported, are submersion in water, shining of bright lights, burning, blindfolding and hooding, use of manacles, pharmacological torture, dental torture, and assault by animals. (Refer to Appendix H for details of incidence reported in recent research.) Psychological procedures most frequently used include verbal abuse, solitary confinement, threats of execution, threats to family members, mock execution, false accusations, witnessing torture of others, nakedness and a number of other humiliations. (Refer to Appendix I for details of incidence of psychological forms reported in recent research.) Victims in these studies were drawn from countries as diverse as Chile, Greece, Argentina, Northern Ireland and Spain, yet broad patterns of torture were quite similar. Certain regional differences have been noted though: falanga is more common in Greece and Latin America, while sexual assaults and rape are more prevalent in Latin American than European countries. In Northern Ireland a particular combination of procedures (hooding, prolonged wall standing, subjection to white noise, and food, drink and sleep deprivation along with beatings) appeared to be used as a dominant pattern.[51] Despite such national variations, the frequency of central techniques such as beatings, shocks, solitary and a wide range of humiliation methods is depressingly common.

In considering torture sequelae we should note that they may be direct, such as problems in walking due to falanga and organic brain damage due to head trauma, or indirect, such as gastro-intestinal problems as a consequence of poor living conditions, nutritional deficiencies, lack of exercise or physical exhaustion. Somatic symptoms reported at the time of examination (between two to seven years after torture) in one study of 135 victims included the following: headaches (35%), gastro-intestinal symptoms (32%), cardiopulmonary symptoms (22%), pains in the joints (19%), difficulties in walking (17%), reduced hearing (15%), vision disturbance (14%).[52]

All empirical findings have agreed, however, that the most severe and most common sequelae are psychological. Furthermore, psychological problems persisted and caused considerable stress years after the events of torture. Cathcart and colleagues and Warmhoven and colleagues, in separate Canadian and Dutch studies of 11 and 43 tortured refugees (respectively), agreed that all victims had severe psychological problems characterised chiefly by anxiety-related symptoms and labile emotions. Other problems concerned difficulties with concentration and memory, sleep disturbances, and psychosomatic symptoms. Headaches are frequent in all research findings.[53]

In the most comprehensive study to date (135 victims from a number of countries), 80 per cent of subjects complained of symptoms which arose after imprisonment and torture. At the time of examination, 62 per cent evidenced pathological signs, sometimes a number of years after release. A total of 75 per cent reported one or more psychiatric symptoms. Chief among these were sexual problems (49% of the sample), a cluster of emotional symptoms (48%) largely related to fear and anxiety, sleep disturbances (47%) and impaired memory and concentration (45%). In a particular sub-sample (39 per cent of the total), the authors claimed to have found evidence of a symptom complex corresponding to that of the post-traumatic cerebral syndrome. Of the 52 victims who showed three or more of the following problems – headaches, sleep disturbance, memory and concentration impairment, alcohol intolerance, sexual and mental/emotional difficulties – 44 had been subjected to trauma of the head during torture. On the basis of their findings, these researchers did not feel that they could propose a specific 'torture syndrome', but they did find evidence of a symptom cluster in a sub-sample strongly correlated with head trauma.[54] A separate study of 17 tortured Greek men confirmed the finding of a relatively high incidence of sexual dysfunction (29%) as a sequel to torture.[55]

Similar patterns of findings were reported by Allodi.[56] In one study of 41 victims from four Latin American countries, virtually all subjects reported affective disorders to varying degrees (anxiety, depression, labile emotions and specific fears) and psychosomatic disorders, under which Allodi included nervousness, insomnia, tremors, pains, recurrent headaches, nightmares and panic reactions. Approximately half the victims also reported behavioural problems (including aggression, irritability, withdrawal, suicide attempts, severe sexual dysfunctions) related to changes in personality, as well as problems associated with impairment of intellectual activities such as memory, concentration and disorientation. Allodi has suggested that the cluster of symptoms constitutes a clinical entity and warrants the label of 'torture syndrome', similar to or constituting a sub-classification of the generic category of post-traumatic stress disorder.[57] Agreement about the clinical status of the 'torture syndrome' is far from settled, as Warmhoven and colleagues, Rasmussen, and Randall and colleagues[58] do not find evidence sufficient for designation of the label. It is clear, however, that severe psychological sequelae have been found in the majority of torture victims, and that the pattern of symptom types has been remarkably similar across different studies.[59] Incidence of particular symptom types may vary, and is probably due to both specific torture regimes and individual differences. Evidence for the presence of a 'torture syndrome' per se, apart from the post-traumatic stress syndrome, must await further research.

Effects of torture are not restricted to detainees themselves. Research on families and children of torture victims has begun, and the few available reports indicate serious disruptions between marital partners, exacerbated by sexual problems, as well as a range of psychiatric symptoms in children. Allodi reports research showing withdrawal, intense fear and depression among three-quarters of children of tortured parents, with other symptoms, such as sleep disturbances, regression in behaviour and in school performance, appetite loss and over-dependence on parents, in more than half.[60] Cohn and colleagues in a sample of 75 Chilean children found 36 per cent to be anxious and noise-sensitive, 35 per cent to have sleeping problems and a range of further behavioural and relationship problems.[61] In a follow-up study four years later of 58 of these same children, data showed a highly significant increase in the number of children experiencing symptoms, as well as in the number of complaints. The authors concluded that the symptomatology of children of torture victims may increase over time, and that these problems affect the family as a whole.[62]

In conclusion, it is clear that strong evidence has been provided of a pattern of severe psychological sequelae in both victims and their children following imprisonment and torture. Since research in this area is so recent it is not yet clear to what extent further delayed symptoms may appear many years after the event, but research does show the presence of symptoms a number of years following torture events. Rehabilitation work in this area has also recently got under way, particularly in Toronto and Copenhagen, with very promising results.

Concentration camp survivor studies

On the face of it the dissimilarities between the situations of South African security detention and the Nazi concentration camps appear too substantial for any insights to be gained from a study of the latter. On the other hand a study of the psychological sequelae of concentration camp experiences would provide valuable knowledge of psychological reactions to situations of extreme stress. For that reason we touch on it here. The literature in this area is of course vast, and space limitations allow only a brief discussion of the main aspects.

The general concentration camp situation, although it varied from camp to camp, is too well known to require detailed description here. From a psychological point of view the extreme stressfulness resulted from a combination of factors: physical exhaustion from starvation and very heavy work-loads; incredible physical cruelty of almost every imaginable kind; daily humiliations; the constant threat of death; isolation from home, family and friends; confinement under appalling conditions; the indefiniteness of imprisonment and the lack of any certainty about the future. Among survivors a fairly clear and consistent pattern of physical and psychological symptoms was identified, which was seen by many researchers to be sufficiently consistent and regular to warrant the label of 'concentration camp syndrome' or less frequently a 'survivor syndrome'.[63] It is well recognised that symptoms and vulnerabilities may persist for decades after the event.[64] For example, recent work has shown that among Norwegian ex-concentration camp prisoners, morbidity rate of admission to psychiatric hospitals was 40 per cent higher than for the general Norwegian population. Similarly, the mortality rate during the decade 1965 to 1975 was higher than for the general population.[65]

The symptom picture is characterised by signs of emotional numbing and withdrawal or dissociation – a psychological 'closing off'[66] – as well as neurasthenic-type symptoms of extreme fatigue, lack of initiative, irritability and emotional lability. Hoppe found virtually all of 145 survivors he studied suffered from a range of psychosomatic symptoms.[67] Anxiety symptoms, sleep disturbances and nightmares, sexual problems, and intellectual impairment of memory, attention and concentration, were commonly reported with high degrees of frequency. Physical symptoms included pathological exhaustion, persistent underweight, aged appearance, headaches, dizziness, diarrhoea, reduced sexual potency and amenorrhoea.

In one of the most extensive studies of concentration camp sequelae, Matussek provided a good deal of order in understanding the complex picture.[68] He conducted a factor analysis of the fourteen major somatic and twelve psychiatric symptoms, using a sample of 144 survivors. This analysis yielded four types or dimensions of disorder. Two dimensions were purely somatic; gynaecological disorders, particularly amenorrhoea, formed one (almost half the sample reporting such problems) while internal disorders involving cardiovascular and pulmonary-bronchial complaints (half the sample reported strong presence) constituted the other somatic symptom complex. The third dimension was labelled the 'psychophysical syndrome' and included a combination of physical and psychological complaints. Matussek also called this cluster a 'depressive exhaustion syndrome' and noted that this was the combination most frequently recognised as the concentration camp syndrome. Symptom loadings on this factor included head complaints, memory and concentration problems, tiredness and apathy, depressive mood states, anxiety dreams and sleep disturbances, inner agitation and irritability, and disturbed vitality. The final dimension covered only psychological complaints including mistrust, feelings of isolation and paranoid ideation. This was recognised as a 'social disorder' since it disturbed fundamental relationships with fellow human beings. About one-third of the sample experienced this 'mistrust' symptomatology strongly while 43 per cent reported strong presence of the psychophysical syndrome. The psychological symptom clusters were associated with more severe camp conditions than the purely somatic.

On the basis of these findings Matussek presented a strong case against the view of a single concentration camp syndrome. Rather, he argued, response to extreme stress may take a number of forms, depending partly on the precise conditions and severity of stress and to a certain extent upon personality structure prior to persecution. The duration of incarceration did not affect symptomatology in this study. As further support for the argument of a number of different forms of response, Matussek factor-analysed the psychological symptoms of the 39 per cent of survivors who had received psychiatric diagnoses on examination. Four separate psychological symptom clusters were found for this group. They were described as poor social contact, disturbed vitality, anxiety, and depression. Matussek extended his inquiry beyond this narrow clinical sphere by also looking at psychological complaints among the wider sample of 210 survivor cases. Factor analysis of this whole group revealed three different basic forms of psychological disturbance. The first, labelled as 'resignation and despair', was strongly observed in 56 per cent of the whole sample of 210 interviewees. The second factor, 'apathy and inhibition', denoted general passivity and included hypochondriacal complaints. The third was described as 'aggressive-irritable moodiness' and included irritability, dissatisfaction, self-pity and emotional instability. Roughly 41 per cent of the full sample reported strong symptoms of both these second and third forms of psychological symptoms. Matussek found a small group of about 12 per cent of the total sample who were relatively free of these psychological symptoms, and an equally sized group who evidenced strong symptomatology across all three psychological dimensions. The differentiating characteristic between these two extreme groups was found to be that of 'activity'. The symptom-free survivors were physically and psychologically active at the beginning of persecution while the heavy-symptom group were found to be passive and resigned from the beginning of incarceration.

Matussek's work provides a very useful way of viewing categories of responses to stress. While it casts doubt upon the existence of a unitary syndrome, it must be recognised that the symptoms found in this study were the same as those reported by other writers. In addition, like other studies, the number of survivors entirely or almost free of symptoms (psychological and physical) was relatively small. All research is agreed that the majority of survivors were found to be suffering from debilitating disorders that remained persistent. When it is recognised that the survivors are a self-selected group, precisely because they survived, and may thus constitute a psychologically hardier group, then the effects of concentration camps are revealed as catastrophic. Furthermore, as in the case of torture victims, symptomatology has been observed in the second generation of camp survivors. Children of survivors have frequently been shown to evidence apathy, depression, lack of emotional involvement and feelings of emptiness.

In understanding the psychology of survival, the literature on camp survivors has stressed the earliest period of incarceration as critical in selection of survivors. Expectation plays an important mediating psychological role. Fenichel in his theory of trauma stated that unexpectedness increased the effect of a trauma. 'The essence of the ego is anticipation of the future. Consequently, unexpected and unanticipated events are liable to overwhelm the ego.'[69] Thus the initial shock of the first few days or weeks acted as a selection principle between those who survived and those who did not. The suddenness of transition was claimed to subject the mental state to a strong increase in stress in such a short period that the effect could not be assimilated mentally by normal means. The greatest number of suicides and psychotic outbreaks occurred during the first few weeks. In the struggle for self-preservation additional mental energies, a 'mental emergency regime', had to be summoned.[70] This required a shifting of mental energies from the world of objects and reality, to the world of self. Many survivors have described this process as one of a change in emotions, a numbing or killing of feelings. It has also been described as a process of depersonalisation, detachment or of inner estrangement. This process, so important as a survival defence mechanism in the critical earliest phases of persecution, remained subsequently as a major psychological effect in survivors. It would seem that for many survivors the basic psychological senses of trust, of emotional integration and of invulnerability, were never entirely regained. These processes probably constitute the core of the various forms of sequelae found in former concentration camp inmates.

Although we have argued that the concentration camp differs substantially from the detention situation, it is nevertheless possible that some of the psychological processes in reaction to considerable stress, as described above, may be operative in both situations. For example, one study found remarkably similar symptom patterns in war sailors and concentration camp victims although the situations were very different. In common there was the indefiniteness of time, the constant possibility of death, and isolation from home, job, family and normal social fabric.[71] A recent study of 168 Dutch people taken as political hostages also revealed similar short-term negative effects although only a few situational variables were in common with concentration camps.[72] It is these common symptom features that have been recognised in the psychiatric classification of the post-traumatic stress disorder.

Post-traumatic stress disorder

Although reactions to severe stress conditions have been recognised since the late nineteenth century, and following major wars have been labelled variously as 'combat fatigue', 'war neurosis', and 'battle stress' or in lay terms such as 'shell shock', it is only as recently as the third edition of the Diagnostic and Statistical Manual of Mental Disorders (DSM-III) published in 1980 that the disorder has been granted an appropriate recognition and label, and has been associated with stressors other than combat stress.[73] Research on concentration camp survivors played an important part in this wider category recognition. The first (1952) DSM-1 provided the category of 'gross stress reaction', which covered a similar type of disorder, as a reaction to great or unusual stress. But gross stress reaction was defined as a transient and reversible reaction; if it persisted, another diagnosis was to be given. Inexplicably at a time when refinement in the concept would have been warranted, the category was deleted entirely from DSM-II in 1968, and the space left vacant.

DSM-III description of post-traumatic stress disorder, chronic or delayed, defines the stressor as one that 'would evoke significant symptoms of distress in most people, and is generally outside the range of such common experiences as simple bereavement, chronic illness, business losses or marital conflict'.[74] Specific stressors mentioned include rape and assault, military combat, natural disasters such as floods and earthquakes, accidental disasters such as car accidents with serious injury, aircraft crashes, large fires, and deliberate man-made disasters such as bombing, torture, and death camps. It is recognised that some stressors frequently produce the disorder (e.g. torture) while others produce it only on occasions (e.g. car accidents). The disorder is apparently more severe and longer lasting when the stressor is of human design. DSM-III also recognises that impairment may either be mild or affect nearly every aspect of life. Two subtypes are recognised; an acute disorder with good prognosis is diagnosed if symptoms begin within six months of trauma and do not last longer than six months, whereas a delayed onset and long-lasting symptomatology is designated as the chronic or delayed subtype. Thus no official subtype is granted either to the 'torture syndrome' or to the 'concentration camp syndrome', but both are included under the generic label.

No precisely equivalent category is provided in the international nomenclature as given in the ninth revision of the International Classification of Diseases (ICD-9). The most similar label is that of acute reaction to stress, which is defined as a very transient disorder in response to exceptional physical or mental stress, that usually subsides within hours or days. Clearly this definition is insufficient to describe research findings of disorders in torture and concentration camp victims.

The essential clinical features required for a diagnosis of post-traumatic stress disorder are defined as follows:

(1) Occurrence of a stressor that produces significant distress symptoms in nearly all people.

(2) Re-experiencing the traumatic event by at least one of the following: (a) recurrent and intrusive recollections; (b) recurrent dreams or nightmares; (c) suddenly acting or feeling that the event was occurring again in response to some trigger stimulus.

(3) Numbing of responsiveness to, or involvement with, the external world manifested by at least one of: (a) decreased interest; (b) feeling of detachment or estrangement from others; (c) marked constriction of emotional responses.

(4) At least two of the following cognitive or autonomic symptoms: (a) hyperalertness or exaggerated startle responses; (b) sleep disturbance; (c) guilt about surviving, or about behaviour required for survival; (d) memory or concentration impairment; (e) avoidance of activities that arouse traumatic recollections; (f) intensification of symptoms by exposure to events that resemble or symbolise the original trauma.

Associated features include: depression and anxiety symptoms, emotional and autonomic lability, irritability and emotional outbursts, impulsive behaviour, headaches, and alcohol and drug abuse. As depressive, anxiety or organic mental disturbances are so closely related, it is suggested that such diagnoses are made in addition to the post-traumatic stress disorder.

As with any classifications there are advantages and problems with the DSM-III designation. It is important to have a clear definition of the long-recognised reactions to extreme stress, particularly if one bears in mind the likely psycho-legal implications (including compensation settlements) that may follow events such as torture and death camps. It is also obviously important to be able to draw upon definitions of the severity of disorders in the humane struggle towards the abolition of torture.

Two major problems with the post-traumatic stress disorder are evident. The first concerns the conceptual implications of a unitary syndrome, and the concomitant requirement that all four diagnostic criteria listed above should be met before a diagnosis of post-traumatic stress may be made. If Matussek's research findings on concentration camp survivors are correct, then a unitary designation is false.[75] The practical implication is that a number of Matussek's subjects, although suffering debilitating disorders, may not have qualified for compensation on the grounds that their disorders were of a more specific nature than that recognised as the full-blown syndrome. The same may occur for many torture victims. Research has already indicated that sequelae may be somewhat more situationally specific than those currently recognised by DSM-III.

The second problem is that the aetiology and pathogenesis of post-traumatic stress disorder remain largely invisible.[76] In this regard it may be suggested that the treatment of natural disasters such as floods, and human-designed events such as torture, as equivalent stressors could be found to be mistaken. We submit that the meaning and the causal attributions assigned to the two classes of events are highly dissimilar. As a result aetiology, pathogenesis and symptomatology may vary between the two forms of stressors in quite critical ways. For example, pathological mistrust, as found by Matussek, is far more likely to be characteristic of human-designed stressors. Treatment then may have to take rather different forms, as already shown in rehabilitative work with torture victims.

As regards aetiological and treatment theory it may be useful to take note of the psychological work drawn together by Janis.[77] One of the key factors identified by research in a number of different traditions is the loss of a taken-for-granted sense of psychological and physical invulnerability. This sense of invulnerability acts as a core protective mechanism in normal psychological functioning. Once a person has experienced helplessness to protect the self from harm, this basic sense of confidence can no longer be maintained. The earliest phase of internment in concentration camps provided a good description of such processes at work. The essential loss of protective invulnerability may provide an explanatory core for the widely observed post-traumatic stress phenomena, but at this stage it awaits further research.

Interrogation and confessions

The extraction of information through interrogation constitutes the central component of security detention in South Africa. Although a range of other stress-inducing factors may be involved in detention, interrogation itself can involve processes and dynamics that are stress-producing and could lead to involuntary actions on the part of the detainee. Research related to this area is quite extensive and is often referred to under the label of 'brainwashing'.[78] However, this is frequently not the most appropriate term, for interrogation is often concerned with extracting confessions and statements without necessarily aiming to change attitudes in the detainee. The 'brainwashing' label is a leftover from specific situations researched in the 1950s, notably Russian and Korean interrogation techniques.

The problem here is to identify the social-psychological processes operative in the interrogation situation, apart from those involving physical coercion. In this respect research has found that interrogation tactics involving physical assault or threats of violence were less frequently rated as effective than were 'non-coercive' tactics.[79] Biderman provided a useful introduction to the psychology of interrogation in his interviews with USA air-force prisoners captured during the Korean War.

Interaction during interrogation is, like other communication situations, a social encounter. It is primarily the interrogators' manipulative use of normal rules or conventions of social encounter that renders the situation coercive. For example, in everyday conversations it is taken for granted that questions will be answered. Thus POWs found themselves worn down by the difficulties of breaking this convention and refusing to answer. Answers such as 'don't know' and 'can't remember' were used twice as much as outright refusals. Silence by the detainee is furthermore manipulated either as indicating confirmation or as being incriminating – silence implying that the person has something important to hide.

Communicative manipulation of detainees' frustration and hostility is another important source of stress. Frustration builds up in the detainee as a result of false accusations, verbal abuse, personal attacks and unanswerable questions. Prisoners are then faced with the problems of managing pent-up hostility. Outright expression of hostility could lead to retaliatory violence, but blocking of hostile expression is one of various factors leading to subsequent guilt on the part of prisoners. As a result, interrogators are sometimes able to control the deflection of hostility onto other objects or persons that suit their purpose, for example other prisoners.

Further stress is induced by the prisoner's need to shield the inner, more covert aspects of personality, a need to protect against 'losing control' that so obviously gives the upper hand to the interrogator. Similarly the role of a prisoner itself may be used as a manipulative device by interrogators. The need to 'keep face' as a prisoner, in relation to fellow prisoners, is a stressful, demanding task. The psychological needs to maintain a positive self-image, and to maintain a consistent role in the face of a situation where talk itself may be dangerous and where silence is manipulated, constitute a highly stressful situation and at least partly account for the considerable number of persons who have given some statement or information even against their dearest wishes or (in the case of POWs) against military orders.

Communication is clearly central to any captive–captor relationship, and it is suggested that at least some of the 'effects' of detention are due to manipulative and distorted communicative devices.[80] Apart from those already mentioned above (false accusations and verbal abuse), other distorted communications may be used as the stock-in-trade of interrogation:

(i) Contradictory information, as when detainees are given information only to have it denied later. Such information may contain serious, affectively laden information, for example news that fellow detainees have talked or that family members have been hurt.

(ii) Sham total information – a weakening technique in which a false impression, using details of information, is given that all is known to interrogators.

(iii) Counter-effect, of which the most classic example is the variation

of friendly and kind interrogators with brutal and threatening ones.

(iv) Double-bind techniques, whereby contradictory messages or emotional ones are given in the same situation, yet both messages bind the receiver into a trap.

(v) Reinforcers. Low-key verbal and non-verbal reinforcements are probably the most common variety of almost any conversation and certainly are used in interrogation.

(vi) Hypnotic techniques. As hypnosis is difficult to achieve on non-willing subjects, it is unlikely to be a frequently used formal technique. But subtle use of suggestion on subjects already weakened by other means (such as solitary confinement) may well be practised on a wide scale.

(vii) Lack of information, used strategically, is probably the most common of all coercive devices and hardly requires further discussion.

These communicative devices either separately or in combination may contribute to confusion, disorientation, uncertainty, and heightened affect in detainees.

It is usually recognised that the practice of interrogation goes beyond the use of communication devices by themselves, and employs a combination of techniques. Three of the key elements in such combinations have been described by Farber, Harlow and West as those of debility, dependency and dread.[81] Debility is produced by semi-starvation, fatigue, disease, constant humiliation and chronic physical pain through beatings and other physical abuses. This results in loss of energy and incapacity to resist even minor abuses. Dependency is the product of the totalitarian regime imposed by captors and is demonstrated to captives by deprivation of those factors needed to maintain sanity and life. Solitary confinement over prolonged periods clearly strengthens the dependency upon captors. Dread is simply the state of chronic fear induced by captors through a range of threatening devices. The authors, using learning theory, claim that this debilitating DDD package is employed to provide reinforcement for behaviour desired by the captors. Relief of DDD conditions produces greater willingness on the part of captives, and structures the situation so that captives learn that DDD alleviation is a positive reinforcer for desired actions.

What degree of effective resistance may occur under these sorts of conditions? In similar conditions Farber and colleagues reported that 95 per cent of USA prisoners in Korea failed to meet the stringent requirements for 'commendable behaviour'. On the other hand only 15 per cent 'cooperated unduly'. Great individual variability was shown in response to DDD conditions, but two of the most important resistance factors were noted as a state of physical health, and initial or chronic levels of anxiety. In addition, anticipation of possible stressor conditions reduced the shock factor of DDD and facilitated adaptation and resistance. The authors note, however, that under extreme degrees of DDD severity, few may be expected to resist indefinitely.

Even short of such severe conditions it is important to note that the fairly ordinary conditions of incarceration that accompany interrogation place captives under constraints which weaken their resistance. Such constraints include regulation of behaviour in prisons, constant supervision, lowered self-esteem, and humiliation on a daily basis. Compliance with such ordinary, insignificant demands may begin the process of compliance with greater demands. And underlying the process of compliance is a state of psychological helplessness, which is the purpose of DDD-type conditions.

Learned helplessness and reactance

'A person or animal is helpless with respect to some outcome when the outcome occurs independently of all his voluntary responses.'[82] A substantial amount of laboratory evidence, mainly relating to animals, shows that when an organism has experienced trauma it cannot control, a number of reliable consequences follow. Firstly, its motivation decreases and it fails to avoid further trauma, such as electric shocks. Secondly, even if it does respond and the response alleviates the trauma, it appears that the learning process has been disturbed, for the organism shows trouble in perceiving and learning that the response worked. Thirdly, the organism's emotional balance is disturbed. Signs of anxiety and depression predominate.

A good deal of sound experimental evidence by Seligman and his colleagues has further shown that it is not the trauma itself but the inability to control it that is responsible for the condition of helplessness. Although there has been less evidence with regard to human subjects, a number of other studies have given added support to Seligman's thesis. Glass and Singer, for example, in a classic study on effects of urban stress, found that exposure to uncontrollable noise produced deficits in motivation for problem solving.[83] They also concluded that the mere belief that noise could be controlled had beneficial effects. Hiroto found further support for the notion that uncontrollability leads to helplessness in humans. He also discovered that learned helplessness in humans is produced by the contributing factors of cognitive expectation (whether outcome is expected to follow skill or chance) and personality factors as measured by internal–external locus of control.[84]

Does helplessness generalise and become part of a more basic change in personality, or is it situationally specific? Evidence suggests that it does generalise. Findings with humans have shown that helplessness, apart from producing defensive deficits, also retards the solution of cognitive problems. It seems to produce a basic cognitive set, in which people believe that success and failure are independent of their own skilled actions.

Seligman employs a cognitive-learning approach to explain this process. At the core of the theory is the expectation of control or lack of control. It appears that once the original cognitive set of controllability is disrupted, and replaced with the expectation that actions and outcomes are independent, it becomes more difficult to regain the original set. Initial struggling gives way to resignation and a helpless state, whereas initial fear of the aversive stimulus gives way to depression.

It should be noted, however, that the state of helplessness in experiments is a statistical effect, and not all subjects suffer so. In studies with dogs, Seligman reports that about two-thirds respond to uncontrollable shocks with helplessness, while about one-third remain normal. Evidence showed that these differences could be accounted for by past history of exposure to controllable contingencies.

Evidence has been reported showing that uncontrollable shock may produce physiological consequences. Levels of norepinephrine, a neuronal chemical transmitter, were found to be depleted in animals exposed to uncontrollable shock. Uncontrollability also produced weight loss, appetite reduction and ulcers in rats.[85] In related fashion, two experiments by Pennebaker and colleagues with college students showed that uncontrollable noise led to increases in reported physical symptoms such as racing heart, dizziness, short breath and flushed face.[86]

Effects of unpredictable events such as natural disasters may well be due to the basic processes described by Seligman. Although technical distinctions may be made between predictability and controllability, the two are difficult to separate. We may recall that unpredictable periods of confinement produced more serious effects, and the unpredictability of concentration camp and torture situations add to the traumatic effects. It goes without saying that lack of control and unpredictability constitute central elements in situations of political interrogation and torture.

A second, closely related theory dealing with loss of freedom has been proposed by Brehm.[87] In contrast with Seligman's theory, Brehm claims that when behavioural freedom is threatened, motivational arousal occurs, and attempts are made to restore freedom. Although both theories are premised on the same underlying motivational assumption – that persons are motivated to maintain relatively effective control over their environments, the two theories make different predictions. Learned helplessness suggests that persons exposed to uncontrollable outcomes will become passive, depressed and demotivated. Reactance theory suggests that persons react to loss of control by becoming hostile and aggressive towards agents of restriction. A feasible integration of the two could be effected by considering them on a time-scale.[88] It is likely that reactance would precede learned helplessness when initial expectation of control is fairly high. If the actual situation then continues to provide evidence of low control, then the processes predicted by learned helplessness would follow. In the context of detention, it is possible that behaviour of detainees would change over time, as often reported in anecdotal cases of former prisoners. Psychological attempts would be made in the earliest phases to retain and restore certain measures of control, and to retain at least a sense of personal freedom. However, if aversive lack of control persists to a sufficient degree, motivational, cognitive and emotional impairments will follow. Prolonged periods of uncontrollability are then likely to produce the set of sequelae so frequently reported in torture, concentration camp and political interrogation cases. But as with previous findings it is necessary to note that individual variation is likely in responses predicted by both reactance theory and learned helplessness.

Psychological processes and detention in South Africa

Throughout the preceding review of literature we have stressed the need to examine attentively the social context and precise conditions before resorting to hasty analogies or concocting simplified predictions of likely psychological processes or sequelae. Similarly, it has been argued, and evidence has been forwarded to show, that individual differences and other variations may occur in all the situations surveyed above.

Nevertheless, it must also be stressed that fairly reliable and consistent evidence has been shown of typical reactions, of psychological vulnerabilities, or of potentially debilitating physical and psychological outcomes right across the areas reviewed. As a very general interpretative rule of thumb one may say that the stronger the traumatic conditions, the more predictable the typical psychological processes and outcomes, with concomitantly less individual variation.

What is the applicability of these findings to detention without trial in South Africa? From the legal survey provided in Chapter 3 it is clear that detention in South Africa involves at the very least a closed system of incommunicado internment, social isolation and in many cases solitary confinement for varying but potentially prolonged periods. It certainly involves lengthy periods of interrogation with the high probability of distorted communication techniques and debilitating factors that usually accompany interrogation. Detention may or may not involve all components of REST, although for those held in solitary confinement the monotonous stimulation component is certainly applicable, and this may have effects similar to those of sensory deprivation. Though it depends upon precise conditions, alteration of usual perceptual levels may also be applicable. Because of the closed system of detention, with no statutory protection available from agents outside, it is further entirely reasonable to expect the DDD elements of dependency and dread to be salient for detainees. The widely held knowledge of substantial numbers of deaths in detention is certainly likely to add to the fear held by detainees. Katz, in probably the only earlier empirical psychological study of detainees, involving assessment of attitudes and feelings of twelve former detainees held for periods of 3 to 41 weeks during 1981 and 1982, found that the third DDD element, debility, was not particularly applicable to the South African detention situation. Her results reported symptoms including detachment, hyperalertness, insomnia, restlessness, nervousness and tremor, which show congruence with some of the symptoms expected of a post-traumatic stress disorder.[89]

These likely conditions of South African detention form a formidable list of stress-inducing combinations. While individual variations in response to these conditions are of course possible, the general research findings would suggest a high probability of debilitating psychological effects as a result of such a combination of stressors. This combination in itself almost certainly meets the criteria for torture as defined above, and moreover we have not yet considered physical aspects of torture.

The repeated allegations of physical torture and abuse of detainees in South Africa found annually in security trials, the local and international press, and in many other publications,[90] are too well known to require further comment here. Needless to say, state officials consistently deny these allegations. The courts have also seldom made findings of systematic assaults perpetrated by security police. What is the case, then, regarding torture?

In 1982 the Detainees' Parents Support Committee (DPSC) collected 70 statements and affidavits from South African detainees claiming that systematic and widespread torture was used by the security police.[91] Some 54 cases (77 per cent of the sample) claimed to have been beaten, kicked or otherwise assaulted. There were 28 cases of enforced standing, 25 cases of claimed suffocation, 25 cases of being kept naked during interrogation, 22 cases of electric-shock torture, 20 cases of substantial sleep deprivation, 19 cases of hooding, 14 cases of genital assault, 11 cases of enforced suspension, 11 cases of death threats, and further details of physical and psychological abuse. Nobody would doubt that such actions constitute torture. The Minister of Law and Order attacked the DPSC, claiming that it was seeking sensational publicity by handing the memorandum to the press.[92] The torture allegations were apparently not investigated any further.

In another recent study of torture allegations under South African security laws, Geldenhuys searched press clippings from English-language metropolitan newspapers over the period 1975 to April 1982.[93] Although this search cannot be claimed to be exhaustive, and newspaper accounts themselves are subject to numerous biases and limitations, not least because of wide-ranging legislation curtailing the South African press, the study does offer further information of torture claims during detention.

Altogether 161 cases of torture allegations were found, many emerging during political trials of former detainees. The majority were South African rather than 'homelands' or Namibian cases, though this finding reflects the clippings sampling more than anything else. The frequency of reported allegations increased during periods of heightened political resistance, notably during the years 1976, 1977 and 1980. While it is not possible to quantify the findings in a formal manner, a close scrutiny of the data reveals a fairly clear picture of the relative frequency of claimed torture forms. As regards physical torture the methods were (listed in order of frequency):

> beatings and general physical assaults, including severe beatings with a range of implements, kicking, punching, slaps in the face, head knocked against wall and other assaults;
> forced standing and enforced strenuous exercises;
> electric shocks applied to various parts of the body;
> food and sleep deprivation;
> enforced nakedness;
> shackling, including chains, leg-irons, handcuffs;
> a few cases of genital assault;
> unreasonably long periods of interrogation.

Among the alleged psychological forms, in rough order of reported frequency, were the following:

> threats, including cases of interrogation at gunpoint;
> pressure to make false statements;
> humiliation methods, including withholding of toilet facilities, stripping and derogatory language use;
> solitary confinement;
> blindfolding and hooding.

No clear details of psychological sequelae were available, but reports indicated that a number of cases were referred for psychiatric treatment and anxiety symptoms. Furthermore, numerous deaths of security detainees occurred during this period.

The general picture obtained from Geldenhuys's study provides support for the DPSC claims of systematic and widespread torture of security law detainees, as does the comprehensive United Nations report of 1973.[94] Covering the period from 1963 to 1972, this report provided 74 typed pages of details about torture during detentions. Reported methods of torture were remarkably similar to those described in the above-mentioned studies. Of particular note was the widespread use of 'statue torture' (lengthy periods of enforced standing in a demarcated place under threat of assault) among women and white detainees during the mid-1960s.

Virtually no systematic research on physical or psychological sequelae has been conducted in the South African situation. However, one further hardship imposed upon former detainees has been suggested in a recent study investigating the stigma attached to detention by the wider public. Questionnaire responses from nearly 600 employers showed that former detainees were as stigmatised with respect to employment opportunities as ex-convicts and former mental patients.[95]

Although the above work is invaluable in providing insights into conditions of detention, and seems to give incontrovertible evidence of widespread practices of torture in South Africa since the inception of detention provisions, a more systematic scientific study of both conditions and sequelae is still lacking. It is the purpose of the present empirical work to investigate further the conditions of detention and interrogation in South Africa as well as psychological processes and sequelae both during and following detention. The following chapter provides details of the study and the main empirical findings.

5 The empirical study

As indicated in Chapter 1 the intention of this study is to examine in detail the events, conditions and psychological processes associated with detention practices in South Africa. Although a considerable amount of information pertaining to conditions of detention has been assembled over the years from court records, inquests, newspaper reports, and investigations by churches and other organisations, no large-scale empirical study of such conditions has yet been conducted.

With respect to psychological aspects of detention in South Africa even less work of a formal nature has been done, as the final section of Chapter 4 indicated. It is well known that a number of detainees and former detainees have been admitted to psychiatric units, and press statements, journal articles and the like have criticised detention as being psychologically damaging. The MASA Report made similar claims from a theoretical perspective, but virtually no attempts have been made to investigate empirically psychological processes during detention and claimed effects following release. As previously stated the Rabie Commission failed to provide detailed information on conditions or practices during detention, or any information on psychological aspects.

The aim of the present study is therefore to investigate claims from former detainees regarding conditions, events and actions prior to and during detention; as well as to investigate systematically claims by former detainees of psychological states and symptoms during and following detention.

Procedure

The study was conducted by means of personal interviews with former detainees on a countrywide basis. A semi-structured questionnaire formed the basis of the interview. Certain sections such as modes of harassment prior to detention, physical conditions of internment, physical and psychological treatment during detention, health symptoms during and following detention, as well as standard demographic information, were asked in a structured fashion. For other areas, covering general description of detention experiences, forms of arrest, and modes of coping with detention, directed questions were alternated with open-ended requests for discursive information. This was encouraged in order to facilitate a less stilted exchange during the interview and also to gain a picture of more candid descriptions of events and psychological states.

Interviews were conducted by a total of nine interviewers at or around the major centres of Johannesburg, Durban, East London, Port Elizabeth and Cape Town. All the interviewers were trained and thoroughly briefed on the use of the interview schedule, by either one or both of the principal researchers. Further written instructions were provided to all interviewers. Additional checks and visits were made by principal researchers during the course of fieldwork.

Fieldwork was conducted between the period from mid-1983 to November 1984. It should be mentioned that for certain periods during that time, particularly the months leading up to and subsequent to the elections of August 1984, access to former detainees was considerably hampered by the generally difficult political climate, widespread security clampdowns involving substantial numbers of arrests and detentions, and military interventions which virtually sealed off access to many townships.

Each interview required roughly an hour and frequently longer for completion. Interviews were held at venues most suitable for respondents and interviewers. All interviews were conducted in English, although a few cases required the use of interpreters. With the permission of respondents, all interviews were audio-taperecorded, excluding only those sections covering demographic information, which was collected by hand. Interview material was subsequently fully transcribed from audio-tapes, and coding of information for quantitative purposes was done from the typed transcriptions. Transcriptions were also used for the purpose of obtaining detailed descriptions of experiences and events, and for the purpose of qualitative analyses. Coding for quantitative purposes was all completed by one person, thus promoting consistency. As a check on coding reliability, a 10 per cent sample of transcripts was also coded by a second person. Excluding demographic information (which was straightforward), agreement on all remaining questions was 90 per cent; this may be regarded as quite satisfactory.

Quantitative data were largely treated descriptively, by means of frequency tables and cross-tabulations. In addition, some comparative analyses using inferential statistics were also conducted.

Sample

The sample consisted of 176 cases of detention. As 12 persons reported multiple detentions (7 persons describing two detentions each, 4 persons reporting three detentions, and 1 person who was detained four times), accounting for 30 cases of the total, the number of persons actually interviewed was 158. However, in the data which follow, each case of detention is treated as the unit of analysis. In certain cases not all information was supplied whether because of unwillingness on the part of the respondent, interviewer error or indistinct taperecording. Therefore the number of cases used for different areas of analysis may vary. When data are expressed as percentages, they are calculated on the basis of the number of cases answered, deleting missing cases.

In demographic terms the sample was made up as follows (full details of sample composition are given in Appendix A): 145 were males (82,4%) and 31 were females (17,6%); political category or 'race' comprised Africans 127, coloureds 18, Indian 18, white 13; mean age at time of detention was 25,3 years while mean age at time of interview was 29,3 – a difference mean of 4 years; 61 cases failed to provide religion and of the remaining 115 cases, 93 (80,9%) gave their religion as Christian, 11 as Moslem and 5 as Hindu; in terms of marital status 120 (70,0%) were single, 27 were married and 22 were in steady relationships at the time of detention; the majority lived in family arrangements (85,1%) or with friends (7,8%) at the time of detention. In terms of year of detention the sample consisted of 23 in the period 1974 to 1976, 71 in the period 1977 to 1980, and 78 in the period 1981 to end 1983. Only four were 1984 detainees.

As regards area of political work at the time of detention, the majority (92 or 53,2%) were connected with student organisations, trade unions (25 or 14,5%), community work (21 or 12,1%) and political organisations (15 or 8,7%). In order to gain some idea of the representativeness of the present sample with regard to work area, present data were collapsed into four main categories and compared with data collected by the South African Institute of Race Relations and other bodies for the years 1980, 1982 and 1983. Data for these three years were combined and expressed as percentages. These comparisons, as percentages, are given in Table 1.

Table 1. Areas of work: comparison of present sample with combined population data from years 1980, 1982 and 1983.

	Present sample (%)	Combined population (%)*
Student, youth, teachers	57,2	65,8
Community and political	20,8	15,6
Trade union and workers	14,5	10,8
Other work, e.g. church, lecturers, journalists, etc.	7,5	7,8

* *Source: Survey of Race Relations in South Africa, 1980, 1982, 1983.*

Although the present sample is slightly underrepresented with regard to student, youth and related work area, and slightly overrepresented regarding unions and community work areas, in general the pattern is rather similar. The present sample may be taken as adequately representative in terms of area of work.

As regards employment categories rather than general area of political work, the present sample was distributed as follows (main categories only are given): student (99 or 52,2%), skilled worker (18 or 10,4%), professional (14 or 8,1%), clerical (8 or 4,6%) and unemployed (7 or 4,1%). These figures represent employment status at the time of detention.

With regard to education level, the sample consisted of the following: high-school level (110 or 63,6%), university level (54 or 31,2%) and a small sprinkling of other categories. The sample of detainees was therefore of a relatively well-educated level. No comparable data of education level among the general population of detainees were available, but the present sample may reasonably be viewed as representative.

Information pertinent to the geographical distribution of the sample was collected in a number of different forms concerning the (a) respondents' place of origin, (b) place where detained, and (c) place where finally held, and these categories were collected in terms of cities and wider geographical region. Here only the distribution in terms of region where detainees were held is reported (for a full breakdown see Appendix A): Transvaal (54 or 30,9%), Eastern Cape (43 or 24,6%), Border (34 or 19,4%), Natal (24 or 13,7%) and Western Cape (20 or 11,4%). Again, no population distribution information is available, but from common knowledge of detention patterns this sample seems reasonably representative of the general pattern.

The sample in this study was restricted to detainees who were held under South African security legislation, and therefore excludes those detained in the so-called 'independent states' such as Transkei and Ciskei, and also excludes those detained in Namibia. Further sampling procedure guidelines were to exclude as far as possible detainees who were subsequently convicted and imprisoned (although a few such cases were finally included), and to target the sampling largely towards those who had been detained for purposes of interrogation. Table 2 provides the sample breakdown in terms of legislative Acts, which in turn have been combined into categories expressing the purpose of interrogation. Data are complicated by the fact that many detainees were held under one Act, then transferred to regulations under another Act. Therefore Table 2 expresses figures in terms of first, second and third legislative procedures. The more detailed breakdown is given in Appendix D.

From Table 2 it is clear that a substantial majority of the present sample of cases were interrogation detainees: a total of 130 cases (76% of the sample). It is also clear that a sizeable number were initially held under 'short term' legislation, then transferred largely to interrogation sections, with a few transfers to preventive or witness sections.

Apart from the sampling guidelines and limitations mentioned

Table 2. Distribution of sample in terms of type of detention

Type of detention	Legislative sections:	first	second	third
Interrogation	s.6 and s.29	75	54	1
Preventive	s.10 and s.28	12	18	2
'Short term'	s.22 and s.50	85	2	–
Witnesses	s.12 and s.31	–	3	4

1. Data are given as raw numbers, not percentages.
2. Sections 28, 29, 31 and 50 are of the Internal Security Act 74 of 1982; Section 6 is of the Terrorism Act of 1967; Sections 10 and 12 are of the Internal Security Act of 1950; Section 22 is of the General Law Amendment Act of 1966.

above, respondents were obtained wherever possible and willing, and therefore no formal claims may be made about representativeness of the sample in relation to the general population of South African detainees. As we have indicated, however, the sample closely approximates the wider population in terms of work area, and there is no reason to suspect that it is substantially unrepresentative of educational level and geographical location. To gain a further idea of the representative nature of the sample, data on 'race' and gender of South African detainees during the two-year period July 1980 to end June 1982 are compared with data from the full sample here, which covered the period 1974 to 1984. Although such a comparison is not without problems, the paucity of official information on detention renders it the only one possible. Comparative data are presented in Table 3.

Table 3. Gender and 'race': comparison of present sample with data of South African detainees 1980 to 1982.

		Present sample (%)	Total S.A. detainees July 1980–June 1982 (%)*
Gender:	male	82,4	82,8
	female	17,6	17,2
'Race':	African	72,2	75,2
	coloured	10,2	15,9
	Indian	10,2	3,1
	white	7,4	5,1

* Original figures from Annual Report of Director-General of Justice, reported in *Survey of Race Relations in South Africa*, 1982, p. 206, and 1983, p. 523. Figures from 'homelands' were excluded.

Although some slight differences are apparent for the racial composition, the global distributions of both race and gender are highly similar for sample and for 1980–2 population. This lends substantial further support to the claim that the sample is reasonably representative of South African detainees in general, with the one obvious exception that the present sample overrepresents the interrogation-type detainees as a proportion of all detainees. Yet even in this respect the sample may not be entirely unrepresentative. A calculation of relative proportions of the major types of detention taken from official figures[1] for the periods July 1977 to end June 1979 and July 1980 to June 1981, reveals the following as percentages of all South African detainees: interrogation 45%; preventive 26%; 'short term' 16%; and witness sections 13%. In these terms the present sample with a preponderance of interrogation-type detainees would not be wholly unrepresentative of the general pattern. However, calculations based on a different set of figures given by the Minister of Law and Order for whole years 1980 and 1981[2] reveal a rather different pattern, where the majority of detentions were short term (61%), followed by interrogation (25%), then preventive (9%) and finally witness sections (5%). It is not fully clear what may account for the differences in official figures given, but it is feasible that the first set excludes detainees held in police cells and reports only those held in prisons.

To gain some rough idea of the total population of South African detainees over the decade covered by this study, official and unofficial figures were surveyed. (See Appendix L for summary of detainee numbers, 1974–84.) No official figures at all were available for 1974 and 1975. From about mid-1976 to late 1983, the period in which the large majority of our sample cases (96%) fall, official data indicate that there were in excess of 5 500 people detained in South Africa under all provisions. It is likely that the figure is really in excess of 6 000 as both sets of figures surveyed showed gaps of certain periods. Expressed as a percentage of the latter detainee-population estimate, the present sample of cases constitutes roughly 3% of the total population, yet as we have seen there are reasonable arguments to suppose that it is acceptably representative of the whole. It is therefore possible to argue that generalisations may be made from present results with sound justification, particularly as regards detention for interrogation purposes.

Results

Results of the quantitative empirical work, which largely take the form of descriptive frequency tables, are presented in a number of sections, following a rough logic of the time sequence of detentions. Results therefore begin with pre-detention events, then cover details about patterns of arrest, before moving to a third section describing general statistical patterns of detention. Within the process of detention itself, results are further presented for physical conditions of detention, interrogation patterns, personal contact with both authorities and non-authorities, as well as details of claimed physical and psychological torture. Health problems are examined in terms of symptoms experienced during detention as well as upon release. Finally a few exploratory analyses of relationships between certain detention conditions and sequelae are presented in the form of inferential statistical analyses.

(1) *Pre-detention aspects.* As we have already seen in the discussion on the sample, involvement in certain areas of work predisposes people to the possibility of detention, to a greater extent than for other types of involvement. In recent years certainly, black students' organisations have constituted the most vulnerable work area. If we cast the net wider it is clear that involvement in student, youth and education-related aspects is associated with the highest rates of detention, followed by community, political organisation and trade-union-related activities.

The high detention rate of students is obviously due to the almost continuous unrest and organisational activity since Soweto 1976. Detention figures peaked between mid-1976 to mid-1977, in 1980 and 1981, and again in 1984. The first two peak periods are strongly related to activities in black education including protests, school boycotts, stayaways and organisational growth.[3] The 1984 peak has yet to be fully analysed, but on the surface it has clearly to do with continuing activity in black education, as well as with resistance to the new constitutional proposals and the August 1984 elections for the tricameral parliament.

It has frequently been alleged that police harassment is a standard part of the wider aspect of political oppression in South Africa.[4] It may be expected if this was the case that a reasonable number of detainees will have experienced such harassment prior to detention. Table 4 gives an abbreviated summary of results, cross-tabulated by gender and racial categories. Fuller details are given in Appendix B.

Table 4. Pre-detention harassment by gender and racial categories (%)

Harassment type n = 157	Male 131	Female 26	African 112	Coloured 15	Indian 17	White 13	Row total 157
No harassment	41	46	41	27	47	54	41
Raids/visits	28	35	30	33	29	15	29
Tailing/following	26	15	21	47	24	31	24
Short-term detention	12	8	11	13	18	–	11
Intimidation family	9	4	7	20	6	8	8

Results expressed as rounded-off percentages.

Results from Table 4 show that almost 60 per cent of the 157 cases, for which full answers were available, claimed to have been harassed by the police or officials prior to detention. Apart from those forms listed in Table 4, a range of infrequent forms were mentioned, including phone-calls and tapping, harassment by riot police, detention of close comrades, visits to bosses at work by security police, being banned, attacked, called to report to security police, questioned at roadblocks, threatened with arrest, and having mail opened.

From the breakdown by gender and race in Table 4 it is apparent that substantial variations in forms of harassment were not strongly evidenced, apart from slight suggestions that whites were less harassed than blacks. Reference to breakdowns by age and regional area given in Appendix B suggests that the youngest age group, below the age of 20, from the Eastern Cape region were the most harassed. Least harassed were the older groups, over the age of 35, and those from Natal and the Western Cape.

What was the mental state of detainees prior to detention? Because of the theoretical importance of such aspects as mental preparation and expectation, cited in the literature reviewed in Chapter 4, interviews covered questions of this sort. Of those who answered (14 missing) the question 'Did you expect to be detained?', 55 per cent answered 'yes' while 45 per cent answered 'no'. It should be admitted that this is a fairly crude way of measuring expectation, which is a rather subtle psychological state involving among other things denial and blocking as well as variations over time and in retrospect. There is also a sharp difference between a vague, diffuse expectation and a quite clear and specific expectation, fuelled possibly by warnings through increased harassment. A psychological hypothesis is that a state of vague expectation or non-expectation of detention would be associated with greater coping problems and possibly more severe sequelae, tempered of course by individual variations.

To gain further information about detainees' mental states prior to detention, questions were asked about forms of preparation, if any, and respondents' knowledge of the law. Results of these questions, in simple frequency form, are provided in Table 5.

Scrutiny of Table 5 shows in general that respondents were not particularly well prepared mentally for detention; 27% claimed no sort of preparation and 58% claimed poor or very poor knowledge of the law. The dominant pattern appears to be that general information is heard from other activists and former detainees, or general thoughts occur about the matter. From these results one may hypothesise that of the 55% who expected to be detained, a considerable number held diffuse rather than specific expectations. Only a small minority had read information or held a good knowledge of the law.

The majority of the 'other' responses regarding forms of preparation in Table 5 referred to the condition of having been detained before. This would appear to be the best form of mental preparation for coping with detention. However, conditions may vary from one time to another,

Table 5. Respondents' claims regarding forms of preparation and knowledge of the law.

Forms of preparation	n	%	Knowledge of law	n	%
No preparation	41	27	Very good	4	3
Hearing information	90	58	Quite good	12	8
Speaking to ex-detainees	53	34	Reasonable	47	31
Thinking about detention	35	24	Poor	31	21
Reading information	14	9	Very poor	56	37
Legal consultation	10	7			
Physical preparation	5	3	26 missing cases or no response. Percentages calculated on total of 150 cases.		
Medical checks	1	1			
Other	35	23			

Respondents could provide multiple answers. As 22 cases were missing percentages were calculated on total of 154 cases.

and if different techniques are employed detainees may still be relatively unprepared. This was shown to be the case in two courageous personal accounts by Albie Sachs of his experiences in detention during the mid-1960s.[5] During his second period of detention he was subjected to severe sleep deprivation, which he had not encountered previously.

(2) *Patterns of arrest.* A number of questions were directed towards obtaining information about the pattern of arrests. Questions covered the place and time of arrest, the number of police and other persons present, the method of transport used, the place detainees were taken to, and the manner of detention. (See Appendix C for full details.)

The most common single place of arrest reported was the respondent's home (55%). Other places of arrest included work (6%), home of other persons (7%) and schools, meetings and gatherings, the street and places of unrest. The reported number of police involved ranged widely from one to estimates of more than ninety. Between two and four police was the most usual occurrence. The large number of police, for example ninety plus as sometimes reported, may seem surprising, but less so when it is pointed out that arrests are made at schools and gatherings where truck-loads of police arrive and arrest people in considerable numbers. Most detainees (95%) report that other people were present when they were arrested, the most frequent occurrence being the situation where between one and three other people were present. The majority of detainees reported that relatives were informed (88%) while 12% claimed that this was not done. The most common mode of transport used was a police car (86% of cases), less commonly by police van (12%). Detainees were usually first taken to either a police station (53%) or to security headquarters (45%) although a minority of other occurrences, such as being taken to a house, were reported. The distribution of time of arrest and the descriptions of manner of arrest are given in Table 6, as rounded-off frequency percentages.

Table 6. Time of arrest and manner of arrest.

Time period of arrest	%	Manner of arrest	%
00–06 hours	44	Violent	7
06–12 hours	31	Rough	6
12–18 hours	13	Aggressive	45
18–24 hours	13	Calm	32

11 missing cases. Percentages based on 165 cases.   Percentages based on 167 cases. 9 missing or unclear.

Results from Table 6 indicate firstly that arrests were distributed right through the day and night, but secondly, as expected, that the most frequent period of arrest was between midnight and 6 a.m. Frequency distribution of each hour of the 24-hour cycle shows that the modal time was 4 a.m., while the next most frequent hour for arrest was 5 a.m. As regards manner of arrest, almost 70% of the sample described the procedure as aggressive, rough or violent.

(3) *General patterns of detention*. In the section under 'sample' the general pattern with regard to 'section detained under' was described. It may be recalled that a frequent event was to detain persons first under one section then to transfer them to another section or a different Act. In 1982 all detention provisions were of course drawn together into the single Internal Security Act. The pattern of sectional shifts for this sample showed that nearly half of the sample were initially detained under 'short-term' provisions and then shifted to other sections, largely interrogation sections, but a minority to witness or preventive sections. Further interview questions elicited information on the period held in detention; whether detainees had experienced multiple detentions and, if so, how many detentions; and the number of times detainees were transferred to other places during the period of detention. Full details of

Table 7. Time period of detention and number of times transferred during detention.

Period detained	n	%	Number of transfers	n	%
00–60 days	44	25	One	27	17
61–120 days	52	30	Two	66	41
121–180 days	45	26	Three	41	26
181–270 days	22	12	Four	20	12
271 days or more	13	7	Five +	7	4

Percentages based on all 176 cases.   15 missing cases. Percentages based on 161 cases.

these frequency results are given in Appendix D.

The results for period of detention, grouped into time categories, as well as the number of times physical transfers took place during detention, are presented in Table 7. Results are expressed in terms of raw frequencies and as rounded-off percentages.

The majority of detainees (81%) in this study were held for periods ranging from a few days to six months. The full range was actually between 6 and 550 days. Reference to Appendix D shows the modal period as between three and four months, with the second most frequent period between four and five months. It is noteworthy that 9 detainees were held for more than a year. The mean period of detention was 132 days.

The geographical transfer of detainees from place to place is the norm rather than the exception. There are undoubtedly many reasons for this, some of them purely administrative, and the authorities would be in the best position to explain such actions. From a psychological perspective however, it is also quite clear that such procedures would be disorientating to the detainee and may be used quite intentionally to reduce morale and separate detainees to break group camaraderie. Results show that the modal number of transfers was two, but that as many as 42 per cent of cases answering this question (n=161) were transferred at least three or more times. (See Appendix D.)

Approximately half the case sample had experienced multiple detentions (51%) at the time of interview, and half (49%) not. Of the 86 out of 89 multiple-detainees who provided details, 43% had been detained twice, 27% three times, and as many as 30% had been held four times or more. Therefore it would appear that multiple detentions are also a fairly standard part of the general process of detention in South Africa. It is possible in this manner for the state to detain persons for years without ever laying charges. Although it may be a shade problematic to generalise this result to the wider population it is certainly clear, even if only for this sample, that multiple detentions are a more frequent occurrence than may have been generally understood to be the case.

(4) *Physical conditions of detention.* In many countries the 'gatehouses'[6] of the legal system frequently fall somewhat short of providing luxurious accommodation and facilities for those who are required to inhabit them. South African prisons and police stations are by all accounts no exception. Numerous published accounts of personal experiences in detention or in South African prisons have painted in general a grim picture of life and conditions.[7] Questions in this section were directed towards obtaining a description of seemingly peripheral but nevertheless important immediate details of conditions under which detainees were held. Accordingly, detainees were asked about cell conditions, exercise, food and clothing parcels, medical treatment, and access to reading and writing facilities. Full details of these questions and results are to be found in Appendix E; here the main features will be high-

lighted.

Cell conditions may be generally described as fairly poor in the sense that most respondents described sleeping conditions as poor (74%) and claimed that they had no means of switching the cell lights on and off (95%) – which although a relatively small detail nevertheless facilitates a sense of dependency and helplessness; and a surprising 39% claimed that cells had no access to external light. A similar proportion (38%) claimed that they had no formal opportunity to exercise, while a further 25% claimed that exercise was irregular. Therefore a clear majority of respondents, 64% in all, claimed that formal exercise was either non-existent or irregular.

With respect to exercise, it is instructive to note the 1982 Directions about treatment of detainees under Section 29 of the Internal Security Act.[8] Paragraph 16 reads that a detainee shall be afforded ample opportunity to sleep and to do physical exercise. Unfortunately it is not at all clear what may be meant operationally by 'ample opportunity', and the direction leaves every possible room for a wide range of interpretations. In any event, the bulk of present respondents were in detention prior to the 1982 Directions, which would not then be applicable to them. However, from evidence in the Aggett inquest it appears that an earlier set of instructions dated 1978, issued by the Commissioner of Police, covered treatment of Section 6 detainees and included the direction of one hour's exercise per day, taken in two periods of half an hour each.[9] If this is correct, and considering that nearly 75% of the present sample fall into the post-1978 period of detention, then results obtained here, with only 36% of the sample reporting regular exercise, suggest that police were largely not complying with directions. Of those 67 respondents who replied to the question on time allowed for exercise, 36% claimed that they were usually granted less than thirty minutes.

The majority of respondents (58%) claimed that they had not received food parcels at all, while clean clothes were received at a higher rate – 57% claiming to have received clothing from friends or family. With respect to respondents' claims about medical and dental treatment it is rather difficult to evaluate results. For example, 25% claimed to have received no medical treatment, and this could mean that none was granted or that none was required. The latter seems more likely in that for dental treatment, which one would expect to be not as often required, 87% said no treatment was received. Nevertheless the medical profession did not come off too well, since for those who received treatment, a greater number (43%) claimed the treatment to be poorer than those (30%) rating it to be sound. These ratings of course should be interpreted as simply the impressions of detainees who are not usually likely to be medical experts themselves; nevertheless they raise the possibility that official definitions of medical treatment adequacy may not correspond with subjective evaluations of detainees in this regard. The Biko inquest in particular put into question the clinical independence of doctors in practice, as opposed to the assumptions held within regulations.[10]

Results further show that exactly half the responding cases claimed that they had had access to some reading material while half claimed not; only 9% claimed access to writing materials – obviously excluding writing materials made available for producing statements. Legislation has been silent on such details as the right to reading and writing facilities in detention. The 1982 Directions state only the following: 'A Bible shall be supplied to a detainee at his request. Where a detainee's religious convictions are such that he regards a book other than the Bible as his holy book, reasonable steps shall be taken to supply him with such book.'[11] Nothing is said of writing materials.

The earlier Appellate division decision in *Rossouw* v *Sachs*[12] relating to conditions of 90-day detention reversed a decision of the lower court, which had held that to deprive a detainee of a reasonable supply of reading and writing material constituted a form of punishment. The judgment concluded that 'it was not the intention of Parliament that detainees should as of right be permitted to relieve the tedium of their detention with reading matter or writing materials'.[13] The intentions of parliament have undoubtedly not changed subsequently in this matter; it remains to be seen whether the courts will change their interpretations.

Results in this section provide only the barest bones of a description, yet taken together they do offer a hint of the degree to which detainees are dependent upon officials for even the minimal necessities. Such dependency is, as we have seen, a precondition for psychological vulnerability. Results in this section also indicate that in a number of respects, detainees experience inferior conditions in comparison to convicted prisoners.

(5) *Conditions of interrogation.* Questions were directed towards obtaining information on detainees' experiences of interrogation conditions. In this section, results are reported for length of interrogation sessions, estimated number of interrogation sessions, the average number of interrogators present as well as other details. More extensive details covering these results are to be found in Appendix F.

Clearly the time period of interrogation sessions, as well as the number of interrogators present, may vary from one session to the next, and so the situation as reported does not necessarily reflect in detail the situation experienced. The picture reported here reflects the average or the typical situation as experienced by detainees. Table 8 presents the frequency results, given as rounded-off percentages, for number of sessions experienced, typical time-length of sessions, and average number of interrogators present.

The number of sessions ranged quite widely between 1 and over 40, with the majority of the sample distributed almost equally over the smaller category of sessions as well as more than 11 sessions. The

Table 8. Interrogation: number of sessions, length of sessions and average number of interrogators present.

Number of sessions	%	Time length of sessions	%	Average number of interrogators present	%
0–5 sessions	40	1–4 hrs	33	One	10
6–10 sessions	24	5–8 hrs	48	Two	30
11 or more	36	9–12 hrs	13	Three	23
		Over 12 hrs	6	Four	14
				Five or more	23
N = 155		N = 153		N = 155	

distribution as presented is somewhat misleading in that the range is shortened; the mean number of sessions was 11,0.

The variation was similarly wide in results of typical time-length of sessions, ranging from 1 to 24 hours. The modal value was 6 hours, closely followed by 8 hours. The mean length of interrogation per session was 6,6 hours. It is noteworthy that some 6% of the sample claimed typical interrogation sessions of between 16 and 24 hours in length. It may be recalled that the inquest of Dr Aggett also revealed that he was subjected to very lengthy periods of unbroken interrogation.[14]

The modal value for the average or typical number of interrogators present was 2. The range was effectively from 1 to 10, with a further one respondent claiming more than 10 interrogators. The mean value was 3,5. The majority of respondents, some 75%, claimed to have been faced typically by between 2 to 5 interrogators.

Further results showed that the majority of respondents claimed that teams of interrogators were not used (83%). This is rather surprising in the light of evidence from the Aggett and Biko inquests, and the recent Van Heerden civil case,[15] which all suggested that teams were used, apparently on a fairly regular basis. Perhaps the contradiction may be resolved by hypothesising that teams are restricted to the more 'important' cases. Some 27 cases, or 17% of the responding sample, did claim that teams of interrogators were employed.

Finally, the majority of cases (67%) claimed that a statement was made. A bald figure such as this tells us little of the nature of the statement, why it was given, how much information was revealed, or under what duress it was given. One third of respondents claimed on the other hand that no statement was given, yet that does not mean that certain information was not gained by the interrogators.

As with the previous section on physical conditions of detention, results in this section simply provide broad outlines without giving any deep understanding of the processes involved. Yet it is not entirely insignificant to know that respondents in this sample were most typically subjected to 6–8 hours of interrogation, conducted usually by 2 or 3 interrogators at a time, for an average of about eleven sessions, and that two-thirds of detainees claimed to have made written statements. Given the assumption that virtually no detainees would have made statements to the security police entirely out of free will, for example if not faced by the system of detention, it is possible to speculate retrospectively that some degree of coercion – physical, psychological or both – was highly likely in drawing statements from as many as two-thirds of respondents.

(6) *Interpersonal contact during detention.* A distinction was made here between contact during the period of detention with authorities such as security police, magistrates and inspectors of detainees, and non-authorities, such as fellow detainees, ordinary prisoners, family and friends, and legal personnel. Full details of results for each of these categories of contact, cross-tabulated by the variables of gender, 'race', age group, and geographical region, are given in Appendix G. The main findings only are sketched here.

Hardly surprisingly, virtually the whole sample, irrespective of demographic variables, reported contact with the security police. The next most frequent contact was with magistrates and medical officers (who in most cases may be presumed to have been district surgeons), with roughly 66% and 64% reporting such contact respectively. A surprising feature of the results was the low frequency of claimed contact with inspectors of detainees, particularly in the light of state rhetoric which has stressed the importance of inspectors as protective mechanisms against abuse within the system of detention. Appendix G shows that 17–18% of detainees claimed contact with inspectors. It should be recalled however that inspectors of detainees were only introduced during 1978 following Biko's death in detention, and were only statutorily introduced with the Internal Security Act of 1982. To gain some idea of the reported contact variations over the historical period covered by the present sample, cases were separated into three periods, 1974 to 1978, 1979 to 1982, and 1983 to 1984, and then cross-tabulated with reported contact with authorities. Results are reported in Table 9 as corrected whole percentages.

The trend of percentages in Table 9 indicates clearly that reported contact with inspectors increased considerably over the three periods specified, with 34% of the most recent years of detainees reporting contact with inspectors. Yet it is noteworthy that even for the 1983–4 period of detention, contact with inspectors was less than with any other single group of authorities. It is amply clear from such findings that inspectors could not provide the safeguards for detainees that they are expected to do, on the simple grounds that they do not get to see the majority of detainees.

Viewing the sample in totality, only two-thirds of detainees reported

Table 9. Periods of detention and contact with authorities (%).

Authorities	1974–8 (53)	1979–82 (82)	1983–4 (38)	Total (173)
Security police	100	99	97	99
Magistrates	66	62	74	66
Medical	49	66	82	64
Police	68	59	47	59
Warders	49	45	42	46
Inspectors	2	20	34	17

contact with other so-called 'protective' personnel such as magistrates and medical officers, although Table 9 does show that contact with medical personnel increased steadily over the period surveyed, and that 82% of the 1983–4 detainees claimed some contact with them. Contact with ordinary police, interestingly, seemed to decline steadily over the three periods. When viewed overall, there is little from these results to dispel the view that detainees are predominantly in the hands of the security police, with visits from time to time from other officials.

The most striking demographic differences in official contact (shown in Appendix G) are that females systematically claimed greater contact with all officials other than security police, and that Eastern Cape and Border regions claimed least contact with inspectors of detainees. The Eastern Cape region also reported considerably less contact with magistrates and medical officers than did respondents from other regions. This suggests that official 'protection', such as it is for detainees, was less in the Eastern Cape and Border regions than elsewhere.

As regards contact with people other than authorities, 23% of cases reported no contact at all. The most frequent reported contact was with fellow detainees (54%), while a quarter (26%) reported contact with family and friends – notably lowest of all again in the Eastern Cape and Border regions. As would be expected from the provisions of legislation, there was virtually no contact at all with legal personnel. Little else of note emerged from cross-tabulated results with gender, 'race' and age groups, apart from whites reporting more contact generally than other 'race' groups, particularly greater contact with family and friends.

The figures describing contact are quite gross and may be misleading in the sense that they fail to depict either the quality or the absolute time spent with these various categories of people. Such qualitative aspects will be dealt with more closely in the following chapter. Nevertheless, quantitative results do support the widely hypothesised view of detention as a situation in which most contact is with security officials and least contact is with supportive or protective persons. Furthermore, nearly a quarter of cases reported no contact at all with anyone other than state officials. The description of detention as a closed system is supported by the data presented here.

(7) *Incidence of claimed physical torture.* Despite the widespread allegations of physical torture during the now almost standard trials-within-trials relating to security offences, as well as in a substantial number of publications and media reports, and in the numerous civil actions against the Ministers of Police and of Law and Order,[16] the South African authorities have consistently denied that torture occurs in South African prisons, police stations or security police headquarters. Notwithstanding such denials, numerous cases for damages have been settled out of court, indicating tacit admissions of irregularities.[17]

Questions here were directed to ascertain former detainees' claims and experiences of physical abuse during their period of detention. Respondents were asked to reply to a list of various forms of physical abuse, and report which of the items they had experienced during the course of their period of detention. Results in the form of corrected whole frequency percentages are presented in Table 10, cross-tabulated with gender and racial category variables.

Table 10. Incidence of reported physical torture (%).

Forms of torture	Male (144)	Female (31)	African (126)	Coloured (18)	Indian (18)	White (13)	Total (175)
No physical torture	17	19	7	50	17	69	17
Beatings	78	61	86	39	72	23	75
Forced standing	49	55	58	28	33	23	50
Maintain abnormal body position	35	26	38	22	33	8	34
Forced gym exercises	31	13	34	6	22	8	28
Bag over head	26	16	30	6	22	–	25
Electric shocks	27	13	32	6	6	8	25
Food deprivation	22	19	24	11	22	8	21
Strangulation	20	7	23	6	11	–	18
Suspension	16	3	19	–	–	–	14
Cold water	14	3	15	6	6	–	12
Water deprivation	9	7	11	–	6	–	9
Applications of cigarettes, chemicals	9	–	10	–	–	–	7
Bright light	4	3	5	–	6	–	4
Excess cold	3	10	5	–	–	8	4
Excess heat	1	3	2	–	–	–	2
Walk barefoot over glass, stones	1	–	1	–	–	–	1
Other torture	29	23	34	6	17	8	27

Only 17% of cases claimed no form of physical torture; in other words 83% reported some form or other of physical torture during detention. The most frequent form of torture (75%) was beating, which included punching, hitting, kicking, slapping as well as beating and whipping with a variety of implements, and other forms of assault. The next three most frequently reported forms of physical abuse were forced standing (50%), maintaining abnormal body positions, which included crouching, standing on toes with arms upstretched, holding chairs or other objects above the head, and holding a position as if sitting in an imaginary chair (34%), and forced gymnasium-type exercises (28%). In addition 25% reported having been subjected to electric shock, 18% to strangulation either by hand or by means of a cloth or towel, and 14% to suspension in various forms.

Other forms of physical torture were reported by 27% of cases. Hand analysis of these other descriptions revealed the following most frequent forms of abuse: manacling (including handcuffs), legs constantly chained and chains placed round neck (15%); pulling out or burning of hair or beard (5%); genital abuse (3%); placing pins or needles under feet or into the body (3%); use of cold-air fan (3%); and falanga, which involves beating on the soles of the feet with some implement (3%). A further range of abuses was reported by one or more cases and included: being wrapped in canvas, kept barefoot, having burning matchsticks placed under nails, or sand in shoes while doing exercises, being thrown into the air and allowed to fall, given salted water to drink, having hands cut with knife, being placed in boot of car, having nose twisted, fingernails crushed by a brick, petrol poured over body and set alight, or breasts squeezed, being held out of a moving car, tied to a tree, and scrubbed on face and body with a hard brush. Even this substantial list does not entirely exhaust the range of abuses reported.

If one considers variations in forms of abuse associated with demographic variables (see Table 10 for gender and racial variables and Appendix H for cross-tabulations by age groups and region) the following general patterns are apparent:

(i) The frequencies of females claiming physical torture was generally lower than those of males for all forms, with the exceptions of forced standing and excess heat and cold.

(ii) Whites made notably fewer claims of physical torture than did blacks. Some 69% of whites claimed no form of physical torture whereas only 7% of African and 17% of Indian respondents reported no torture. Higher frequencies for blacks of virtually every particular form of torture were evidenced.

(iii) Results in Appendix H show that the youngest age group, below the age of 20, were apparently the most heavily tortured, only 7% claiming no physical torture.

(iv) Results by region show that physical abuse of detainees was most severe in the Eastern Cape and Border, only 5% and 9% respectively claiming no torture, thus supporting previous results obtained for conditions of detention. Respondents from the Western Cape region claimed the least frequency of physical abuse.

Despite such demographic variability the general rank-ordering of the separate forms of physical abuse in terms of frequency was remarkably similar for the whole sample, indicating the commonality of procedures used. Appendix H also provides a table comparing forms of torture reported in other studies. Although detailed descriptions of forms of torture used were not as extensive as the present study, certain similarities emerged across national boundaries. In all cases physical beatings were evidenced as the most common form, showing a distinct lack of originality on the part of torturers from countries as diverse as Chile, Argentina, Greece, Spain, Northern Ireland and South Africa. Electric torture is relatively high on a rank-ordered list while forms of abuse such as food deprivation and suspension appear less frequently. There are also some apparent differences. Viewed in terms of an overall sample, physical torture in South Africa appears to be marginally less frequent than in the case of other studies. The frequency comparison however is somewhat spurious in that other studies reported data only from respondents who were already established as torture victims, whereas in the present study the sample criterion was detention, and not torture per se. The major differences occur with respect to different specific forms of torture employed. It would seem that in Latin American countries and in Greece the forms of falanga, sexual abuse and rape, and direct trauma to the genitals have been more frequently employed than in South Africa.

These results provide clear and definitive evidence that physical torture occurs on a widespread basis and constitutes a systematic and common experience for those detained for interrogation purposes under South African security legislation. The range of forms employed and the frequency of use make distressing reading, and challenge and contradict in no uncertain terms the standard utterances of state officials who claim that torture does not occur in South Africa apart from a few isolated errors of judgment. These data on the contrary show that it is a standard form of treatment meted out during detention, particularly in the case of young black detainees.

(8) *Claims regarding psychological forms of torture.* We have seen earlier (see Chapter 4) that psychological forms of abuse have been recognised as torture by the United Nations, the European Commission on Human Rights, and Amnesty International as well as by other international bodies concerned with legal, medical and criminological ethics and aspects of human rights.

It has been recognised that the precise operational definition of what constitutes psychological torture is less than entirely clear, but definitions usually include the criteria of 'cruel, inhuman or degrading' treatment. We may suggest here that definitions of psychological torture should additionally include some notion of distorted communication techniques, vicarious forms of abuse such as those involving witnessing other persons' maltreatment, and psychological devices that have been shown to weaken or disorient basic mental and emotional function and so render the person more vulnerable and less capable of rational or emotionally stable forms of thought or action. This third criterion would include treatment such as solitary confinement, sleep deprivation, hooding and blindfolding, and administration of drugs.

Table 11. Respondents' claims regarding psychological forms of torture (%).

Psychological forms of torture	Male (144)	Female (31)	African (126)	Coloured (18)	Indian (18)	White (13)	Total (175)
False accusations	83	81	84	67	94	77	83
Solitary confinement	77	87	75	94	89	85	79
Verbal abuse	69	81	71	72	89	54	71
Threatened violence	63	71	63	67	83	46	64
Good/bad interrogators	57	58	56	50	67	62	57
Misleading information	53	42	48	44	72	62	51
Witness/knowledge of others' torture	49	29	56	17	28	8	45
Threats of execution – self or family	44	26	48	11	50	8	41
Offer of rewards	34	36	39	6	44	15	34
Forced to undress	31	10	30	11	22	23	27
Constant interrogation	22	29	21	22	50	15	23
Blindfolded	15	19	19	6	6	8	15
Sleep deprivation	15	19	14	17	17	23	15
Threat of prolonged detention	8	13	7	6	11	23	9
Knowledge of abuse of family or friends	6	7	5	–	11	15	6
Sham execution	4	–	3	–	6	–	3
Drug administration	1	10	2	6	6	–	3
Excrement abuse	2	–	2	–	6	–	2
Use of animals	1	3	2	–	–	–	2
Other forms of psychological torture	8	29	7	22	17	31	11

The list of psychological forms of torture employed in the current study consists of those types listed as psychological torture in previous research (see Chapter 4 and Appendix I for details of some other studies), all of which meet the criteria as specified in the paragraph above. Table 11 gives the frequency distribution for various forms of psychological torture expressed as percentages, for the total sample and in terms of gender and racial categories. (Cross-tabulations by region and age are given in Appendix I.)

Results from Table 11 show that a high proportion of the sample claimed to have been subjected to various forms of psychological abuse. No cases reported an entire lack of psychological abuse. Over half of the cases reported having been subjected to the following forms: false accusations (83%), solitary confinement (79%), verbal abuse (71%), threats of violence to self (64%), contradictory styles of interrogation (57%), and being given misleading information (51%). These results are broadly similar to those obtained in other recent studies of psychological torture forms in South America and other countries. (See Appendix I for details of these comparable studies.)

The various forms of psychological torture could be viewed in terms of four main classes of techniques. (a) The majority of types involve communication techniques of one sort or another. These in turn could be perceived as constituting sub-classes in terms of their aims. Some for example aim to distort or confuse the situation. False accusations, misleading information and offers of rewards are of this sort. Others such as verbal abuse aim at humiliation or degradation. Threats are intended to instil fear and thus to weaken cognitive resolve of resistance. Misleading information about family or friends, or knowledge of others' torture, is directed at heightening emotionality. (b) A second class of devices such as solitary, prolonged interrogation, blindfolding, sham executions and administration of drugs could be described broadly, and rather imprecisely, as mental weakening devices. Some of them involve perceptual distortions and reductions, whereas others (for example, sham executions) involve extreme stress and anxiety. All of these are likely to induce cognitive, affective and motivational vulnerabilities and disorientations. (c) A third group may be labelled as psychological terror tactics. Sham executions and threats of violence or execution to self, family or friends, as well as witness of others' torture, would fall under such a label. All of these would induce extreme degrees of fear, anxiety and debilitating emotional arousal. (d) A final category would include those techniques which primarily involved humiliations, degrading actions and acute embarrassment before others. Excrement abuse, verbal abuse including swearing and name-calling, being forced to undress or hold ridiculous physical postures, are all exercises of this type. Use of dogs to bite detainees may also partly be considered in this class, whereas use of other animals such as snakes or spiders may be classed as a form of terror induction. All four classes may be considered as cruel treatment.

In practice the forms of psychological torture do not only fall into discrete classes but overlap across classes to a considerable degree. We may also note that psychological forms of abuse may conceptually be divided along the lines of those directed primarily at the self, and those directed primarily at the dissolution of social bonds of group or communal solidarity. We may also agree with Suedfeld[18] that the majority of forms seem to involve an increased or heightened stress rather than a reduction of stress, but it is ultimately the conjunction of a range of forms that is likely to be responsible for psychological debilitation.

Breakdown of results in terms of gender and 'race' categories as given in Table 11 does not evidence quite such consistently variable patterns as was the case for results of physical torture. Nevertheless there is a tendency for females to report greater frequencies than males in a number of the psychological forms: solitary, threats, rewards, blindfolding, sleep deprivation, prolonged interrogation and others, although the differences are not particularly substantial. Whereas blacks received systematically more severe physical torture, the differences were less substantial in respect of psychological forms, and in certain forms such as knowledge of abuse of family, threats of prolonged detention, sleep deprivation, whites' responses were marginally more frequent. In categories such as violence and verbal abuse, however, blacks were apparently somewhat worse treated.

Variations in terms of age groups (see Appendix I for details) were similarly not clearly systematic, although close scrutiny of the data suggests that the youngest age group less frequently reported the more subtle forms of psychological techniques such as solitary, offer of rewards, undressing, blindfolding, contradictory interrogation and so on. Though perhaps slightly overinterpreting the data, it does nevertheless seem reasonable to assume that the general picture is one of more severe direct physical abuse of the younger group, and thus less need or less attention is given to more sophisticated psychological forms.

Results for regional differences also suggest this somewhat complementary relationship of physical and psychological forms. In the Border and Eastern Cape regions where physical violence was more frequently reported, solitary confinement and constant interrogation seem relatively less frequent. The Western Cape region appears generally less severe, as was the case with physical abuse, except that solitary confinement was frequently claimed.

Roughly 11% reported 'other' forms of psychological torture. Hand analysis of these additional responses found that most of them involved threats or fears regarding other persons (5% of responses, calculated in terms of the total sample), and physical threats (3%). Remaining 'other' responses involved forms of humiliations, such as spitting in the face (1%).

If these results are seen in combination with those for physical torture, the prevalence of torture in general is very widespread indeed. As with the physical torture results, despite some slight demographic variations, the general rank-ordering of psychological forms of torture was remarkably similar for the different groups of people. The combined 'package' for detainees must be viewed as very similar, and a most severe combination of treatment forms. The mean number per respondent of physical torture types experienced was 3,3, while the mean for psychological forms was 6,4. Although the two forms have been separated artificially here for purpose of analysis, there is no doubt that the modalities operate together in terms of effects upon the victims of such treatment. It is to the sequelae of these methods that we now turn.

(9) *Reported health problems during detention.* In keeping with the focus on the process of detention, respondents were asked about their health problems as experienced during detention. This distinction between

Table 12. Reported health problems during detention (%).

Health problems	Male (137)	Female (31)	African (121)	Coloured (17)	Indian (17)	White (13)	Total (168)
No health problems	4	–	3	6	12	–	4
Difficulty sleeping	59	61	64	47	47	54	60
Headaches	52	58	57	53	47	23	53
Excessive fantasy	39	74	44	59	35	54	45
Weight loss	44	48	51	35	29	15	45
Appetite loss	43	45	48	12	41	46	44
Difficulty concentration	43	48	46	41	47	31	44
Nightmares	39	45	49	12	24	24	41
Tiredness	34	48	40	24	35	23	36
Difficulty memory	36	26	40	12	30	15	34
Stomach pains	26	36	31	18	18	23	28
Restlessness	27	29	31	18	24	15	27
Depressed	26	32	19	14	35	70	27
Constipation	22	39	25	29	18	31	25
Shivering	21	39	31	–	18	8	24
Crying	19	45	26	6	24	23	24
Rapid heart beat	14	23	17	6	29	–	16
Nausea	17	23	21	18	6	8	18
Sweating	15	26	19	12	24	–	17
Trembling	10	23	12	6	24	15	13
Diarrhoea	12	13	11	6	18	23	12
Uncontrollable laughter	8	10	12	–	–	–	8
Hyperactivity	6	7	7	–	6	8	6
Other health problems	35	23	35	24	35	23	23

problems during and following detention may be regarded as particularly important in the light of questions about admissibility of detainee evidence, for statements are clearly demanded during the period of detention, not following it.

The former detainees were asked to respond to a presented list of health problems and say which of them had given them particular difficulty during detention. In addition they were asked to describe any other problems they had experienced but were not presented on the checklist. Results for the list of presented health problems during detention, expressed as corrected percentages, are given in Table 12, which also includes cross-tabulations by gender and racial categories. Additional results including cross-tabulations of health problems by age groups and region, and details of 'other' response analysis, are provided in Appendix J.

Only six (3,6%) of the 168 cases that provided responses to this section claimed no problems during detention. The most frequently experienced health problems were: sleeping difficulties (60%), headaches (53%), excessive amount of fantasising (45%), weight loss (45%), appetite loss (44%), difficulties with concentration (44%), nightmares (41%), tiredness (36%) and problems with memory (34%). It is clear that the dominant symptoms are largely psychological. Although it is difficult to make direct comparisons with other research, as processes during incarceration are seldom explored, the present pattern is generally similar to those reported in earlier studies of torture victims. For example, Randall and his colleagues in their study of 44 torture victims found reported symptoms immediately on release as follows: difficulty in sleeping (62%), headaches (52%), weight loss (35%), decrease in concentration (59%) and tiredness (43%).[19]

Women detainees were specifically asked whether they had experienced any gynaecological problems during detention. In response, 47% claimed to have experienced such problems while 53% said not. Of the sample of women detainees, 33% claimed to have experienced irregular

Figure 1. Number of health problems during detention: distribution expressed as percentages.

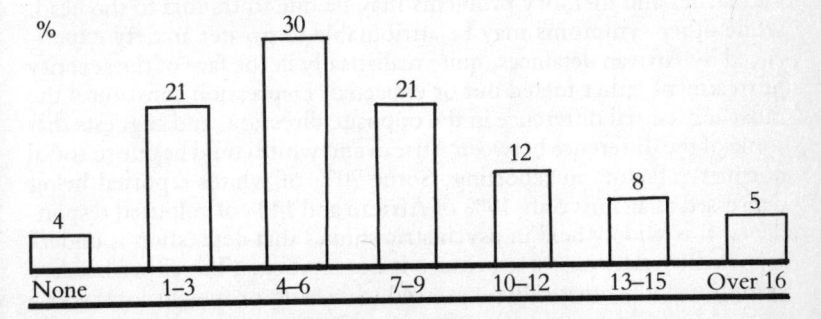

None	1–3	4–6	7–9	10–12	13–15	Over 16
4	21	30	21	12	8	5

periods, while 13% said that they had no periods. It may be surmised that the gynaecological problems claimed by roughly half of respondents were due to stress experienced during detention.

The number of reported symptoms varied across individuals and ranged from 0 to 20, with the mean number of symptoms 6,8 and the mode 6. The frequency distribution, expressed as percentages, of the number of claimed problems is given in Figure 1.

While the majority of respondents claimed between four to six problems it is noteworthy that roughly a quarter of cases claimed to have experienced ten or more health problems during the period of detention.

Manual analysis of responses coded as 'other' problems (see Appendix J) showed that psychological problems (10,7%) and body pains, either general or localised (8,3%), constituted the majority of 'other' responses. If we view results across both structured and unstructured responses, it is clear that problems were primarily related to the following types of psychological disorders: stress anxiety, depression, cognitive functioning and psychosomatic problems.

Examination of demographic differences in claimed health problems shows the following:

(a) Females show higher frequencies in virtually all listed problem types; the single exception was 'memory problems'. Although the differences are often not particularly substantial, it is the consistency of results that is striking. The greatest differences are found for excessive fantasy, crying, shivering, trembling and constipation. Whether these differences are due to actual experiential differences or to differences in social norms in respect of health reporting for males and females is not entirely clear, but this pattern is a common finding in the literature of general health problems.

(b) A similar pattern is evidenced for 'racial' category differences, with African respondents showing a greater incidence on most health problem types. The greatest differences are for weight loss (36),[20] headaches (34), memory problems (25), nightmares (25) and shivering (23). It seems reasonable in this case to attribute the differences to the more severe physical torture experienced by Africans, as found above. Headaches and memory problems may be due to trauma to the head, while other symptoms may be attributable to greater anxiety experienced by African detainees, quite realistically in the face of the severity of treatment either meted out or expected. Depression constitutes the most substantial difference in the opposite direction, and suggests that some of the difference between African and white could be due to social normative factors in reporting. Some 70% of whites reported being depressed as against only 19% of African and 14% of coloured respondents. It is widely held in psychiatric studies that depression is underreported by Africans, not because it does not exist but either because symptoms are somatically expressed (shivering or weight loss would be examples from the present findings) or because the concept of depression is not understood by Africans in the same way as whites.[21] This remains a possible explanation, although caution should be expressed about an over-hasty emphasis upon cultural differences in explaining psychiatric disorders.[22] An alternative explanation may suggest that these differences are due to actual differential treatment received during detention. The relatively milder physical torture experienced by whites associated with periods of solitary may lead to a predominance of depressive-type symptoms, while blacks may show symptoms associated with head trauma and anxiety to a greater degree. This matter cannot, however, be finally settled here.

(c) Age-group differences are not sufficiently systematic to draw clear patterned results, although the youngest age group, below age 20, almost without exception showed slightly lower frequencies for problems than the next two older groups, covering ages 21 to 30. It is not quite clear what this may be due to, although it is possible to speculate that the youngest group, while severely treated, were detained for shorter time periods and less subjected to psychological manipulation than the older groups. One can equally argue that this youngest group may be more robust both physically and psychologically. Viewed overall, the slight differences in respect of age groups is, however, probably less significant than the similarities found across groups in this variable.

(d) The most systematic pattern emerging from results by regional area is that problems were least frequently reported from the Western Cape region for 15 out of the 21 listed characteristics. This undoubtedly reflects the earlier finding that the Western Cape was the least severe region in terms of torture. The Border region showed the highest frequencies for serious health problems such as headaches, nightmares, tiredness, memory and concentration difficulties, again probably reflecting the earlier finding of the severity of physical torture in this region.

Like earlier findings however, demographic differences notwithstanding, the general rank-ordering of health symptoms is reasonably similar across groupings, though showing slightly greater variability than was found for torture types. The commonalities are sufficient to suggest a relatively similar set of health problems during the course of detention, but the severity of problems do seem in part to be associated with the severity of torture forms. Methods used here however are descriptive, and more sophisticated methods of analysis would have to be employed before anything approaching definitive results could be drawn. But there can be no doubting the frequency and commonality of psychological problems that have been shown in this study to be associated with detention.

(10) *Reported problems on release from detention.* A further set of questions was directed at examining claimed problems that were experi-

enced during the period soon after release from detention. Qualitative findings suggest a common (and hardly surprising) period of great euphoria upon release, accompanied by warm solidarity on the part of friends and family, and frequent expressions that the experience had

Table 13. Reported problems on release from detention (%).

Release problems	Male (132)	Female (28)	African (115)	Coloured (15)	Indian (17)	White (13)	Total (160)
No release problems	4	–	1	7	12	8	3
Easily tired	42	61	58	7	6	31	46
Relating to friends	36	50	40	40	35	31	39
Change eating habits	36	36	44	20	12	15	36
Relating to family	33	43	34	47	41	23	35
Getting to sleep	30	54	32	47	29	46	34
Nightmares	32	39	37	27	18	23	33
Irritability	30	36	30	47	18	31	31
Depression	21	39	23	27	18	39	24
Problems of concentration	23	29	24	27	18	23	24
Scars left on body	21	11	26	–	6	–	19
Relating to other people	17	18	16	20	6	46	18
Changed tobacco consumption	21	7	19	27	18	8	19
Problems of memory	17	18	17	33	6	8	17
Fear/nervousness	11	21	10	27	18	8	13
Changed alcohol consumption	15	–	14	27	–	–	13
Want to be alone	13	11	13	27	–	8	13
Headache	9	18	12	13	6	–	11
Easily woken up	8	18	12	–	6	7	10
Fear of detention/ban	9	7	6	13	24	8	9
Anxiety	7	11	7	–	12	15	8
Physical disability	7	7	10	–	–	–	7
Interrupted sleep	5	11	6	13	–	8	6
Hyperactivity	6	7	6	7	–	15	6
Passivity	3	7	5	–	–	–	4
Reduced hearing	5	–	5	–	6	–	4
Relating to authorities	2	4	2	–	–	8	2
Other release problems	33	36	33	40	18	46	33

increased the resolve to oppose apartheid – which, it needs to be recalled, is not in itself a crime, though often enough is taken to be so. The euphoric spell does not necessarily overcome entirely other sequelae of detention, which appear to be rather longer-lasting than the immediate exhilaration. It is these deeper sequelae that are reported here. Results of responses to a list of release problems are given as percentages in Table 13, along with cross-tabulations by gender and racial categories. Further details of cross-tabulations by age and by region, and of analysis of 'other' release problems elicited by interview, are presented in Appendix K.

The scope of listed problems on release was broadened to include a number aimed at assessing social or interpersonal problems. Results from Table 13 show that social difficulties were indeed one of the most frequent outcomes of detention; 39% claimed to have experienced difficulties relating to friends, 35% to family and 18% relating to other people. Interaction with authorities on the other hand did not seem to present much of a problem. As was the case for problems during detention, sleeping difficulties and concomitant tiredness, as well as symptoms of depression, were fairly frequently experienced. Depression was claimed as a problem by nearly a quarter of respondents, with far less substantial differences in this case between Africans and whites, a finding which tends to support further our earlier caution against the glib culturalist-type explanations of differences in symptomatology. The hypothesised presence of a depressive-type sequel to detention is further supported by claimed problems, though less frequent, of social withdrawal (13%) and passivity (4%).

Anxiety-type problems are indicated by a number of different problems, and behavioural or personality changes are also strongly indicated by the social problems and reported frequencies of changes in eating-habits (36%), and tobacco (19%) and alcohol (13%) consumption. Physical and psychosomatic problems, while not entirely absent, were less evident than the other psychological problems. Cognitive problems, as in previous studies of torture and stress-related sequelae, were evidenced here but with somewhat less frequency than in other research.

Examination of the breakdown of 'other' responses elicited by non-structured means (see Appendix K) shows a further 14% of reported psychological problems, mainly psychosomatic, anxiety- and depression-related, as well as further evidence of social and interpersonal problems, such as aggressiveness (8%), excessive talking (5%), feeling alone in a group (5%) and less trust in people (3%). Other symptoms further suggest difficulties related to social withdrawal, tension and anxiety.

Overall the types of problems experienced following detention are very similar to those of previous research findings of stress sequelae, with the exception that frequencies in this study were generally lower than those of other studies concerned with torture victims.[23] But a number of points should be made in this respect. Firstly, as already mentioned the cited studies selected only torture victims, whereas this study of detainees included about 17% who claimed no physical torture, though all claimed some form of psychological abuse. Secondly, Matussek has shown that the methodology employed may produce differences in frequency.[24] As full psychiatric examinations plus use of interview schedules were used in some previous studies of torture victims, whereas only an interview by non-medical interviewers was used here, differences may have been partly due to methodological aspects. Thirdly, and most important, the number of different symptoms reported in this study is rather wider or more finely differentiated than in previous research. There is no doubt that were these symptom types to be grouped together into more inclusive clusters, the frequencies would be considerably increased. Finally, examination of the frequency distribution of number of problems per person given in Figure 2 indicates that two-thirds of the sample claimed experience of four or more symptom types. Data were based only on the presented list of problems, and not of 'other' problems, for this analysis.

Figure 2. Number of problems on release from detention: distribution expressed as percentages.

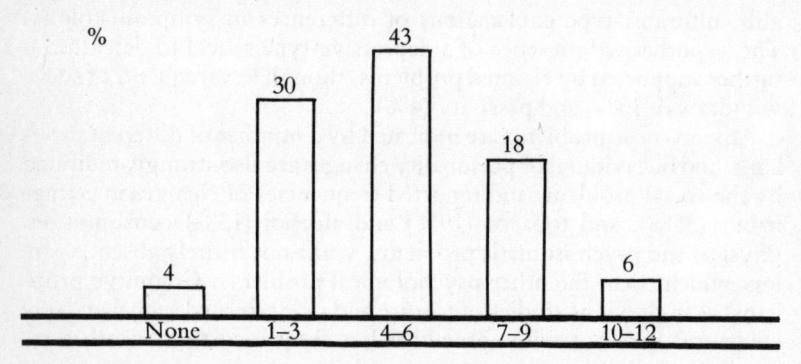

None	1–3	4–6	7–9	10–12
4	30	43	18	6

The number of release problems reported ranged from none to twelve, with a mean of 4,8 problems per case and a mode of 5 problems. Some 54% of cases reported between five and twelve symptom problems following detention while only five cases reported absolutely no problems. Viewed in the context of these points raised above, the evidence clearly shows a majority of cases experiencing relatively serious problems following detention.

Results from cross-tabulations by demographic variables support the earlier findings of health problems during detention in the case of gender and racial category variables. Females systematically showed higher frequencies on almost all release problems. Exceptions to this pattern referred only to physical problems such as scars on body and reduced hearing, and behavioural patterns such as change in tobacco and alcohol consumption. Africans again showed generally higher frequencies of problems than did whites, exceptions being 'getting to sleep', 'depression', 'relating to other people', 'anxiety' and 'hyperactivity'. It may be reasonable to attribute the greater frequency of release problems evidenced by the African and coloured detainee sample, in comparison with whites, to the harsher treatment received during detention. It should be noted that coloured respondents reported higher frequencies on many attributes than did Africans. No systematic patterns emerged from the comparative groups of age or regional variables. Although differences were evidenced, they varied in terms of specific attributes, so no clear results can be drawn from these analyses.

A last set of findings in this section relates to efforts to assess objective changes following release from detention. It may be recalled from the section in this chapter on the sample that respondents were asked a number of questions pertaining to their status before and after detention (see Appendix A for raw data from these questions). None of these questions showed substantial changes, but the few observed changes are suggestive of a pattern. The majority did not claim a change in marital status, but of those who did, the shift was in a direction of an increase in proportion of those who were married. Very slight shifts in educational status indicated greater numbers with university experience following detention. The most substantial objective changes were in the area of employment. Prior to detention 4% were unemployed while 26% were unemployed following detention. This provides some support for the recent study showing the employment stigma of detention in South Africa.[25] There were also increases shown in the numbers who claimed professional or organisational work and trade unions as their employment area. Despite these interesting trends, results in this more objective area do not allow one to conclude that there was much evidence of change.

Severity of detention and sequelae: some explorations

There is a consistent assumption in a study such as the present, of a relationship between events during the course of detention and psychological or other sequelae. A wide range of events in detention may be involved, and includes the time period held, the exact nature of the physical and psychological regime experienced, the severity of interrogation sessions, experience of solitary confinement, and the degree of mental preparation or anticipation of the stressful events. In the following analyses, the earliest beginnings of such explorations are presented. While hardly constituting definitive results, the data suggest some trends and thought for further research along these lines.

In order to assess whether the period of time in detention was associated with greater symptomatology, the sample was split into three groups, those detained for less than 90 days (n=63), those detained between 90 and 180 days (n=71), and a third group held for longer than 180 days (n=34). For each detainee case a rather crude 'symptomatology index' was computed by simply summing the numbers of health problems reported. Table 14 gives the means and standard deviations of this 'index of health problems' for the three subsamples. Health problems in this case refer to those reported as occurring during the period of detention.

Table 14. Index of health problems by length of detention period.

		Length of period detained		
		0–90 days	91–180 days	Over 180 days
Number of health problems	Mean:	5,54	7,48	7,61
	sd:	(3,9)	(4,5)	(4,3)

To compare the three groups, a one-way analysis of variance was computed, which yielded the following results: $F = 4,35$, df 2/167, $p<0,02$. Both the Scheffe and Student-Newman-Keuls procedures showed that groups 1 and 2 differed significantly at the 5% level. Although only these two groups differed significantly it is clear that the general trend is one of an increasing number of health symptoms with longer periods in detention. While this result would require an adequate control group to be definitive, it is nevertheless suggestive of increased health dangers associated with prolonged periods of detention.

To explore whether solitary confinement was associated with health problems during detention, the sample of those with computable health-problem indices was divided into solitary (n=133) and non-solitary (n=34) groups. An independent t-test yielded a score of 1,22 (df=165), which was significant only at the 10% level (one-tailed). The mean number of symptoms reported by the solitary group was 7,0 and by the non-solitary group 6,0. Although in a technical sense this result may be considered to be only marginally significant, given the fact that most detainees were harshly treated in all sorts of ways, the result is strongly suggestive of an increase in the number of problems particularly linked to solitary confinement.

The number of release problems was similarly compared across the three groups of increasing time in detention. Means and standard deviations of release problems are given in Table 15. A one-way analysis of variance found a highly significant difference between the groups, $F = 7,27$, df = 2/159, $p<0,001$. The Scheffe procedure for comparison of means found that groups 1 and 2 and groups 1 and 3 differed significantly at the 5% level. It may be concluded that an increasing number of health problems accompanies longer periods of detention. Although the index employed in these analyses was not a particularly sophisticated one, the results taken together strongly indicate that detention constitutes a health hazard.

Table 15. Index of release problems by length of detention period.

		Length of period detained		
		0–90 days	91–180 days	Over 180 days
Number of release problems	Mean: sd:	4,05 (2,2)	4,82 (2,8)	6,19 (2,4)

As a further exploration of detention effects, correlations were computed for the association between the number of interrogation sessions experienced (for those cases where such data were available) and (respectively) the number of health problems reported during detention and the number of problems on release. The hypothesis is clearly that a greater number of sessions may be positively related to health problems experienced. It should be noted however that the mere number of interrogation sessions is by no means an adequate indication of the qualitative severity of treatment. For example, two very lengthy sessions involving physical torture, teams of interrogators and sleep deprivation could not be equated with ten relatively mild sessions of questioning.

The Pearson-correlation for number of sessions with health problems (n= 135) was r = 0,25, p<0,002; while for number of sessions with release problems (n=131) the obtained correlation was r = 0,20, p<0,02. The correlations are certainly rather low but both were significant and in a positive direction. Such results suggest, albeit tentatively, that there is some association between interrogation practices and health problems.

Taken together, results in this section, although individually somewhat unsophisticated and tentative, all point in the same general direction, and overall provide rather strong evidence that greater health problems are associated with greater severity of treatment during the process of detention.

Summary and concluding comments

This chapter has described the empirical investigation of conditions, processes and sequelae of security detention in South Africa. Although field research of this nature is usually less controlled than either formal psychometric tests or full psychiatric examinations in terms of both procedures and findings, there can be no doubt of the importance of the descriptions obtained. Viewed overall this work offers clear evidence of the extreme severity of treatment handed out to political detainees. Results provide clear evidence that both physical and psychological methods of torture are employed on a widespread and fairly systematic scale in South Africa. The number and range of health problems, particularly of a psychological nature, both during and following release from detention, indicate the severity of treatment at the hands of security officials. These data of sequelae compare quite closely with those obtained from torture victim studies elsewhere, and while not as severe as sequelae of extreme conditions such as concentration camps, nevertheless are of a similar clustering and are also similar to symptom patterns from other highly stressful situations. Finally, some evidence was presented to show links between certain practices in detention and health sequelae.

6 The process of detention: detainees' descriptions

How is the process of detention in South Africa experienced by those people who are its victims – the detainees themselves? While statistical data as reported in the previous chapter are certainly important in depicting the process, they provide only the skeleton or outline of the process. Statistical procedures, being rather dry, analytical and abstract, cannot adequately convey the feelings, thoughts, reactions, interactions and hopes and fears of persons in this situation. Qualitative data constitute an equally important source of information in the effort to understand and describe the mental and emotional state of detainees.[1] Such an understanding is, as we have previously argued, a prerequisite for legal interpretations, grounded moral evaluations, and the appropriate provision of adequate safeguards and protection of human rights. This chapter gives accounts by detainees of their experiences, expressed in their own words.

It is necessary to describe briefly the methodological basis of this qualitative section. The excerpted passages were all obtained from full transcriptions of the audio-taped interviews with detainees. No formal selective method was employed in obtaining the passages and descriptions presented here. Neither can the claim be held that selections were made entirely at random. The final selections were based on the combined grounds of typicality, clarity and, in certain cases, psychological insight. No charges of witting or systematic bias in selective procedures can be sustained.

Transcribers of the audio-taped research material were instructed to produce transcripts as accurately as possible from the original in order to minimise interpretative bias. However, minor errors in transcription cannot be ruled out because of the inaudibility of sections of taped material, or language difficulties. As regards the matter of language it should be noted that English was not the home-language of the majority of respondents, although they kindly assented to being interviewed in English. This should be taken into consideration when reading the detainees' statements. Further minor editing was conducted only for purposes of clarity and readability or of deleting unnecessarily offensive language. On occasions, interviewers' questions might have been omitted. The identity of security policemen who were named in certain passages has been protected throughout. The same procedure was applied in the case of detainees.

The descriptions of events, feelings and thoughts are presented in separate sections below, roughly following the sequence of detention, beginning with descriptions of arrest, moving through interrogation and descriptions of torture, methods of coping, and finally release. The purpose of setting out these descriptions is not only to depict details of events within detention, but also to provide some insights into the psychological processes involved in such an experience.

Arrest

As shown from quantitative data in the previous chapter, arrests most frequently take place in the early hours of the morning, and at home, and involve between two and four policemen, who characteristically behave in an aggressive manner. However, results also made it clear that the range and variation in forms of arrest are far wider than this most typical manner. Furthermore, statistical description catches nothing of the meaning or flavour of the aggression which typifies these events. The accounts given below should add to the fullness of descriptions. (The dash beginning paragraphs denotes the start of a new interview.)

– I was detained in the course of a march. We were all arrested by riot police with machine guns and taken to the police station. Four of us were called out of the mob and taken to X police station. I waited there about a week. During the course of the week somebody came and woke me up early one morning and said, 'You'd better cooperate.'

– About 5 o'clock in the morning, I guess, ja.

Can you describe how many people were there? Was anyone else around?

Ja, I was asleep in bed, somebody else from my house answered the door and came into my room, and started calling me in quite a scared tone of voice, so when I woke up I knew there was something going on, I didn't know what it was. I think there must have been about five cops, who told me just to get up out of bed and get dressed, which I did. I snapped awake immediately and realised what was going on and got quite angry; my immediate thing was anger, obviously mixed with – obviously apprehension, fear – just not knowing what was going on and why they were there and what was going to happen. And then I got up and dressed, and they started searching my room. I don't remember if they told me what they were there for, I presume they did, and Captain X would have identified himself, I think – ja, he did, that's how I knew his name. And they just started searching my room, going through everything, and leaving me sitting there, and I again was going through quite a lot of confused feelings, because on the one hand there were a couple of things around that I didn't want them to find, so that made me a bit apprehensive, but on the other hand I was feeling quite angry and feeling important to actually be quite – not show any kind of fear. I had one altercation with them, because my dog tried to come into the room, and Captain X was trying to push it out, he pushed it out with his foot, so I shouted at him and told him not to kick it, so he turned on me, and told me he wasn't kicking it and I mustn't cause trouble with him, and so on and so forth. So I kind of felt there was a huge air of tension in the room, but I was very angry and trying not to show the anger and sense of outrage rather than what they were doing, because they wouldn't explain anything to me, they just went through everything.

– I was at work, and we just arrived from our tea time when two gentlemen, one white and the other one black, came in, and they went to the employer and they asked the employer as to who is X and then the employer pointed at me, saying, There he is, and then they called me. Then I went to them and they said to me, Are you X?, and I said, Yes, I am X, and they said, We are police, we've come to fetch you, and then I said, Okay, can I go and wash my hands and change my clothes?, and they said that the black man should accompany me. So I went to wash my hands and from there I went into the change-room to go and change my clothing, and then when I came back I just asked the black policeman from which police station they come from and then they said it's John Vorster but they are working in Springs but they are working for John Vorster, so I just shouted at the other workers, Tell them I'm at John Vorster Square, so that my parents should know my whereabouts.

– We were four. And then on the way there we met with the parent of one who was arrested there, warning us not to go there, because it is bad, the situation is bad. The police are beating up the people. They are chasing them away from the court. So, then we decided not to continue our journey to the court. So, on our way back home, we have met – by the way I didn't see that kombi which was coming along to us. It's one of us who have seen it. Then he fled away and shouted, Here are these whites coming. I can't run away because there is nothing that I have done. I've got nothing wrong. Why must I run away? Well, the other three did run away. Well, I have seen now this yellow kombi stopping and I have seen a white man alighting from this kombi, having a rifle in his hands. Then with fear I try to run away because I am seeing that this chap is going to fire at me. So I have got to run now. So when I have jumped a fence there, trying to run away, and I have heard a shot that is shot. At the same time I have heard this thing – the shot – on my head.

You were shot at your head?
Yes. Those pellet shots.
Then what happened?
They pick me up and they started beating me up, with these long rubber batons.
Were they all white policemen?
Yes.
– In fact I heard the sounds of the cars. It was early in the morning, round 4 a.m. So I heard footsteps and they surrounded the house and knocked at the doors, kicking the doors and threatening the owner of

the house that they are going to break the door if they do not open. So the owner decided to open. So they harassed everyone in the house and they were armed that time, carrying guns, each of them had two guns.

– *Can you tell us of the pattern of your arrest?*

It was on Sunday night when I came home for feeding my stomach – and a change of clothes. Then, when I was about to move away, I heard cars just halting outside my home, and I peeped out of the window and saw that there's a convoy of police cars surrounding my area and I hadn't a chance to run away, so I just went inside and they came, but I tried to hide myself in a cupboard. Then my father was present that time, and they asked him my whereabouts and he told them I was not at home, so they asked him permission to check the house, and they get inside the house, all of them, checking each and every place, and one of them just opened the cupboard where I was inside and he found me and said, *Ja, this vokking kaffir, kom uit*,[2] and that was my detention.

What was the time?

About eight.

How many cars?

Maybe there were over ten, but there were also some Landrovers.

– *How did they react?*

In a bad way. After they stopped the car they said, Yes, you are the one we are looking for, and then they put me in the car and left the two others. And when we were in the car they started throwing insults at me and telling me that I was going to hell, that they were taking me to hell, and throwing all insults at me, and they were even *klapping*[3] me.

– Yes, I was awakened in the morning in the early hours. I heard a loud bang on the door and the others were knocking on the window, and when I got up I found that it was the police. They shone the light through the window, and when my father opened the door they all got in. They were seven that morning, and they took me up to the police cells at Algoa Park.

– *What time?*

It was twelve o'clock, in the morning.

How many were there?

I think there were over – the security police alone were over eight, and there were also, I don't know whether they were soldiers or police. They surrounded my house, I'm not sure how many were there but I think there were approximately about fifteen, who surrounded the house.

Were they armed?

Yes, they were armed.

Was your wife there?

She was at work. There was only me and a woman who was helping me in the house. My children were present – no, only the younger ones.

What was the attitude of the security police then?

They were very rude. They asked me things I don't know and they

insulted my children. For instance, I was sleeping, for I was not well, and this young kid came and said, Hey, dada, there comes some other comrades, because he saw people and he doesn't know whether it's a security police or not, and these people say, Hey, you fucking son of a terrorist – that is the rudeness.
How did the children respond?
This young fellow started to cry because they were carrying guns, and he started to cry and they took me away.

Early impressions: alone in a cell

As the early impressions of detainees when first finding themselves alone in a cell were not really amenable to quantitative analysis, a few comments upon their thoughts and feelings are included here. Descriptions cover impressions of physical conditions as well as fears and apprehensions about the immediate future. It appears that these early moments of detention, particularly the lack of predictability of events to follow, are in themselves a highly stressful experience. This contention is supported by psychological literature (see Chapter 4). The widespread reputation and symbolism of major security headquarters such as John Vorster Square are an important additional contextual factor in understanding the fearful mental state of detainees at this stage.

– I was interrogated in the interrogation offices at Caledon Square, and I was also locked up there for the first month of my detention. . . . When they decided to detain me, I was taken down and of course the normal procedure – everything's taken away from you, your cigarettes, your matches, your belt, you are almost stripped naked except for the basic clothes you've got on. I think one should spend a bit of time on just the effect of being locked up for the first time in your life. I think that it is probably, if you take the interrogation and detention as a total reality, it is probably one of the most traumatic moments in the whole, that moment of being locked up, being thrown into a cell and that door being slammed behind you. It's indescribable, it really is like a huge punch in the stomach. I remember distinctly as they slammed that cell door closed, it was heavy, it's an old type of cell door, the Caledon Square building is still very old, and it has a thud that's not describable, it's almost like a huge log that's being thrown down from a high distance, or from a big height, and it just knocks into you.
– *How did you feel left alone in your cell that first night?*
Terrible, because I was all alone and the walls were all circling around me, and it was bitterly cold and there were no blankets, no mat. It was winter. I just couldn't sleep, I had to crouch in one corner and sit up from the cold floor and just wait for what is going to happen next.
– *How did you feel when you were left alone in the cell?*
Well, for the first time it is very different, because there are so many questions that you are asking yourself, what wrong have I done, how

long am I going to stay here, particularly after you remember there are quite a number of people who have killed themselves, and you just ask yourself, why are those fellows killing themselves, where do they hang those ropes, and I couldn't identify a spot where a person could hang himself, and I think that brings more fear into you because then you think, no, these people really kill you, so it's very horrible. And you think about the outsiders too, what is happening, what are the people doing, what are the people in organisations doing, and so forth.

How good was your knowledge of the law and your rights?

Well, my knowledge so far was still weak, I didn't know so much about my rights as a detainee.

– *What went through your mind when they kept you inside for the first evening?*

I was feeling so lonely and apprehensive in fear of my fate of what was going to happen to me. Because I had to encounter a lot of threats from the police. I would get so nervous whenever the doors was opened.

Descriptions of interrogation

Occurrences during the course of interrogation sessions are described in this section. They include descriptions of physical events as well as more subjective matters such as the emotional climate and the relationship between interrogators and detainees. Descriptions illustrate quite clearly the interrelated nature of physical, psychological and interpersonal forms of coercion employed during interrogation. They also indicate the historical character of the interrogation relationship, embedded as it is for both detainee and interrogator within the contexts of past detentions, the knowledge of dire events that can befall one under South African security law, or the numerous earlier deaths in detention. The threat exerted by knowledge of past deaths in detention is in itself a highly coercive device.

– There were many, I think there were about ten of them, there were quite a lot of them then. So that now in here, during the course of interrogation, I could actually see that there was one fellow there who sat on the desk there, writing everything that I say, you see. I mean it is quite clear, that is because he blindfolded me, it was quite clear now that his work was only to write the reponses I gave, because every time they were torturing me, he was just looking on with his pad in his hand, flickering the pen in his hand, and every time I blurted out something, he would 'gas' with the others and then he would start writing. And so now at times they gave me some breathing space of about 30 seconds, or 48 seconds or so, and then they would come back later, and so on with this punishment of theirs: kicking, throwing you up, truncheons and so on, so that by the time I left that place I was dazed and puffed out.

– Well, the nature of interrogation depended on group to group; with one group they would appear to be kind to you and say that they are only doing their work, and one cop even said, I'm not going to beat you, I'm not going to assault you, I'm not going to harass you, I'm not going to do anything to you, I just want you to talk, I'm interested in your welfare, if only you would talk; and throughout the interrogation he presented me with that picture, you know, that he is a soft-like person or that he is sympathetic towards me, whereas the others were rude and arrogant and aggressive and they'd beat you and insult you, call you bitch, you must talk, but I thought that this was a tactic to make you uncertain about what was happening.

– What happened is, I came in just before lunch, they gave me lunch, and after lunch I was chained, my legs were chained.

And your hands?

No, just the legs, and throughout that period my legs were chained, every time I went to the toilet I had to go in chains, anywhere I had to take the chains. Oh, I forgot, on the Thursday I was taken back to the prison, because I was complaining that I had 'flu, but when I got there I was taken to the orderly, the warder took me there, and he gave me a couple of tablets and took my temperature, and said I was okay, then I was taken back to the interrogation centre.

– There would come two people at a time, that was the maximum, always there would be two, and they would change, like I counted they were working in four-hour shifts, like two would come from 8 to 12, and then from there they would break for lunch, and then after that the next two comes, and during the period that I was interrogated day and night there were ten of them and they would even sleep at the barracks, they wouldn't go home; two would come and then go and another two would come, and if it was in the evening then two would sleep while the other two are busy with me, and when these two are finished with me then the other two would wake up and come to me.

– Firstly, he would say to me, This is tenth floor and it is John Vorster, many people didn't escape here, so if you are going to tell me lies you won't escape and nobody will know what has happened to you. That was the strategy which he adopted. And then the other one was that of loud banging and shouting at you, and the other was that of being kind, saying that if you can write down a statement and sign it and send it to Pretoria, then Pretoria is going to let you out. And also the strategy of whenever they ask you a question and then they say, But that man said this and this and this, so why don't you mention that in your statement. So in that time you become confused as to whether that person has really said that, so in that case they were able to link our activities. And the other one was that of *klapping* you and shaking you around.

– Actually that's one of their problems in terms of language when they interrogate you, they use English, and most of the people who were interrogating me were using English, so you find that the tactic that I found myself using was just playing with words. Actually you end up not understanding each other just because of the language.

– *What did you do after your interrogation sessions when you were left in your cell?*

Usually I was quite exhausted, I just tried to do some physical exercises to maintain my mental and physical balance, did a fair amount of walking and reflecting, and because I was being interrogated so often I didn't have too much time really, in my cell. By the time I came back, did my exercises, had my food, spent a while reflecting, I was fairly exhausted, it was fairly strenuous being interrogated constantly, and fairly stressful.

– *Can you just describe briefly actually what happened during those sessions, interrogation sessions, what happened to you?*

Actually on my arrival at X they took me out of the jeep. Then they started kicking me. Then there was a sort of tunnel but it is within the enclosure, and so they hit me until I reached the last door, it was opened and so there was a wall, and so I just turned in and entered into that room. So thereafter then they just started beating me, some were hitting and others were kicking. Then someone arrived and told them to stop and told them to go out. And then they did, and then they started asking me questions.

– Well, I was under interrogation effectively for about four to five weeks. That meant that every day from about half-past 7 till half-past 3 till half-past 4, it varied; I would be up on the 10th floor. Through this period I in fact wrote three statements, and it was during this period that I would be periodically subjected to insults, assault and a great deal of mental anguish, pressure.

– The first few days they were just trying to, I got the impression, just to exhaust me. I mean they were making me do exercises and, I mean, giving me the odd beating and all that, but nothing of a heavy, you know. Just the odd jabbing, punching, just exhausting me. But then slowly it started becoming heavier. At one point they gave me alert tablets, which they told me were alert tablets.

– *What else was in that room?*

There was a box like an air-conditioning, it was a long box about one or two metres high. They also use it for the electric shocks, and I also saw it used on one person. There was once a boy who came and he only had a sweater and underwear on, and they told me to turn around and face the wall and I only heard him screaming and calling, Don't choke me, don't choke me, and so I turned around and I was fortunate to see them.

Now when you walked into this room and you saw that happening, what did you think?

I thought that they would do that to me and that I would be lucky to get out of that room still alive, and even if you get out it will have an effect on your body.

– *Now during this period that you were being interrogated, did you have food*

and water?
  Yes, they gave me food and it was fairly decent and they gave me water. But for a day or two I was not washing myself, and of course I smelt. I think on the third day I did go and have a very cold shower, and again I think it was because I was complaining of sleep and they said the cold shower would brighten me up, so every morning from that day they gave me the cold shower, saying that it would brighten me up. It was bloody cold I must tell you.
  – They were about seven and you found that not only one man questions you, they all ask you questions, and they don't give you a chance to respond to one person because they all ask their own questions, and when you answer one then another one is expecting you to answer his question, but you find out that you don't know who is interrogating you, you find that the whole squad is interrogating you at the same time. Then I told them that I won't answer you all, I will only answer one man at a time.
  – *How many black policemen, were there black policemen also?*
  Black policemen didn't interrogate, only white.
  – But the most fearful part of it was I was taken to the rooms where they interrogate you on the 6th floor. They used to tell us that if we did not speak the truth they can easily throw us out the window, then we will crash down, and no one will know that they threw us out the window. They even went to the extent of showing you the height, how high it is from the office – such terroristic methods.

Descriptions of physical and psychological torture

This section speaks for itself. It includes descriptions and details of both physical and psychological torture, elaborating upon such blank labels as 'beatings', 'cold water' treatment, holding 'abnormal body positions' and 'gymnasium-type exercises', as well as illuminating psychological forms such as 'verbal abuse', 'misleading information', 'constant interrogation' and others. In this section the interrelated nature of psychological and physical forms again becomes apparent, as well as the absolute and uncurbed nature of power wielded by the interrogators in South African security detention situations. On the other side, the utter helplessness of detainees is revealed, with the virtual inevitability of compliance with demands. The failure to comply means more severe forms of treatment, some of which are also described here.

  – And while these guys were dancing around with me like that, two massively built guys just came along. They just got hold of me and they dragged me into the adjacent room. And from there a small little room led off that, and they put me in there. Those guys didn't ask me any questions. They hardly spoke with me and they just beat me up – they just beat me up. And they had this thing which they refer to as the imaginary chair: you sit against the wall and you stretch out your arms. And they keep you like that, and they were making a lot of statements. And they weren't really interested in whether I was talking or not, and whenever I was falling down they were just kicking and beating me. And they kept me like that for about 3 to 4 hours. And I was finished after that. I couldn't walk, you know. At some point another guy joined them, he was an African guy. But now we were in this bigger room. They took me to the second big room. And there this African guy joined them. And the effects of that exercise, it upset my coordination. I could not walk. If my mind instructed my leg that I want to stand, then I just fell. I could not coordinate. Not at all. It was completely disturbing. And they were aware of this, because they told me to do frog jumps to sort of regain my coordination. And I couldn't do that, and I was trying, I was really trying to please them. And as much as I was trying and failing, this African guy was kicking me. After a while of course, slowly, I could.

– Then after that they again ask you questions, then I again didn't agree with them up to the time when they took me to another torture. This one is that helicopter[4] but I didn't know what was it, because also it was the first time that I found myself being put across the tables, some of them standing on that side and some of them standing on this side, hitting you so that you can fly over to that one and then to that one.

– Yes, the man was very much rude. Swearing my parents, calling me a kaffir – everything, you see, and accusing me of being a communist.

– Before the morning I was taken from the cell to the place where I was tortured the day before. I was suspended into a jack where I was handcuffed below the knees and my arms, and an iron bar was forced between my arms and legs, and I was left hanging between the two tables. I was being pushed and I was told to tell the truth. They put a rubber tube on my face. And I was bleeding from my nose and somebody was stabbing me with a sharp instrument at my private parts – for about four to five hours. But the process of being stabbed in my private parts took about four hours. There were some intervals inbetween those hours, I cannot say how many times I was stabbed.

– They interrogated almost without any breaks because they would tell me to do some exercises such as push-ups, sit-ups and the rest of the exercises. They would instruct me to do them for as long as I was reluctant to give them any information, and whenever I stopped through fatigue they would hit me until I resume the exercises. That would continue throughout the day from half-past 8 to half 4. It would be the whole of the day throughout that week.

– *Did they undress you during interrogation?*
Yes, they would take off my clothes and I was handcuffed behind my back. They would take the canvas bag – with the canvas bag over my head and my hands tied behind my back, I would stand naked in front of

the police and they would use some lit cigarettes, yes, as their techniques of torture. They would burn me on my chest.

– They kept on torturing me, but they use another method now, which was too desperate. They took my hands and fastened them with the handcuffs, and the legs with the irons, then they put a stick and they had two tables, and they made the helicopter and turned me around. That time they did it they kicked me, each time I came around they kicked me. When I was going so fast they pushed me and I fell on the floor and my head hit the wall and I came to be unconscious. I don't know how long, how many minutes I took to be conscious again, and they told me I must get up, and it was hard for me to get up from there, and they helped me to get up by taking the stick and the handcuffs off, and then when I was up they handcuffed me again, and then X did that thing to me again by pulling me this way and that, and the handcuffs cut deep. And then I asked them if I could go to the toilet, to save myself.

– There were four of them, the fourth one was a black man, he was translating only. They keep on doing the same method, after so many minutes they turned the method, and they ties my legs and I was naked. And they took a bucket full of water, cold water, and they threw this over my head, and they turned on the fan, this water was coming from the fridge, and they had on the fan, then they chucked over me again the cold water. And they took a bag – the money bags – that size, and they put it over my head, and they [. . .] me and they threw me down. Before they put that bag over my head, they showed me something, it was about this size, and X asked me if I knew this thing, and I say that I know about it, and I think it was an electric shock because it was looking like this, similar like a [. . .]. Then they threw me down and at that time I had some shock, they touched me here, they touched me with this thing, they started here, and it goes down, and when it started here I feel shock, and I cried out but in vain. When they had done everything I was almost unconscious, and then after some minutes I felt some kick in my stomach, I tried to get up but it was too hard for me.

– At first they gave me a foolscap and told me to write everything. They told me to start from when I was in Standard 6, and where. Well, I wrote everything I know, then they took the foolscap and they tear it to pieces, say I write lies, they are going to get rid of me. They put canvas on top of me, a wet canvas, they slap me, they kick me. They told me that I had an affair with a woman. Then they hit me like hell. I fall with the chair and he kicked me using a rod, hit me with it, and Mr X interfered. They make me go down like this, handcuffed me and put that rod and put it between the two tables, and make me to spin on my knees, for over two hours. I was naked, they pour water from the refrigerator, it was a cold day, it was August. They make the fridge water to pour over me. They hit me. Then when they see fit to loose me, they give me another foolscap to write it. When they put that canvas over my head, they told me that they are bringing me a man to tell them everything in front of me. They will make a point that I don't see his face.

– Yes, they did that. They told me they are going to kill me if I don't tell the truth.

– They actually at one stage handcuffed me to the chair. Most of the interrogation was done while I was sitting. They were done thoroughly and they even told me that they know me and my background, I'm old, 71 years old, and they don't want to treat me like a boy, they don't want to beat me, but I just have to answer their questions. They did threaten me with assault, to shoot me, to physically assault me, and they kept on saying that people whom they have already arrested have already made statements about me, and that I better make a statement because they know everything about me.

How did you handle it?

I knew nothing, I just answered what I knew. They just kept asking me. Physically I was not assaulted. I was just handled roughly. And also threatened to be shot.

– I was interrogated from 10 o'clock to past 4.

What happened during this?

I was asked where am I going, and I told them that I was going to Sterkspruit for a holiday, and then I was taken to another office where there was a picture of Steve Biko. Then I was asked if I know this guy, and I say, yes, that I know him. And they asked me where is he now, and I told them that he is dead. And they said that I will follow him if I don't speak the truth. I told them again that I am going to Sterkspruit for a holiday. Then they beat me with a sjambok, and with their fists and so on. But the torturing that was very very strong was the electric shock.

Was it applied whilst you were dressed?

No, no, the clothes was pulled off.

You were left naked?

No, not naked. It was a part.

– They put sack on me and they used pipe to me and kicking me because I was too stubborn. They throw chairs at me and I fell – I cried. Then I stand up again and always, Sit up, sit down, sit up, sit down. Had to do exercises. I was beaten with a hose pipe.

– It was not pleasant. I was slapped. A motor car tyre was put round my neck, some bricks inside to make it heavier. Kept on my neck for about fifteen minutes, only to find that I knew nothing. They poured ice-cold water on my face, trying to squeeze the truth out of me but don't find anything, as I do not know anything. Kept on telling me to speak the truth. They took tyre off when I was exhausted. I collapsed and then they threw cold water on my face. They beat me with clubs.

– There was just the one experience that might be worth sharing – is once when I was interrogated by nine people. They all stood around me in a circle, five in front, four behind. I was seated in the centre with another very big size cop sitting in front of me. He was always looking aggressively, and it seemed that at the turn of my head that he would punch me or react violently to anything that I said that they didn't want to hear. Examples of these are many. For example, where a person in the front would ask you, Were you involved in this?, and you'd say no. The person at the back would produce a pamphlet and say, Didn't you produce this for that organisation? So it was difficult to look back and face the person eye to eye. This was repeated quite often, where easier questions were asked from the front and the people at the back whom you could not see were asking the more difficult questions.

– One of the impressions they tried to give was that they already know of you. They tell that everyone is spilling the beans, so you must say yourself. They used to say that everyone is telling the whole story so there is no point in holding back. They detained me on Thursday, and on the following day, the Friday, when they were taking me to my cell, this guy told me that they had told everything. They would try to give you the impression that the thing you had got involved in was hopeless, and at times it would be quite persuasive. At times there were also assaults but they were careful not to leave any marks – hit you on the chest – keep you standing for a long time.

– Now the first day I wasn't allowed to sleep, the second day was Tuesday and I wasn't allowed to sleep but I was dozing off, and every time I dozed off, they would shout at me. The Wednesday again I just dozed off about 3 in the morning, and they just let me doze off on a chair. The first day that they actually allowed me to sleep was on Thursday, but again it was only a couple of hours. Friday night again just from sheer exhaustion I dozed off until they woke me up for breakfast, I was completely exhausted at that time, so that the interrogation was interrupted by those little sleeps.

– With the verbal abuse they used to call me a kaffir, saying, Do I know and agree that I'm a kaffir? Then I used to say no and they would come to me and threaten me and grab me and tell me to be careful, you bloody bastard – you know, such language. And with the false accusations they used to say you are a terrorist and also that Tambo is using you as his puppet, and also that I'm a member of the ANC. And with the threat of violence they used to *klap* me a bit, or just go and show me the electric tubes, the shock machines, and say, You see this thing, nobody has escaped this thing.

– How they did it initially – they came with a whole lot of information. And they told me that they knew in fact that I had done this and that with so and so, and what is my response? What do I say about that. So it was either reject or approve of what they say. In most cases, where I had to disapprove was when the torture or the beatings would come in. And in some of the instances one was forced, through the torture and the beatings, to admit that, Okay, I was involved; although I knew very well that I wasn't really involved in those activities. But through the pressure and the torture which was exerted on one, one eventually has to admit to some of the things. But now some of the methods they used really were quite painful. Like at some stages, one was made to kneel on the concrete floor for hours on end whilst being interrogated. I had to remove my clothes and had to kneel naked, and I was interrogated whilst on my knees – without sleeping. That used to happen for the whole night. They used to change the guards, have one for a certain period and then after some hours they would change.

– They put a kind of canvas bag over your face and then they close your nose and your mouth, and by that time actually you are sitting on a seat and then they take a bag, the one which they normally use for belts for the convicts. So they put it here, then they call it the handcuffs – they put the handcuffs here as well as here. Then they tie them to a seat and you sit like this. They put on that bag and then they close it and they close your nose, your mouth, and while you're trying to breathe then somebody hits you in the stomach, so as a result you cannot breathe. What you need most by that time is air, therefore they are always doing this until you tell the truth and they tell you that they are going to do it again. And so I keep on telling them what they want to know. And so that was continued on several occasions until I lost count. Then I fainted. Thereafter then they revived me. After reviving me the one who chased them away came in again and then asked me whether I wanted any form of security from him, and guaranteed that, if I gave them a correct statement – not the one that I've already told them. I said that is the best I can do – I know nothing further than that. He said, then he'll come later. Then they came again. Then on coming back they put me – actually they had two tables – and they put a broomstick between my feet. At the time the handcuffs were still here, so they tie them to my feet and they insert the broomstick here – they call that chicken.[5] And then they put you on top of the table. They start kicking you while others are hitting you with sjamboks, hands and so forth.

– They threatened to shoot me, take me to one of the borders of the country to show that I was on my way running out of the country, and somewhere around there they would shoot me.

– *Do you remember crying out?*

I was crying all the time. When a shot comes, you know, and he hits me then I cry 'yaa'. He was called the panel beater. And that session – that session is called panel beating,[6] he's the panel beater in terms of bending a man with a fist. And then they came with another thing now – sticks, you know. I was beaten on the toes and ankles, you know – elbows.

On the joints?

Joints, all the joints.

Are you handcuffed all the while?

No, you are made to jog. They chase you all the way round the cell, like they are chasing a ball, you know. But the parts which they are

looking, these hard parts.
Do all of them partake in that?
No, four – there are four of them.
All of them are armed with sticks?
Ja, they are armed with sticks. You run, you know, you run to this direction.
Are you dressed all the while?
No, you are undressed, in underpants.

– Then when they returned I smelt liquor from the police who was interrogating me. He started hitting me and throwing objects before he could even interrogate me, just provoking me – that I must not forget him, I must face the facts that kaffirs do not sit on chairs. Then he started with the interrogation. He started to tell me what X was trying to get me to agree on. He told me that I had received military training, and myself and a friend had been recruited to leave the country. I also declined to that. He grabbed me by my shirt and flung me across the office. I struggled. He was also hitting me against the wall. As time goes on he sees he can't get anything out of me, he devised another quote. Then he left, and a different cop, this Y, came, together with 3 men, tried to get me to enter into a contract. I denied and then they took out something they claimed they confiscated in my room. They then produced a pamphlet issued by the ANC and also made me to sign that. Then I refused to put my signature there. Then the other bloke produced a picture of a black man whose face was battered and full of blood, and there was some stitches on his face and asked me if I want to be like that. I said no, and then he said I must sign it or else my mother will see me like that person if I don't do that. Then I started signing there.

– Yes, they're all there. About five or six chaps, sitting around you all the time, and then all the time crowding you, all over you, so it's a very threatening position you're in. There were other things, like standing with your arches on inverted bricks – they turn 2 bricks towards each other like an inverted V – and you have to stand on that narrow edge while you are being interrogated, and you've got to balance yourself on your arches, which are killing you, and eventually you either step off the thing or it collapses.

– Fists, slapping, knee in the stomach and groin, punching in the stomach, my hair being pulled, beard – on a few occasions I was laid out on the table or laid out on the floor and my testicles were then manhandled – a question would be directed at me, usually a question which I couldn't answer, like for instance, We know that you are a member of the ANC; and I would say 'no', because I'm not; and if my response was not the desired one then this would go on. On one or two occasions if I can remember, I was again laid out on the ground; when this kind of thing was happening a number of them would hold you down, and my shoes were then taken off and I was beaten with a thick slab of wood on my feet, the toes of my feet, and if I tended to move then my shins would be kicked with the bottom of the heel which is quite painful. My throat – it's a variation of the sack thing, the effect is exactly the same, because on a previous occasion I had gone through the sack treatment, but they would get hold of the front of your throat and press so that you couldn't breathe. I remember after that happened I couldn't talk or eat comfortably for days. I was threatened with electric shocks. On the occasion which that happened I was more or less through with my third statement – the assaults frequently came after a statement – the first two statements were not complete, I'd write say ten pages, and they would come and say this is not good enough, give me a good hiding, and then instruct me to write another statement.

– In fact when they applied the electric shocks I felt as if some muscles were moving away from my body and because of a certain thing that they put on my private parts – it was as if they were tearing apart and I'd sweat all of a sudden. Actually after that, after I felt pain, I don't know what happened, all I remember is that I woke up from collapsing, and they were sort of asking me some more questions.

– They tried to tell me that Mandela is a spy, he is no longer in prison, he is kept around Cape Town in a beautiful villa.

– They used to beat you if you don't tell the truth. He used to press my breast and all that.

Press it with what?

With his hands. Squeeze it, very tight, and then after that they take that hose pipe and beat me up. After that take this brush and scrub me on the face and everywhere on the body.

– They brought me in on the Tuesday morning and interrogated me on Wednesday during the day, on Wednesday night, carried on through Thursday, went into Thursday night, they gave an hour's sleep on the floor of the cell of the interrogation room and woke me up so I don't even count the sleep I had with this interruption. They carried right through Thursday night until the following morning and right on to Friday evening – about 60 hours, which is a pretty long time. Normally, I've seen intensive interrogation – they don't normally keep people on a 60-hour shift without a 4-hour break.

Can you describe what you went through?

I remember, although it's difficult for me to recall the most poignant moments – as I said, that there was that moment of triumph when I established that thing that was after about 60 hours but I had to – it was like playing chess – they were trying to manoeuvre me, which was an incredibly intensive experience. I'd say one thing, they allowed me to smoke, and they allowed me to drink Coca Cola. Both of those were valuable in keeping me awake for 62 hours. One of the guys apparently said to a person who was detained at the time, they never met someone who would last for 62 hours. And I think it had something to do with the fact that I had a really healthy injection of caffeine going right throughout the day and night. But it was towards the end of the third day of interrogation – I was just talking slowly and I could hardly follow what they were saying. It wasn't a painful experience, it was actually like drifting. I went at some stage – they took me to the lavatory – looked at myself and felt I must have been 15 years older, unrecognisable. There were little things they did – I remember on the third day one of the guys in interrogation picked up the phone and phoned his wife and said to her, I was just coming to breakfast and what was she doing, he was going to take a walk on the beach and how were the kids – it was an effective little gimmick. This was a very soft kind of guy, very open who tried to be helpful and so on. They let me sleep after the third night – a full night's sleep, and then they kept me going through the Saturday, Saturday night, Sunday, right until late on the Sunday night.

Another 60 hours?

It was about a 40-hour stretch. Then I got another night's sleep, then they let me out the next day.

– When I was transferred after two months from section 6 to section 10, I was told to strip. And I [a woman detainee] will never forget that. A policewoman was standing next to me, but it was unfair. I had to strip everything. Searched in my hair. My armpits. Then I had to stand with my legs apart and jump. I asked them, But why do you do this? They said to me, It's my job, I must do this. And I said, I should know why I am doing this; and I was made to jump like that, lie down with my legs apart, and she went into my private parts with [. . .]. And I thought, what is happening? And that's another thing that I will never forget. It was humiliating for me, even though it was done by a woman. I don't think she had any right to do that.

– *There was no chance for you to say anything?*

No, in that state you wouldn't, because they themselves, whenever they want you to talk, they would reduce their pressure and give you a chance to say something, and if they don't agree with what you say then they would go on. What they did later, as they were saying '*praat*' and I tried to *praat* but they didn't agree with what I was saying, then one of them said, Laat hy vlieg. Now when they say, Laat hy vlieg,[7] I was just held by them, pulled by the legs, and another one, two of them, held me by the arms – they started swinging me. They swung me for a very long time and I was tossed right up and I came down, tumbling. I think they did this about twice or thrice. There I went flying and back to the floor, and I would always try to break the impact of the floor, but I would always fail – I mean, either fall on my back, fall on my head, and so on. Fortunately this was a wooden floor, so fortunately it wasn't cement. It's very easy for one to break your leg, to break your neck, to break your arm, but they used it, and whenever you tried to break that fall, you'd fall in a more awkward way and you'd start screaming. They would laugh, look at you and say, *Ag, hy's nie net 'n student leier nie, hy's ook 'n akrobaat.*[8] You see . . . the amount of pressure they are putting on you, the amount of punishment they are meting out, for the first time in your life you are subjected to this type of torture. But to them it's something quite simple, something to laugh about, they'd so much got used to torture, that they are no longer feeling themselves when they mete it to another person. Surely, even yourself, you can be a coward but when you see a person hitting another person, hitting him with a kierie, even see blood flowing at one stage or another, you try to intervene, because you can't expect one person to deliver that type of treatment or that type of torture to another human being. You'd try one or other sympathies.

Did this horrify you at the time?

It really did. I was shocked in fact. I thought perhaps one of them would say, No man, it's enough, this fellow has had enough; but no, there was nothing like that. They were so unanimous in this agreement of theirs, torture after torture, because some of them would come very free, deliver lots and lots of punches on my stomach here, some would hit you on the back there, and some would just crack you, and some, when I'd laid down and helpless there, they would start with the kicks, always kick you on the stomach. When you are tired you can no longer stand up, then they themselves would lift you up, one would hold you this side, and one would hold you this side and one of them came with one of these big rifles of theirs, and they would start *stomping* on your foot with the butt, just like that.

Solitary confinement

The arguments about the effects of solitary confinements presented above in Chapter 4 should be recalled. One line of argument suggested that solitary confinement in itself was not particularly stressful. The alternative argument claimed that effects of solitary confinement were dependent to a large extent upon the context in which it was utilised. In this respect we agree that it is not particularly useful to speak of isolation or solitary confinement without reference to its contextual setting. One of the advantages of the descriptions that follow is that reference is frequently made to the environment beyond the immediate conditions of solitary.

The following descriptions also provide some indication of ways in which detainees managed to cope with their being socially isolated. In this respect both an active use of fantasy and exertion of control over time-structuring appeared to be facilitatory activities. However, virtually none of the respondents described the experience as a positive one. Given the full context of dependency, helplessness and social isolation common to conditions of South African security law detention, there can be little doubt that solitary confinement under these circumstances should in itself be regarded as a form of torture.

– I was kept in solitary throughout, but before my first interrogation session, by that time I had already been held for three weeks at least. I'd had the experience of solitary confinement before. But I was extremely anxious and I can't really recollect how I coped, but I remember sleeping for long periods, not eating, being aware that I should try and keep up my physical strength through doing exercises but finding it quite difficult to be consistent about it. I remember my memory starting to stretch back very far to the details of my experience with people, family – you know, things that had really receded from my consciousness came back. There was a fair amount of fear but also a fair amount of determination to survive.

– That period was shattering. After detention, after interrogation there was nothing happening. I'd wake up in the morning, make my bed up, wait for people to bring me food, that was almost the only thing to look up to because that would be the period when things were happening. At least there was a person who would at least say hello to you, that's all, and he goes out. That was almost the only contact that you had with people and the rest of the day you would spend listening to cars driving outside, peep through the window, listen to whatever sound is going on outside.

– Solitary confinement was a tough experience as the detention itself was causing me a great deal of anxiety, and being left alone in the cell wasn't a good situation 'cause I didn't know what to expect and what would be happening next. I spent a lot of my time taking a great deal of interest in the ants which inhabited my cell from time to time. I would feed them with my food and watch their behaviour carefully and this took up a great deal of my time. My second pastime was to count the bricks and just take a general interest in the bricks with which my cell was constructed. I also tried to regularise my routine for the day. My only indication of time was when various meals – breakfast, lunch and supper – were brought to me.

– I just used to, when I wake up in the morning after eating, when they gave me food, I used to eat but in a very slow process to pass time by, and then after doing that I used to sit down and just think about things outside – I mean social things, my family and the progress of my organisation. And at times I used to keep on gym-ing or sing very loud but if there happens to enter a fly in my cell then I will have company and try to play with it, chasing it around my cell.

How did you cope with loneliness?

It was really a problem but I had to sort of adopt a strategy, that is always singing and doing that so as not to feel alone. And I had to talk to the warders even if I talked petty issues.

– *So did you find yourself doing things that were quite strange? Do you want to say what sort of things? Don't be embarrassed, everyone says so.*

I thought I'd go mad because I thought about one thing after another, and eventually my thoughts kept repeating themselves and I was scared being all on my own. I thought I'd end up shouting, talking to myself and I just wanted to see one face, even if it was a policeman. If he came in I would have been happy. That actually made me quite anxious and worried about what was happening outside the world. I felt like a person who was totally cut off from everything – like a person who was left alone on an island.

– I couldn't keep track of time – what day it was. To me it was just the same. I was sort of getting mental disorders, because I remember one day I just jumped up and screamed. I just wanted to get out of the cell, at least to the outside, even in the yard. Because I was thinking too much, thinking Why am I here, I haven't done anything wrong, I haven't committed murder? Why should I be treated like this? And I even found common prisoners much better off than we were. At least they could talk to each other. But I was alone in the cell and it was hard.

So how did you keep track of time?

I was lucky because when I was locked inside the first day, though they were searching me, there was a pin inside my coat, a safety pin. So one day I asked one of the warders who were getting fresh with me what time it was, and what date it was. And he told me, so I went to the wall and started making a calendar.

– I walked around a hell of a lot, I managed to get hold of my watch as well, I watched my watch for hours on end – you think about everything, you tend to afterwards lose concentration, so your mind flits from subject to subject, from issue to issue, from incident to incident, you constantly worry about when are they coming to interrogate you. I did a hell of a lot of exercises in my cell, I also laid and tried to sleep a lot. You try to maintain your – you actually have a feeling that you are losing control, what is happening in your head, and so you try to do things and think of things that – that keep some sort of grip on reality. You also do a hell of a lot of fantasising about escapes, and also you – I mean you live in fear of your life as well, so I think I had an obsession with exercises, you know, first twelve, fourteen days. . . .

– It had terrible effects because I just couldn't believe that it was myself that was being detained and I also made a vow to myself that I would never again be involved in the struggle, this is a shit place, you don't have any access to anybody, you are totally under their control and in their hands. I was totally isolated and we couldn't even talk to the other detainees. They used to warn us not to communicate with each other; whenever we go and wash we are under police guard, each one with his own police. So you find yourself completely lost from the outside world, thinking of whether people are thinking of you, are they doing any campaigns maybe to highlight your detention, do they do any means to contact the lawyers to find out what is happening, what are our conditions. So I mean it is very terrible, this solitary confinement.

– *The period in solitary, could you discuss that?*

Ja, well, I think basically I had to organise my life, I had to accept that I could be there for an indefinite period, but I had geared myself to stay there for a period of 2 years, I knew that I would be kept in solitary confinement for that period, I knew that I had to survive, and the way to survive would be to maintain my physical and mental well-being, and to organise my life in such a way that I did that. So therefore I organised a fairly rigorous exercise schedule for myself. I tried to avoid becoming lethargic and sleeping longer than was really necessary, yet at the same time seeing the need to get adequate rest. I was allowed to have a Koran two weeks or so after my detention, after making a lot of noise about that, and I found that doing some kind of reading on a programmatic basis, going through that and breaking that up with exercise and reflection periods, helped to keep me going. Basically to keep a balance between physical and intellectual exercise and stimulation, using the limited resources available.

– *Tell us about solitary.*

Well, I managed – I was going a bit dilly – I was starting talking to myself, and then I realised there is no point in that so I start singing as much as I can. Then I tried to manage, it was frustrating. You can't think for long, you think of so many things. I used to do lots of funny things, like refolding my mat and refolding my blanket, making sure no dust on my hair, just keep myself fully occupied like that. Just pace around floor. Then I found a good idea when I had three holes in my cell window, which was painted black, and the sun rays used to come through those three holes, and I used to mark them on the wall to know exactly what the time of day was, and by that method I became quite used to knowing what was the time of the day.

Did you develop a routine?

Well, it was to get up, clean up the cell, fold the blankets and mat, and I had a piece of cloth I shined the floor with. Then I would wash my teeth in that pan, then wait for breakfast, sit down, take long time to eat. After breakfast, clean up and manipulate my sun rays, and walk about, sing, then by lunch time the food is there again, clean up again.

– There is no violence comparable to solitary confinement. I think it's the worst type of assault against an individual. I have found it a thing very difficult to cope with – a thing which renders you completely supine, you're on your back. You must remember to pass, to while away the time, and it's not ordinary whiling away your time, it's whiling away of time impregnated with the fear of imprisonment, the worry of the family, the worry of your wife and child, the longing for these people, for intimate contact with people – the longing for people in general. It is an on-going anxiety with which the whiling away of times goes hand in hand. So it is not a matter of just being locked up and left there. Now you try and manage the time, which is 3 months, in which you feel that it's better to be interrogated than to be left there, and it is during that period of time I believe that most people decide to give evidence against their comrades. It is in that time that I think your whole personality is transformed. You discover all your inner weaknesses. You discover even your ability to betray other people. You – one morning you get up and say to yourself, I'm not going to stand for this any more. I am going to tell them, I'm going to give evidence, providing they just let me out. You're prepared to do anything to get out of that condition of solitary confinement. It is something I find very difficult in describing. It is something I always tell people, that you first have to experience before you can know what it is all about. You know, I've told this lady who is going to be my colleague, Miss X, she's in the legal department, and I told her, you know, what they should do, they should lock up judges as part of their apprenticeship. They should lock them up just for three weeks, they don't have to go very far, just for three weeks, they must lock up judges in solitary confinement and I'm sure that judgments given against or in favour of people would completely change. They are beginning to think of this type of punishment for people who have other civil offences, speeding and killing someone, they think in terms of sending them to work in the casualty department of hospitals on the weekend where they can see the results of their type of behaviour. I believe that they should do something similar with judges and with magistrates. You'll have a different legal system within a matter of months.

General conditions of detention

Conditions described here cover the size and state of cells, exercise facilities and opportunities, sleeping conditions, food, washing and toilet facilities, and other minor aspects. While the stock response to such descriptions is likely to claim that prisons or police stations are not intended to be luxurious, the importance of excerpts in this section is to act as a reminder that physical conditions also form a central part of the debilitating process of detention.

– We were put into small maximum security cells, which must have been about 15 feet by about 8 feet. There were two very small windows. All the windows had thick wire gauze over it. The entire room was not clean at all. It was quite untidy. I could switch on and off the lights. The sleeping arrangements were a few blankets left with one pillow. You had to use a few to sleep on and one to cover yourself with. Exercise time was provided both during Section 22 and Section 6. The first part of the cell where we slept in was completely locked up. The second part was much more open, with there being walls around and again very heavy gauze around the windows.

– *What were the toilet and washing facilities like?*

There were no toilets because they give you a bucket and a pail of water, and you change that once a day when you are going to wash in the bathroom. There is only cold water, no hot water, and very wet on the floor, always cold, running water on the floor. And the bathroom is very, very filthy. They give you a bucket, and the following day when you go to wash, you empty it, there's a hole in the bathroom, and fresh water for drinking. Those were the day-to-day events.

– Man, I remember that it was just very, very dirty. As we came, it was cold that night, I just remember that it was so cold that night and we came in and there were a whole lot of people sleeping in that cell, people awaiting trial, and they threw those people out, and there was some vomit on the side. The blankets were so dirty, the one blanket actually tore in my hand with the filth and how old it was, but I had no option but to put the blankets over me because it was so cold. All I can remember was the filth all around and the stench. I put the blankets over me and I slept.

– When I was in Maitland police station it was a horrifically filthy cell that I was in, the blankets were covered with excrement, no drinking water, there was a flush toilet with a wire that you pulled on the wall; and I was very thirsty and I wanted to get water, and they gave chips and fish as an alternative, and I had to get water from very unhygienic circumstances [. . .] that had little scratches, and it all turned very septic and my fingers swelled up and in fact family and lawyers got to see me afterwards and they thought that I had been tortured. So that was quite grim but that was just the first night. The second night I was switched to another cell, to the white cell in Maitland where Haron had been killed.[9] In both cases my lights were outside and I was sleeping on one of those mats. Then in Pretoria I was in the old Pretoria local, which is quite an old prison, quite dirty but not nauseatingly dirty, sort of toilet buckets in the corner, there was a bed, smallish but not enormously small, nothing particularly unusual to report.

– Ja, firstly the cell was 4 metres by 4 metres. There was mattress there, and some very dirty, dusty blankets. My nose got clogged immediately after sleeping under those blankets. There was a pillow. There was a slight, low bedstead. There was a toilet attached to the cell, but no toilet paper. I asked for some, and they provided it. There was no shower, but I was allowed to shower after five days, because I demanded it. It was very damp and dark, the light was on 24 hours a day, and a copy of the Bible. This young warder asked me what I was in for, and I told him I was a student, and I was in for making speeches. So he said, Oh, politics! So the next day he came and took the bedstead away, and swore me. Then a SB came, and I told him about it, and he said it had nothing to do with him.

– There were no windows, just I wouldn't refer to those things as windows because firstly they are small and secondly they were just like ventilators – they are small windows with just some perforated sort of fencing but it serves as a –

The lighting in your cell, could you switch it off from inside?

No, they control it from outside.

Would they switch it off every time you wanted it switched off?

No, they would just leave it on and they would say I've got to have a bit of patience. Once you are in that position they would say there's suspicion – so they just say that they have been instructed to keep the light on.

– The conditions in John Vorster – there were just about two mats on the floor and about three blankets, these grey blankets. There is nothing else in the cell, and the floor is painted dark, and the walls were cream-white, not pure white, and the roof was painted dark, I think. The cell in John Vorster was quite big. Now as soon as you enter the cell, facing you are the bars and that mesh wire, and then on your right is the toilet and the wall opposite the toilet, and then on your left is that cement table or bed or whatever, that cement bench that they have there. Further there is nothing. The minute you get into a place like this, it is quite empty, and it leaves you without any protection whatsoever, you see here you are actually exposed. You can't even think of hiding yourself from the security police in your cell, because you are so conspicuous, and you don't feel entirely free, because that peeping hole, anybody can just peep at you. And there are particularly those moments where you might have your own strolls or go on singing without actually being consciously aware of your surroundings – where you are actually trying to relax, and you sing as loudly as you can as you are moving around. And then it would always be irritating, or it would be encroaching into your privacy as soon as someone peeps on the wall here.

Could you see they were peeping?

Exactly, because if you could have a look at your own peephole, it is quite light because there is no shade over it during the day. Now the minute there is a shade, obviously there is somebody there. It's only when you go nearer, closer, that you can actually see that there is somebody there. But obviously at all times when you move around, you become so much acquainted with each and every corner of your cell. . . .

Relationships with authorities during detention

The nature of interpersonal relationships with state authority personnel, in particular those between detainees and magistrates, inspectors of detainees and medical officers, constitutes the core of the 'safeguards' granted to persons held under security detention provisions. Government authorities have proceeded on the grounds that visits by state officials are sufficiently adequate to guard against abuse of detainees by the police, a claim which in part depends upon an assumption that detainees are able to trust and place confidence in the said officials. Empirical data presented in Chapter 5 has already questioned the sufficiency of visits by authorities; the statements which follow further open to question the assumption that detainees have faith and confidence in magistrates, district surgeons and inspectors of detainees. The behaviour of medical personnel in relation to the whole system of detention, severely questioned at the Biko inquest in 1978, is particularly troublesome in the light of the fact that South Africa is a signatory to the 1975 Toyko Declaration of the World Medical Association, a declaration that forbids medical personnel from being party to torture or cruel and inhumane punishment. Some of the following statements re-open the doubts regarding the clinical independence of official medical officers whose responsibility it is to see to detainees.

– Shabbily. Very shabbily. The prison doctors are horrible men. At John Vorster the doctor – X, I think, he is the person in charge there – okay, he is okay, but I mean he doesn't give you the necessary treatment that you get from any doctor. You know, it's very shabby treatment. Okay, you tell him your problems, you've got this problem and sometimes he'll even pass remarks like – these people are against the establishment, this is the type of problems they must expect. Because I remember in one instance actually I'd gone there for consultation and then we ended up talking about my position, my political position, why can't people like us, you know, join Inkatha[10] – you know the type of thing. I mean, it's a bit difficult because the district surgeon is here and the cops are here, you know; you cannot relate fully well to a doctor for fear of the cops as well. Because, I mean, they are part and parcel of the same thing. I'm sure you get some of the fears, this inherent fears in detainees – detainees are not given the chance to converse freely with doctors. I mean, it becomes difficult to take your doctor into your confidence and discuss your problems with him because you somehow one way or the other link him up with the policemen. He is part and parcel of the establishment of the security system.

– *Did you request to go to the doctors at any stage while you were in solitary?*

Ja, there was one stage when I had a terrible headache and I requested them to take me to a doctor, and I was taken to a doctor.

And he gave you the medication?

Ja, although I was not satisfied with that because they took me to the doctor . . . and after some time he said, No, you don't have any problems but I can just use some Disprin. Actually the way he was talking – that chap – I think he thought I was just cheating, you know, because after that he called one of the security policemen outside and he talked to him something.

– The magistrates used to go out and I don't quite remember how often, but it was once a week, and when he asked me whether I had complaints or not I took it he was part of their strategy to demoralise me – to make me a mockery out of me – making a fool out of me – and should I tell them of the complaints, then I would be giving them the feeling that I was really deprived, desperate and do whatever they want me to do, so I never complained to the magistrate or whoever visited me. Whenever they asked me whether I had complaints I would say I had nothing.

Did you have contact with the inspector of detainees?

Yes, he used to come.

How did he treat you?

He was okay. He would make you feel that he sympathises with you and then you can rely on him and you can take him into your confidence.

Did you take him into your confidence?

No, then I didn't trust him or anybody. I felt that no matter how softly he spoke, maybe he is one who has been sent to come and have a look at me and assess how I was.

— *What contact did you have with authorities?*

This so-called detainee inspector, he used to come and take my complaints of which – they seemed to have fallen on deaf ears. But some of the demands, he would speak to the security police and they would come and tell me, Why should I tell him that kind of story, I'm not supposed to do that. But in the process – when I told him about having been punished, having bad food, that I had to see a doctor, well, they availed a doctor, a district surgeon, and I got better food, after my three-day hunger strike. But on torture he could not do a thing, and he told me that.

— At the least, I would say the relationship was a cold one. At the worst, I think it was quite a hostile relationship. So far as the surgeons and the magistrates and the inspectors are concerned, we never expected much from them because right away I just took them as part and parcel of the same system, because even if the magistrates come, you give them your complaints. The next thing the security police come with all those complaints and tell you, It's bullshit, and you talk too much and so on, just stay where you are – they start intimidating you. So eventually the worth of the magistrate just withers away.

— The only authority with whom I had some dealing was the magistrate, whom I met once a fortnight. In the initial period I discussed with him the problems I had and made my complaints and requests to him. After a while I found that he was unable to meet the kind of requests I was making and we had a number of arguments. The police and inspector of detainees and other authorities, although they visited me from time to time, I had no relationship with them, and basically we would just look at each other and the relationship can best be described as very cold.

— *Did you ask to see a doctor or a lawyer?*

No. They said to me that I was not allowed to see a doctor. The only thing they said is they will allow a magistrate to hear our complaints. But when he arrived at our cell he didn't ask any questions. He just passed through the door.

— *Then you were taken to a doctor?*

I was taken to a doctor – back to Algoa and the doctor was called when I was in the cells, and the doctor came to look at me and he just moved my eyelids and looked right in the eyes and he said I must turn around again. I turned around. He just felt my pulse here and said there wasn't anything wrong with me, I must just relax. I was never let to relax. I was taken back to Sanlam again. They started then with the questioning.

How was the attitude of the doctor?

I don't think he looked like a doctor, he looked more like a security policeman, that kind of situation.

– Okay, there are magistrates who come there from time to time and ask you if you're okay, whether they beat you up and do you wish to bring a case against them, you see; but we've had experiences of this very policeman who would come to you and pretend to be the magistrate and come and take statements from you and then the next time they beat you up. Or even cases of magistrates would come to you, talk to you and from there go back to those very people and let them know. I mean the whole story doesn't end between you and the magistrate, it is actually being carried back to these very policemen, you see. And they even threaten you that if you try and bring up a case against them then they either threaten you with indefinite detention. Like it was the case with me, because after I was beaten up I reported that matter to the magistrate, you see, and they came to my room and threatened me that if I go on with this type of thing they won't release me.

– He completely ignored me, he talked to the security police and he told me to open my mouth, my eyes, then he looked in my ears, that was all.

Did he treat you in the presence of security policemen?

Yes. We didn't even go to a place where he had some other medicine.

Was this a surgery?

No, it was an office, a security police office.

Did they come to you after the severe beating-up?

Yes, they did come to me. After being taken to the doctor they gave me two days' rest. Then after three days I was made to write some statements about all that they were questioning me about.

Did you write as they had instructed?

Yes, I wrote as they instructed.

– You only see from the response, as you give him an account of the conditions under which you live, and some of the questions, for instance, like what did you expect to eat, did you expect to eat rice? Sometimes when you are actually pointing out that you didn't get bread over a period of, for instance, a period of two days, three days we didn't get bread, you don't know what is happening. Then they say there might have been a mistake. It is so amazing, the way these people take things so lightly. Even some of the horrifying things they have done to you. When you start telling him that they did this to me, he is not even

[. . .] so that now one wonders of the type of magistrate which they send, whether they are really a magistrate or perhaps a policeman in disguise.

Ways of coping in detention

The evidence shows clearly enough that some people do not survive the process of detention in South Africa, whether the actual reasons be murder at the hands of security police, accidents during torture and interrogation, or induced suicide as a result of the variety of pressures of detention. The respondents in this study are therefore, ipso facto, survivors. Excerpts in this section provide a small sample of descriptions of the manner in which detainees managed to cope with an extreme situation. Some of these recommended devices, whether utilised or not, include the following: a knowledge of detainees' rights, however limited these rights may be; the necessity for physical and mental routine and time occupation; physical exercising; the maintenance of ego control and guards against disorientation; an understanding of the strategies used by interrogators; and a mental resolve to resist. Less clear here but more evident from other transcripts was the notion that appropriate expectation and mental preparation were beneficial in dealing with the situation, as was previous experience of detention. These sorts of strategies are entirely in accord with psychological theories regarding cognitive expectation and anticipation as an important variable in subsequent coping with stress and trauma.

Two of the most important coping devices involve the degree of commitment to the political cause and the necessity to maintain dignity, self-esteem and 'face'[11] in relation to the humiliations and pain of interrogation and torture. However, it should be noted that the range of possible coping mechanisms is both far wider and more variable than the limited descriptions provided here.

– But anyway, there was nothing else to do except train because, look, you are in there all alone. There is no reading material, even at John Vorster they refused to give us the Bible, you know – I mean normally detainees are provided with the Bible – anyway I didn't want it. So you were just in there, there was nothing that you could do – I mean, you've got to try and programme your body, you know. Okay, you sleep, you just sleep, you just wake up, somehow you try and devise a means to get tired so that you can sleep again. I mean, that is the pattern that you go through. So every day in and day out you sleep; in the morning you have breakfast, which is about two to four thin slices of bread with a cup of soup, you know; thereafter you hardly even feel – I mean you can't get more than that; from there somehow you've got to train and sleep, be up for lunch – it's the same sort of thing, from there train and sleep and be up for supper.

– But I think the greatest thing that would stand you in good stead in detention is to be fully aware of your rights under the different sections. To be fully prepared for lines of questioning and how you were going to relate them to the actual work you're involved in and to understand the way in which the security police works – their team approach, what their aim is, what pleases them, what does not please them, what are likely tactics to be used, and how you should survive, and to respond in order to survive under these difficult situations.

– It's difficult to recall all the strategies used. One often responded on a day-to-day or hour-to-hour basis. But generally one's strategy, as I had mentioned earlier, is not to become totally disoriented, not to fall for those kind of manoeuvres that one is aware that they might use. To stick one's ground as one understood one's involvement and to ensure that one didn't become too depressed or despondent. To continuously strive to make one's own position better without any compromises whatsoever. The periods after the sessions of interrogation were obviously periods of reflection, evaluation and forward planning.

– Sometimes if you are lonely and you are being interrogated, feel lonely and depressed and finally you'd come something like a breakup. But at least there is that thing that motivates you, that you are in a struggle, then you – those are things – of hardships of the struggle, from there you get motivated again.

– That depends on what you mean by cope. Because as I say, in the end you get to confirm the story that they give you. And somehow I even get to believe it might be true. You know, you repeat something so often that in the end you even forget what the truth is. Especially when I was exhausted. So I don't know whether you call that coping with interrogation.

– Because it was just after that Biko thing and they also told me, You know how Biko died? So we are going to take it very seriously. After – they say people are trying to escape. So one day after that, I couldn't take it any longer. So I just decided to commit suicide. But I was also worried about my people, that they don't know my whereabouts and what is happening to them. I was not allowed visitors. So I just decided to commit suicide. I just thought I am going to jump out of that window. And I think somebody [. . .] and when I went running to the window, already they had me. They grabbed me.

– I think the best way I found to cope with it was to objectify my situation wherever possible, so that even if I was in a difficult situation, if say someone was hurling abuse at me which was meant to undermine me, which was meant to make me feel degraded, dehumanised – right, what I would attempt to do was to objectify the situation totally. Step out of this and almost watch as an observer what was happening, to subject everything to a sort of critical and vigorous analysis. I think that it is important to do that all the time so that one doesn't get locked into a situation where they're trying to undermine you emotionally, psychologically and every way, you see. But it's difficult, though, to sustain because they can use some dirty things on you, and you get worn down after a while and you actually get weary of resisting after a while because it's an on-going – it's a war of nerves, it's a war of emotional strength, it's a war of personality a lot of the time, and it's a war of tactics. And what is happening is that the shifting tactics are also creating a confusion, it creates a complexity of responses that is needed on your behalf. You actually have to respond to the good guy and the bad guy in a very quick succession, respond to very different sorts of contrived forces that are acting on you all the time – it wears you down.

– *How did you cope with all the torture that you went through?*

The one thing I do is sort of say, Okay, just survive the next five minutes, just try and handle the pain for the next five minutes – there were times you could not actually cope with it but you screamed as mental anguish. Eventually you – I mean – you just – you were just so revolted by being so humiliated by the fact that people can stoop to such low levels.

– *How did you cope with all this physical torture and interrogation?*

There's the question of commitment to the whole political struggle and so when you're sitting there you would, rather to save many people, you'd usually die and let other people stay. I just told myself, Look, these guys are treating me very hard and I've gone through a very bitter experience, so at no stage that I could tell them who was involved with me and where and how and what. That's just my conscience told me that. I said I was not moving anywhere and I was not going to tell you or anyone what happened and how. Let them kill me if they want.

– What you find is that the police like any other bureaucracy has good guys and bad guys and that there are genuinely guys you can relate to. Now what happens to guys whose naive perception of security policemen is only malevolent, is that they can be confronted with bad guys whom they really hate and in contrast good buggers they can open up and relate to. Now in a sense if they haven't got a facility in dealing with people on a relatively day-to-day basis, they don't know how to maintain an even approach or an expedient approach to those relationships, so they're then left in a sense with some kind of relationship with security policemen which is a closed and very dependent relationship rather than being affable on a day-to-day-basis – making that kind of assessment – not confusing that – knowing when you're going to detention some security policemen are going to be good guys and there are going to be some that are bastards and there's something that you should know – but being able to exploit. Because there are some guys who actually protect you from others. They're subject to human interaction as well. People who set themselves high standards which they can't maintain eventually build up a self-loathing – they didn't choose to go into detention – close their eyes and refuse to talk. That of course is not a response that should be ruled out if it's appropriate in certain circumstances, and I considered it in my last detention. I don't know how effective it is but if you can't maintain your own standards you stand in a terrible position of losing your self-image, and your self-image is quite important in detention because you're in a hostile environment and if they get the chance they put you behind bars. You've got to resist a range of strategies and one of the ways you do it is in a sense your self-respect, your political beliefs and so on. And the other thing I want to say is that there are various approaches to interrogation – some of the things I've said is that people maintain a variety of techniques and tactics to cope with it. My own, though, is never to deny my beliefs – I think that's quite important. It's not only important for my self-image but it's important for my own image projection. Listen, I'd say, I believe that South Africa should be ruled by all those who live in it, regardless of race or whatever it is. Don't try and pretend you're actually more conservative than you are.

– *Your general strategy towards the security police?*

Initially I was just like terribly cross with them, and I just was being unreasonable. But later when I began to realise the gravity of the situation, I was powerless, and they were powerful, and I realised my own limitations and ability to cope with the situation. If I could have I would have maintained that position, but I just definitely couldn't. My response then was to be friendly to them but to maintain some dignity.

Problems on release

Instead of attempting to cover a full range of statements on impressions, feelings and health problems after release from detention, an area more appropriately dealt with in terms of the empirical data presented in Chapter 5, the selection of excerpts here gives central focus to discussion of difficulties of a social or interpersonal nature – a stress outcome relatively under-reported in the general literature.

The dominant pattern of release problems presented in the following statements is quite clear. On the one hand there are numerous statements referring to emotional lability – mood changes, irritability, short temper, aggression, depression and increased emotional sensitivity. On the other hand there are a number of reported problems concerned with interpersonal relations, predominantly referring to withdrawal, problems with communication, and expressed wishes to be alone. These two areas may be perceived as linked psychologically by a third commonly raised problem – a general sense of insecurity, lack of self-confidence and reduced trust in people. From the quotations below it seems clear that in general the respondents themselves perceived all three of these problems to be interrelated.

The very last statement in this set of quotations, which concludes the chapter, summarises poignantly and more eloquently than any research statement the destructive impact of this inhumane process upon its victims.

– When I came out I felt quite strong, you see. I saw my family, I saw my friends and I felt quite strong, although I was still feeling quite bitter about what happened to me. What I can say really is detention – it's also having some effects mentally, more especially with the case of torture, that thing always have effects on people. More especially with me. I found that when I went outside I started to be someone who is, although I was quite friendly with people, but I find that now at some stages, for no reason, I just lose my temper, I want to fight with anyone who is speaking to me. At a very, very short time I just get angry, you see. I couldn't control my temper, you see. Those are things that I've noticed, since I've been subjected to torture.

– I also need to have private space whereas before I shared a common sense. I've grown less gregarious, get less from people and less from relationships – I put less into relationships.

Do you think that relates to your detention?

Yes.

– Sometimes I just felt that I wanted to be on my own. Especially the first few weeks. So I used to chase people out of the house, asking them to go somewhere else. Then I was very short-tempered. My mother was understanding. I lost some of my friends because I didn't want to be with any friends at the time.

– Yes, I get problems. I did not want to talk to a lot of people. I did not want to meet people, I would never answer two questions from one person. They had it tough with me. I could not walk even in the streets, I ran when the car comes from that very corner, I could run like a mad cat.

– I was just totally alienated from anybody. You could not relate to that, I mean it's just such a huge experience. That people actually did not understand or you thought that people did not understand, you were totally alienated from them and you couldn't really relate to them, you couldn't speak to more than one person at a time without feeling overwhelmed. I mean, it's also related to how you can concentrate.

– *What about your moods, did you find that your moods changed rapidly, were you irritable, very depressed, passive or did you find you're still the same person basically?*

No, I'm not the same person. I'm highly sensitive. I easily get depressed and at times I just have a feeling of not wanting to see anybody – just to stay alone. When I just look at a person I just get suspicious – maybe this one is being sent by the system. I just don't trust anybody anymore. I think it is the same. Some other times I don't want to see other people, I just want to be alone.

– I had a serious problem with communication after spending so much time in solitary confinement, that even in company I would find myself sitting quietly by myself and not communicating as much as I used to before. Unlike before, I became generally more aggressive, and over petty issues would lose my cool and became a very short-tempered person. I became more susceptible to depression – each time I would hear of problems at home or anywhere else concerning the family it would depress me, and it would take me a long time to recover from these things. My eating pattern did change although for my period in detention I had suffered a loss of appetite. On my release the fact that I was in company encouraged me to eat and in fact began eating more than I used to before. I had serious problems about sleep although some nights I would be able to get a full sleep. There were times very often I would only be able to sleep three or four hours a night.

– There is a general sense of insecurity and lack of confidence. I think that when they actually strip you down, humiliation during the detention, for the interrogation process, it's sort of really lasting effects on you. That, because they strip you of all your dignity and your self-respect, in the sense that they attempt to do that, that causes you to lose your confidence.

– Anxiety, irritable and depression – those I still have problems with, even now. And the tendency of, you know, withdrawal – say you're seated with a crowd of people, everybody is just outgoing, even the person, the people you're used to, you know, you feel kind of insecure to be there and happy and so on. You keep to yourself most of the time – a thing which never used to happen to me before I went in.

Did you observe that before your detention your alcohol intake and your smoking intake has changed from before you went into detention?

No, I didn't take alcohol, but my smoking definitely has changed.

Are you smoking more or less?

More.

– That is the main thing that I noticed when I came out of detention, I've been taking quite a lot of cigarettes and alcohol. Say, for instance, before I went to detention I was not smoking neither drinking but when I came out of detention I was already smoking, and of late I have started to drink. More especially when I think very hard, then I start looking for something to drink.

– No, I don't have problems now. The only problems I have now is after that electrical shocking my muscles were jumping – my whole body would jump. So I would sit, then all of a sudden I would hold my breath in my sleep – I don't know that one but that was what my wife was telling me. I'll first hold my breath then I would just shake and I always wake up after shaking. I have a feeling that I'm falling off the bed or falling off something.

– *Did you have problems relating to your family and friends?*

No, I don't think so, although I don't say I don't have problems. Subsequently I think I'm much more aloof, much more temperamental, sometimes rigid – stress has almost become a permanent part of my make-up.

How do you handle situations where you are faced by the authorities, do you have a different approach now as compared to before?

You know, I don't know how I would react if I was detained again. I mean, I have subsequently had contact with them. I am fearful in the sense that immediately images of my experience are conjured up, but given the fact that I am still politically involved and that I have no illusions to the kind of battle that we are in, my continuing political involvement is a matter of choice, and for me then it is a question of duty to be able to accept those kinds of difficulties again. I don't look forward to them, I fear them, but I am not prepared, at least now at any rate, to make those sorts of considerations stop me from pursuing a course which I am committed to.

– *What happened when you were released?*

After I was released I found that I had muscle pains because of the torture that I went through and also because of the cold where I had to sleep. Also my ear always bleeds. It will bleed for the whole of my lifetime, and I have to go to the doctor for it about twice or thrice a year.

When you came out how did you sleep?

In the first days I used to sleep not normally until after about three weeks, then I sleep normally.

Did you have nightmares?

Yes, I'd dream I'm being taken by the police again, and fighting, and that sort of thing.

– *Is there perhaps anything else that you want to talk about?*

All I can say about detention is that detention is a very bad thing for anybody because it breaks one to state of depression. It makes you feel in a state of helplessness. Whenever you come from the detention you see yourself in a more different way. Different in that your moods are changing. You find yourself less social with people and you get to lose a lot of memory, because you feel such a lack of exercise mentally. You see detention – once one has been detained – a hard part of life, because it is beyond comprehension how one feels when one is detained. More especially it is solitary confinement, because that is the one that anybody would dread. To feel alone. Without anybody to talk to, without anything to do. You have to make up your mind as to what you would do, when you come out. But there is the constant worry that whenever you are in detention you are liable to be taken further into the location anytime. You are left with no peace of mind even though you are alone, you are not enjoying your loneliness. Taking cognisance of the fact that anytime you are liable for detention. And you are liable to interrogation and the interrogation may amount to your death. Because the extent to which these police are brutal, the extent to which they threaten those people, it makes you feel a dead person already. There is a lot of [. . .] between you and society, then and after detention because you have to make up for lost time. Detention interferes with your personal interests, with your personal preoccupations. I don't know what to say.

7 Conclusions, interpretations and recommendations

Preceding chapters have examined literature pertaining to historical and political contexts of detention, the changing legal situation with respect to security legislation, the issue of admissibility of detainees' evidence in court trials, and psychological or psychiatric evidence regarding outcomes of situations such as those detainees are likely to encounter. In addition results of a large nationwide empirical study into conditions and experiences of security law detention have been given, in the form of both quantitative descriptive statistics and qualitative statements from former detainees highlighting certain aspects of their experiences, and indicating some of the psychological processes involved at the receiving end of a highly coercive situation.

In this chapter an attempt will be made to present an overall review of the study. In doing so, central trends of findings will be reviewed, relating empirical findings to psychological research. A further section will try to provide an understanding of the torture situation and the actions of torturers. Finally, since the present situation in South Africa is such that security detention remains on the statute books and, moreover, the continued practice of torture is highly probable, a number of recommendations are provided.

An overview of findings

Historical and legal

The inescapable and obvious conclusion to be drawn from the historical development of the system of security legislation is that detention is above all a political act. Both emergency and security law provisions for detention were enacted during times of potential threat to the state posed by black political resistance. As the form of political resistance changed and became more militant in the 1960s after the banning of legitimate opposition, so too were the detention laws extended, entrenched and made more draconian. Simultaneously new legislation provided criminal sanctions for politically motivated actions, framed in generalised and expediently loose language.

In the wake of renewed, more deeply structured and more broadly based political resistance during the 1970s the state responded with a series of purportedly reformist policies. At the same time the detention legislation was re-examined, only to be streamlined. All the detention provisions were maintained in the 1982 legislation. The objective of the most recent era of security legislation has been to criminalise, and thus depoliticise, political resistance and opposition to the neo-apartheid forms of domination. Thus, in 1982, new and extended definitions of criminal offences for politically related actions were introduced – still somewhat loosely worded in order to incorporate the widest possible range of oppositional strategies. As broad-based popular opposition increased during the latter half of 1984 and 1985, so too did the state's deployment of detention as a political weapon. In 1985 all five detention provisions were applied in South Africa. During the state of emergency from 21 July 1985 to 7 March 1986, some 12 144 detentions were recorded. Of these 7 992 were held under emergency regulations, 2 262 in terms of the Internal Security Act and 1 890 under the detention legislation of the 'independent states'. In addition 7 777 arrests took place in terms of the emergency regulations.[1]

For these reasons the major conclusion to be drawn from the historical review is that detention is unquestionably a political strategy, designed to quell, contain and eradicate democratic political opposition which could threaten the white minority South African regime.

A second conclusion is that the past 35 years or so have seen a substantial erosion of the independence and jurisdiction of the courts and the concomitant increase in the power of the executive. One of the potential protections of freedom in a social order, an independent judiciary, has been systematically destroyed. The history of detention legislation is one reliable indication of this process.

Along with the diminishing influence of the courts in respect of individual rights and freedoms we have witnessed the increasing powers of the police as agents of the executive. This culminated in the recent (1985) state of emergency when, indemnified against any action committed in 'good faith', the security forces and police in particular have become in the words of Gordon and Davis[2] the 'investigating officers, persecutors, judges and executioners, [who] make their own laws'.

Thirdly, despite the considerable loss of formal ground by the judiciary in favour of the executive, one has to recognise that the judiciary has assisted informally in its own loss of influence, particularly with respect to rights of detainees. Notwithstanding the extension of powers of the executive, the higher courts have still maintained an ability to control executive excesses but until late 1985 generally tended to interpret such choices in favour of the state rather than of individuals' rights. Arguably this failing is not altogether by chance. According to Dugard,[3] of 25 security-related trials in the Transvaal between 1978 and 1982 (inclusive), 21 of these cases were heard by only 8 judges of the possible 45 judges and acting judges during that period. In short, 17 per cent of the Transvaal judiciary heard 84 per cent of cases in question; or, expressed differently, 10 per cent (4 judges) heard 52 per cent (13) of the trials. In a recent review of the courts' records in cases dealing with human rights, D. Basson[4] has shown how the courts are confronted with the choice of adopting an approach in favour of the individual or in favour of the executive authority. In his view the former approach is based upon the value of the freedom of the individual whereas the latter approach reflects an adherence to the values of the status quo, leading to a mechanistic interpretation of security statutes.

In general he argues that South African courts have adopted the latter approach, even during the recent state of emergency. As illustrative of this approach, reference can be made to *Momoniat and Naidoo* v *Minister of Law and Order*.[5] In *Momoniat*'s case the court was asked to decide upon an application for the release of detainees who contended that the emergency regulations empowering the Minister of Law and Order to extend their detention beyond an initial period of 14 days were invalid. They argued that their detention without being afforded the prisoner's right to make representations was so unreasonable that parliament could not have contemplated such a regulation being passed. Mr Justice Goldstone held that the exclusion of a right to be heard prior to the Minister's making an order for the continued detention of a detainee could not be said to be so unreasonable that it must have been made by the State President 'otherwise than bona fide'.

In addition the judge suggested that the detainee could make representations to the Minister after his detention had been extended. This decision indicates the pro-executive approach to which Basson has referred. The emergency regulations[6] prohibited a detainee from writing a letter without the permission of the person in command of the prison, and from receiving a visitor including a lawyer without the permission of the Commissioner of Police. For these reasons it is difficult to see what enforceable right a detainee had to make representations when all the necessary action required to make representations concerning his detention was subject to the consent of the Commissioner of Police or the officer commanding the prison.

Recently there have been signs of a change in the judicial attitude to detention. Most significantly the Appellate division in the case of *Nkondo and Other* v *Minister of Law and Order and Another* held that the Minister must provide adequate reasons for the decision to detain a person in terms of Section 23. Failure to do so would enable the court to release the detainee. Chief Justice Rabie held that 'the legislature intended that the person on whom a notice has been served should have a fair opportunity of dealing with the reasons furnished by the Minister. Merely to be informed of the statutory ground on which the Minister found against him would hardly give the person concerned a fair opportunity of making representations to the Minister envisaged by s28(9).'[7]

Nkondo's case was followed by an Appellate division decision in the case of *Hurley and Another* v *Minister of Law and Order*.[8] As noted in

Chapter 3, the court upheld the right of the courts to inquire whether the police had good reason for making a detention under Section 29, but ruled that once the police stated the grounds on which they were acting, the court could not decide whether it would have come to a different conclusion or whether the grounds were an inadequate basis for detention. Although this judgment provides an extremely restrictive form of judicial control over police decisions to order detention, the government reacted almost immediately by introducing the Internal Security Amendment Bill to empower the police to detain persons for a maximum of 180 days but without the restrictions imposed by the *Hurley* judgment.

Results of study

As for the results of the empirical study, they may be summarised in three distinct areas: general conditions of detention, claims regarding physical and psychological abuse in detention, and sequelae in terms of reported health symptomatology. If we bear in mind that the detainees interviewed were all held under security, not emergency, detention and that most were held under interrogation sections, the general conclusions to be drawn from the data are quite clear.

General conditions: Conditions for those held under security law detention in South Africa are harsh. Even prior to the event of detention itself the majority of respondents reported that they were subjected to harassment in one form or another. Other work has similarly found that harassment of individuals and organisations constitutes a regular form of political disruption.[9] The process and experience of detention itself, quite apart from the issue of torture and psychological forms of abuse, were found to be harsh, from the moment of arrest, through confinement and interrogation. The harshness of detention refers to physical conditions, the fact of isolation from support groups, the threatening attitude of authorities, and not least the mental state of the detainees particularly as regards the unpredictability and uncertainty of the situation. Fears and anxieties about possible subsequent events, including facing serious political charges, prolonged detention, physical abuse, or being coerced to turn state witness, all compound the mental fragility of the detainee.

The limitation on personal contacts in detention merely supports the reality of detention as a closed system in which complete control rests in the hands of state officials. Another disquieting aspect concerns the adequacy of visits by those state officials – inspectors of detainees, magistrates and district surgeons – who constitute the only possible marginal protection against abuse of detainees. Results show that not all detainees are necessarily seen by such officials, although this position does appear to have improved somewhat in recent years. Furthermore, such officials are not necessarily granted access to detainees on demand, as the Aggett inquest demonstrated and as subsequent legislation has failed to make explicit. Finally, detainees' trust in such officials is minimal, as shown in particular by qualitative findings in Chapter 6.[10] As a result, abuse may frequently not be reported for fear of further retribution at the hands of security police.

Torture: Findings with respect to interrogation practices and treatment of security detainees are quite clear, if thoroughly unpleasant. Torture, in terms of both physical and psychological abuse, is a relatively standard procedure. The pattern of forms of abuse are, with some variations, nevertheless broadly similar to those reported in other parts of the world. So too there exist variations in the present study. In conformity with South African stereotypes and discriminatory history, Africans in particular were more severely treated. The majority of the small sample of white detainees in fact claimed that they were not physically tortured. Regional variations showed that physical torture was more frequent in the Eastern Province and Border regions, and least frequent in the Western Cape. Males were more frequently abused physically than females, but the difference in certain forms was relatively slight. On average, detainees claimed to be subjected to about ten different forms of abuse. Viewed overall, the data are consistent enough to warrant the conclusion that as part of the pressure placed upon security detainees, torture is widely and relatively systematically practised throughout South Africa.

A few comments could be raised at this stage to contextualise the results. Firstly, it is not claimed that every detainee is subjected to physical torture. The results themselves are clear on the point that not all detainees arc physically abused. However, all the respondents claimed at least some form of psychological coercion. The possible variations in type and degree of maltreatment are considerable, however. We would not claim that someone subjected to one or two forms of psychological coercion, depending upon which forms, had necessarily been tortured. Similarly a few slaps would not be sufficient treatment, of itself, to justify a definition of torture. It must be granted that the precise line between what is and what is not torture could not be drawn with a great degree of objective accuracy. It is fully recognised that factors of subjectivity play a role in such situations. It must be granted that the internationally accepted definitions of torture, such as those endorsed by Amnesty International and the United Nations, are even by their own admissions not entirely free of difficulties.

It is difficult to define torture in a precise and universally applicable manner. There is no doubt that what may constitute the act of torture is always indexically related or context-bound. This was the approach employed in Chapter 4 in the discussion of solitary confinement.

For this reason, the findings of the present empirical study are all the more serious. It is in this broader framework that the precision of numerical frequency of torture forms, important as these data are in gaining some sense of prevalence, should be viewed as relatively less significant than the full set of findings about conditions of detention and interrogation in general. It matters rather less whether it is precisely 83 per cent who claim physical forms of torture, than the understanding that physical assault and other forms of torture occur within a closed system involving numerous further stressors of both physical and psychological forms. Furthermore, a broader contextual approach would have to consider the purposes, intentions and identities of those involved. This is the strength of the most recent United Nations definition of torture, which takes into consideration not merely the acts but the notion that it is pain inflicted 'at the instigation of or with the consent or acquiescence of a public official or other person acting in an official capacity'; and furthermore that it is purposed towards 'obtaining from him or a third person information or a confession, punishing him for an act he or a third person has committed or is suspected of having committed, or intimidating or coercing him or a third person'.[11]

The findings in the present study do not stand alone. The conclusions of this study are supported by other research. In this respect findings of torture in the present study simply support previous findings, obtained by different approaches, and this congruence enhances to a considerable degree the credence of obtained results. The overall conclusion drawn here, that torture is quite obviously a widespread and common practice in South African detention, is thus based on the findings of a range of studies. We would argue that only a biased or naive observer could any longer deny this conclusion.

Definition of torture: As an aid to further interpretative clarity of the torture data, two definitions of torture have been employed in the present study. The first is that of the United Nations, which draws attention to the criteria of both physical and psychological components and stresses as well the contextual criteria of actors, intentions and purposes. This definition provides the broad framework. The second definition is operational, specifying forms of torture. As mentioned above, it should be recognised that there is no universal and formal operational definition of torture and as used here the procedure followed those categories employed in previous empirical research conducted in Europe and North America. Given the context provided by the first definition – that in South Africa instigation is by public officials, it is aimed at extracting information and confessions, and use is made of coercion and intimidation – we believe that all categories listed in the operational definition would satisfy inclusion as torture. In reporting data by each separate category rather than collapsing categories, the operational definition gives clarity, facilitates possibilities of replication, and provides an open description allowing for varying interpretation by critics. For example, if a certain critic claimed that only electric shocks constituted torture, the corresponding claimed prevalence data could be read off the table. This procedure we believe facilitates openness of debate regarding the issue.

Health symptoms: Results of reported health symptomatology, both during detention and following release, suggest serious sequelae, broadly similar to those patterns reported by research elsewhere. In addition to the importance of the results themselves, the empirical pattern obtained provides a significant validity check for the study as a whole. Since it is highly unlikely that the sample of detainee respondents would be medically sophisticated, and therefore unlikely that they would be able to fabricate demand-cued responses, the fact that the obtained pattern of reported symptoms was in broad agreement with other studies lends substantial support to a validity claim for the results in general.

Further results were presented which suggest an association between reported health symptomatology and severity of detention treatment, thus strengthening a conclusion that detention in South Africa does have serious consequences for the health of detainees, particularly with respect to psychological well-being. Most of the symptoms could be regarded as psychological in either form or origin.

As with predominantly correlative research elsewhere, one has to be most cautious in drawing definitively causal conclusions. Furthermore, the indices constituting measures in this case are rather unsophisticated, and no doubt it would have been far better to have conducted full medical, psychiatric and psychological assessments of detainees upon release rather than rely on self-report methods. The last methodological device was however precluded on a number of grounds, not least the general political climate in South Africa and the lack of trust in general shown by detainees in so-called 'neutral' medical personnel. Despite these necessary cautions in interpretation, results clearly pointed in the direction of an association between detention and a deterioration of psychological health. Since research in this specific area of torture sequelae is in its infancy, these results should be read, despite limitations, as important in understanding the outcomes of such grievously stressful situations.

How are these torture sequelae to be understood? In the present state of knowledge it is unfortunately the case that we do not have a full explanation of processes involved, but from the different strands of psychological evidence reviewed earlier, the basis for an understanding is possible.

Post-traumatic stress: At first glance, the best way of understanding the psychological outcome of detention and torture is in terms of the post-traumatic stress disorder as recognised by the American Psychiatric Association's DSM-III.[12] In terms of this interpretation the psychological response to detention is broadly the same as in other highly stressful situations such as serious motor and aircraft crashes, military combat, rape, prisoner-of-war or concentration camps, and natural disasters. The essential feature is that the person is subjected to psychologically traumatic events outside the range of usual human experience. On the evidence presented in this study of conditions of detention, there is little doubt that the South African detention situation would satisfy this criterion.

The remaining three criteria for a diagnosis of post-traumatic stress disorder also seem to be satisfied to a substantial degree by the empirical evidence obtained from this study. *Re-experience of the trauma* is evidenced in the form of nightmares and fantasy. Numbing of responses or an *emotional anesthesia*, representing detachment or estrangement from people and a loss of emotional feelings for intimacy, is evidenced in the numerous 'release problems', which refer to difficulties in relating to people or a desire for withdrawal. The final set of criteria, involving largely symptoms of *excessive autonomic arousal*, was evidenced in the present data by the high frequency of reported sleeping difficulties, weight and appetite loss, and cognitive problems relating to headaches, memory and concentration. Restlessness and hyperactivity fall within this criterion as well. The DSM-III also refers to *associated features* including depression, generalised anxiety and increased irritability, all of which were notably present in both quantitative and qualitative results here. Furthermore the post-traumatic stress disorder falls within the wider diagnostic category of anxiety states, and the present findings of a range of psychosomatic-type symptoms (stomach pains, constipation, shivering, crying, rapid heart beat, nausea, sweating, trembling, etc.) are all further indicators of anxiety stress and autonomic arousal. In short, there appears to be more than sufficient evidence to claim that the majority of detainees interviewed reported symptoms which would support a diagnosis of post-traumatic stress disorder, with varying degrees of severity.

However, application of this diagnostic category, which represents a substantial improvement upon earlier psychiatric labels, is not entirely without problems. Researchers in this field are not in complete agreement. Some have argued for a specific sub-category of a 'torture syndrome'; others have suggested that the concentration-camp syndrome is a separate entity because of the extreme physical stressors and starvation; while yet another group has claimed insufficient evidence to support either post-traumatic or torture-syndrome categories.[13]

Problems also exist in equating natural stressors (such as floods or earthquakes) with deliberate human-produced stressors in the case of torture and death camps. DSM-III recognises this problem in part by claiming that the 'disorder is apparently more severe and long-lasting when the stressor is of human design'.[14] It also suggests that stressors such as torture frequently produce the disorder, while others (such as car accidents) only do so sometimes. The difficulties still remain however. While surface symptomatology may appear similar for the two stressor types, or differ only in degrees, it is highly probable that attributions of causality, responsibility and blame for the two situations would differ markedly, and would therefore have an effect on the recovery process. Closely related to this is the further problem that the DSM-III does not provide explanatory concepts. Given that attributional processes would be an integral part of causal mechanisms, it may be recommended that separate categories for different stressors be established.

A further problem relates to the nature of evidence provided in the current study. Owing to the research methodology adopted in this study, it may not be possible to draw definitive conclusions supporting a post-traumatic stress hypothesis. Firstly, respondents did not undergo a formal psychiatric or psychological examination. Secondly, data on symptoms are aggregated across individuals, not presented separately for each person as would be the case in clinical examinations. Thus, from presented data it is not possible to be completely clear as to what proportion of cases would meet all criteria sufficient for a full diagnosis. Thirdly, while there is some qualitative data about the presence of re-experience of the trauma in terms of dreams, sudden dissociations or intrusive recollections, and some quantitative evidence in reporting of nightmares and general anxiety, it must be conceded that these diagnostic questions were not adequately posed, and therefore data in this respect are somewhat thin. Furthermore, the formal DSM-III diagnostic criteria for autonomic arousal symptoms require that they were not present prior to the trauma. Unfortunately, although we might assume this to be the case, we do not have such a level of evidence here. In short, while the general pattern of self-reported symptoms does appear compatible with a diagnosis of post-traumatic stress disorder, a strict consideration of methodological issues precludes a definitive conclusion.

The most substantial problem with respect to the post-traumatic stress disorder is the possibility that noxious stressors such as torture may not produce a unitary syndrome, but rather separable disorders dependent upon the precise nature of stressors involved, on factors of resilience and support, individual differences in coping, and so on. In one of the most authoritative studies on concentration camp survivors, for example, Matussek found different clusters of symptoms, in part associated with differing forms and severity of stressors.[15] If his analysis is correct, then by analogy it is quite conceivable to expect similarly clustered symptom patterns as the outcome of detention and torture, rather than the unitary post-traumatic stress syndrome.

This issue of a unitary versus a differentially clustered model as best-fit descriptions for torture sequelae is not only a concern with scientific accuracy, important as such a quest is. It also relates to matters of legal evidence, particularly in cases of compensation for suffering from torture, or claims against the authorities for criminal violations. Given the great difficulty in proving torture, because of the closed and secretive nature of the practice and the habitual denials on the part of torturers, such cases are almost always likely to be retrospective – that is, evidence of current symptomatology will be employed to infer the presence or absence of coercive stressors.[16] If the post-traumatic stress disorder is seen as the standard or predicted outcome of torture situations, a question remains in the case of persons not thus diagnosed.[17] Would it then be argued that such people were not victims of torture?

If, on scientific grounds, the post-traumatic stress syndrome does not fully and adequately cover the symptomatology displayed by torture victims, which we hypothesise to be the case, then certain people who have been tortured and who show (for example) psychosomatic symptoms, though these fall short of the full criteria of post-traumatic stress, will run the serious danger of not being properly compensated. An adequate solution to these scientific problems remains therefore a most urgent priority. In the meanwhile we caution against a stance that regards the post-traumatic stress disorder, in and of itself, as the most valid diagnostic category accounting for torture sequelae.

To summarise our conclusions: Health symptoms of South African detainees, both during detention and on release, seem in general to accord with those required for a diagnosis of the post-traumatic stress disorder. This DSM-III category is at present an important heuristic device in describing the symptomatology of torture victims. However, both methodological and other scientific considerations preclude our reaching a definitively supportive conclusion about the post-traumatic stress disorder. Nevertheless, we must remember that, irrespective of the future standing of post-traumatic stress, health problems of the detainees were grave, warranting the conclusion that the system of detention presents a grievous health hazard to those who become its victim. Problems, mainly of a psychological nature, were related primarily to the following types of disorder: stress anxiety, depression, cognitive functioning, psychosomatic and emotional anesthesia with difficulties in interpersonal relationships.

Individual differences: Questions remain about individual variability in response to highly stressful situations such as those found here. It is of course a standard scientific acceptance that such variability exists. A glance at tabled frequencies of reported health symptoms in Chapter 5 and in the appendices shows that in general women and African respondents reported higher symptom frequencies. In the case of African detainees, as well as the regional variations, it is probable that a good deal of the variability is attributable to more serious abuse during detention. This was not so in the case of women, and interpretation of results is not quite so apparent. Frequencies were so consistently higher for women than men for both 'during detention' and 'on release' that it strongly suggests bias in reporting, rather than a veridical reflection of actual occurrence of symptoms.[18] A social normative account would hold that women are taught to respond more readily to symptoms, while men deny and repress recognition. It is also feasible that through social learning women are more sensitive in their recognition of both physical and psychological ailments. If correct, both of these interpretations would lead to a further conclusion that given the preponderance of men in the sample, the overall frequency of reported symptomatology in this study is negatively biased, and should in reality be higher than reported. An alternative hypothesis also remains open: that women may be less likely to expect such grim treatment, or may be less trained to cope with it, and therefore the obtained data are an appropriate reflection of reality. No definitive conclusion could be reached here.

Group-based variations such as these still leave the question of individual differences unanswered. This is a complex issue since coping strategies may vary with different stages of the detention process. For example, dealing with solitary confinement may differ from coping with interrogation or physical torture or humiliations. In general it appears from the psychological literature reviewed in Chapter 4 and detainees' experiences described in Chapter 6, that one of the most effective ways of coping with solitary confinement involves imposing some sort of active structure on time.

Related to this strategy is the notion from psychoanalytic literature that sound coping involves utilisation of fantasy material in the service of the ego to ward off engulfment by primary process impulses. Active mental activity seems thus to constitute a key coping device. Commitment to political beliefs and service to a greater cause also appear to be important strategies. It is now well recognised in the general stress literature that social support by others is of considerable importance in coping with stress.[19] So too for detainees. Isolation from social support is of course one of the major stressors. Thus, use of such support in reality, in terms of other detainees where possible, or in imagination and fantasy, is likely to be an important variable factor.

While it is far-fetched to assume that a single model could incorporate all the factors involved in explaining individual differences, one recent approach does seem to draw together at least some of the apparently central factors. The notion is that of a 'hardy personality'. This is hypothesised as comprising three component factors making up a personality style that facilitates resistance to stress.[20] The three components are as follows. Firstly, *commitment* involves an overall sense of purpose and belief in the truth, importance and value of what one is doing, this purpose being rooted in a sense of community. Indeed, this sense of community or accountability to others has been regarded by some writers[21] as the most fundamental interpersonal resource for successfully coping with stress. *Control* refers to the tendency to believe and act as if one could influence the course of events. It involves strategies of actively seeking explanations for events as well as taking personal responsibility. *Challenge* is based on a belief that change rather than stability is a normative way of life, and involves being practised at responding to the unexpected. While emphasis among the three components may vary, the overall pattern is regarded as describing an orientation or style of 'hardiness' which enables more successful coping with stressors.

Research into this hypothesised 'hardy personality' has not extended to extreme situations like detention and torture, so its use here is conjectural. It does seem, however, to offer some possible set of constructs with which to explain individual variance in response to torture. The hypothesis awaits testing in extreme conditions.

Explanation of stress: To this point there has been little effort to explain the stress symptomatology. We noted in passing that the DSM-III label describes a pattern of responses but does not give an explanation for them. Neither is it possible to do justice to a full explanation here. If we cast back to the review of psychological literature in Chapter 4, it appears that (i) cognitive mediating factors are highly significant in explaining response to stressors, and that (ii) the two factors of predictability and controllability emerge as important variables.

A feature common to all the psychological literature surveyed in Chapter 4, from sensory deprivation through concentration camps and torture research to learned helplessness theory, was the notion that effects of stressors were mediated and exacerbated by variables that have been labelled as ambiguity, unexpectedness, lack of preparation or unpredictability. A number of approaches – in particular learned helplessness, experimental work on urban and noise stress, and the DDD view of coercion – also emphasise the variable of controllability, or helplessness. Both of these factors, predictability and controllability are also emphasised in the literature on the psychology of police interrogation. For example, in an analysis of standard police interrogation tactics as laid down in police training manuals in the USA, Driver argued that stress was chiefly located in the ambiguity and unpredictability of events, as well as in the victim's helplessness in escaping from or reducing the threats or implied threats inherent in the interrogational situation.[22] In a more recent British study of police interrogation, Irving and Hilgendorf claimed that 'ignorance, little or no preparation, and an unexpected sequence of events all conspire to increase the level of stress resulting from confinement and isolation'.[23]

These variables are not, of course, the *cause* of stress; it is quite apparent that physical pain or psychological terror will produce stress via physiological, cognitive and affective mechanisms, irrespective of their predictability or controllability. However, neither are these factors separable from the stressors themselves. For example, to be beaten or humiliated is to be placed generally in a relatively passive and non-controlling situation. But controllability and predictability become particularly relevant in understanding debilitating outcomes such as those described by the post-traumatic stress disorder or learned helplessness condition.

The 'causal' stressors are of various kinds, as we have seen throughout this study. The following is a brief categorisation of the important stressors:

(a) *Physical stressors:* severe bodily pain; deprivation or excesses of life supports (food, water, air, light, sleep).

(b) *Psychological stressors:* sensory (deprivation, monotony, unpatterned, overload); emotional arousal (terror, fear, anxiety, threats); learning mechanisms (behaviour control); cognitive (communication and linguistic techniques, degradation, ambiguity, contradictions, general appraisal of situation); motivational (dependency, helplessness).

(c) *Social-psychological stressors:* isolation and confinement; compliance and dependency; self-threats such as humiliations; threats to significant others or ingroup; threats to beliefs, values and worldview; communication techniques (distortions, contradictions, false information); captive–captor relationship.

(d) *'Institutionalised' stressors:* a regime of total control and manipulation; factors of physical and geographical location, time-space and ecological manipulation including physical conditions of confinement; manipulation of symbolic devices and rituals.

In conclusion, it is necessary to emphasise the widely accepted psychological argument that if the stressor conditions are sufficiently severe, with the deployment of a wide range of variable, unpredictable and uncontrollable stress, then it would be expected that anyone might concede at some time to demands made for information, confessions, denunciations, admissions, renunciations and the like, despite all efforts through preparation, readiness, training or commitment to resist such demands. In other words, the greater the stressor factors, the less one may expect in terms of individual variability in response and the less the likelihood of resistance. It is unlikely that psychological technology is sufficiently advanced at present to be able to make accurate predictions about the degree of resistance of any particular person.

Admissibility of evidence: One of the most urgent and disturbing implications of our empirical findings relates to the issue of admissibility of evidence from detainees in courts of law. The system of security detention in South Africa is designed to manufacture information in terms of confessions, admissions and evidence regarding the activities of other persons. This information is used for general politically motivated security policing, but also for legal processing in order to produce criminal convictions.

On the basis of the empirical evidence in this study, it is submitted that statements from detainees who remain within the closed system of detention should be regarded as unreliable and therefore legally inadmissible as evidence. The empirical evidence relates to harsh general conditions of detention as well as the highly coercive methods employed in interrogation. These coercive devices are both physical and psychological in form. While South African law prohibits the admission of statements extracted under physical coercion,[24] it is often difficult to prove that the detainee's statement was made under duress. The defence is confronted by the corroborative denials of a number of security policemen against the single claim of a detainee. This is an inevitable product of the very legal nature of security detention.

Psychological forms of abuse and coercion are not normally taken into consideration by the courts as formal criteria for admissibility, yet our study has found such abuse to be epidemic in scale. As described earlier, the forms of psychological coercion may be grouped into four main categories: communication techniques (false accusations, misleading information, and others), mental weakening devices (solitary, sleep deprivation, prolonged interrogation, blindfolding and hooding), psychological terror tactics (sham executions, threats of violence, knowledge of torture of others), and humiliations and degrading actions (nakedness, verbal abuse, sexual abuse). At very least, courts should direct themselves to establishing, in a serious and *systematic* manner, the presence or absence of these modes of coercion.

However, the distinction between physical and psychological coercion is rather arbitrary, and one of the important findings of this study reveals that they are used in combination. Results showed that detainees claimed on average to have been subjected to ten different forms of coercion.

In respect of the legal recognition of psychological coercion in the American case of *Miranda* v *Arizona*, the Supreme Court warned against taking insufficient heed of psychological factors in judging the validity and reliability of evidence. Subsequent to that case, E. D. Driver,[25] in a thorough analysis of existing police interrogation manuals in the USA, argued that even the *Miranda* warnings were insufficient to provide adequate safeguards against the general social psychological rigours of arrest and detention in respect of obtaining statements rendered freely and voluntarily. By contrast South African courts have hardly begun to consider the implications of the *Miranda* approach.

Additional evidence for rejecting detainees' statements as legal evidence derives from the present study's unique data on symptoms experienced *during the course of detention*. While this material was obtained retrospectively, there is nevertheless sufficient evidence to support a conclusion of severe and wide-ranging psychological disturbances of a cognitive, psychosomatic, anxiety-related and depressive nature as well as sheer physical debility.

These empirical findings provide more than sufficient evidence to suggest that detainees will be disorientated, and cognitively confused and impaired, and are likely to comply with interrogators' demands, even if this means giving false or at least not wholly true and reliable information. There are thus sufficient grounds to recommend that detainees' evidence, at least while they remain within the system of detention, should be regarded as inadmissible.

The question of detainees' evidence once they are released from detention remains more problematic. Empirical results here show that they still suffer from a range of psychological effects. They are free from direct coercive constraints, but because of the possibilities of being redetained as well as other psychological inhibitions, evidence may still fall short of the full requirements of being made freely and voluntarily. It is recommended that such evidence be treated with appropriate caution.

While the courts are unlikely to forgo traditional rules, most notably the piecemeal or particularistic approaches to the merits of each individual case, it is strongly suggested that they take into account the empirical findings of this study as background information. For we are confident that these findings constitute the reality of experience in South African detention.

The overall conclusion of this study is that the systems of security and emergency law detention in South Africa are inhumane, and fall far short of institutional criteria demanded of a civilised nation. The laws are in urgent need of drastic change. Towards this aim, recommendations for change are provided below. Before turning to them, however, some brief consideration is given to the issues of the torture situation and the psychology of torturers in order to place the recommendations in an appropriately contextual framework.

On torturers

Not a great deal is known about the psychology of torturers. However, from some important experimental work and preliminary field investigations we can begin to sketch the explanatory parameters to account for such extreme action. There is a growing recognition that an understanding of torturers' behaviour is not separable from the wider situation in which it occurs – that is, the social and political context.

A widely held hypothesis argues that torturers must be grossly disturbed personalities. If there were substantial evidence to support such a notion, we may perhaps have greater reason to be optimistic about the rapid demise of torture, since the relative proportion of such abnormal personalities is not likely to be very substantial, and they could be weeded out by means of careful and appropriate selection. Available evidence however tends to point in an alternative direction; that torturers are not particularly abnormal. They are far more likely to be quite ordinary people in an extraordinary, abnormal situation.[26]

An important line of evidence gained from Milgram's set of dramatic experiments[27] suggests that psychological processes involved in the obedience to authority may be one of the major factors in explaining torturers' actions. For it is generally recognised that members of the ruling class do not themselves participate much in the torture situation per se, even if they are giving the instructions; the task of torture itself is frequently 'sergeant's work'.[28]

In Milgram's laboratory experiments it was found that most subjects delivered what they thought to be dangerous levels of electric shocks to innocent, helpless victims. The key explanatory notion appeared to be obedience to an authority figure – a white-coated scientist who was conducting the experiment. A better understanding would be that obedience was not to the experimenter himself but to the situation, the authority being legitimated by the ideology of science. In other words, the participants in a scientific study found it difficult to challenge that authority, despite limited coercion on the part of the scientific experimenter present, and even although they were committing what appeared to be terrible assaults upon the victim.[29] It is notable that Milgram's studies were expressly conducted to throw light upon the Nazi atrocities.

Further findings from Milgram's work, which may lend additional insight into the torture situation, showed the importance of 'buffering' processes. That is, the degree of obedience in his experiment increased when greater psychological distance was created between the 'aggressor' and the victim. For example, if the 'aggressor' was required merely to give instructions to an assistant instead of pressing the switches himself, the degree of obedience increased. Conversely, if the psychological distance between the two participants was reduced – if the 'aggressor' was required to take the hand of the victim and press it to an electric plate – the degree of obedience was reduced; less people were prepared to follow such instructions.

Surveillance was a further variable factor. Under close surveillance, not surprisingly, obedience increased, whereas when the experimenter was not physically present, many subjects did not fully carry out the instructions. Social support was a third variable factor. When there was social support available to resist the authority situation, the degree of obedience dropped. Finally, the legitimacy of the authority plays a significant role. When the same study was replicated in a run-down office in town, rather than in a prestigious university, thus reducing the legitimacy of 'scientific authority', obedience was not so substantial. It is quite conceivable that all of these factors contribute to the explanation of the torture situation. However, the crucial understanding to be gained from Milgram's experiments is that the great majority of participants in his studies, quite ordinary and non-pathological people, went along with the horrific situation, despite evidence of substantial internal conflicts. In short, the results strongly suggest that personality factors, while not being entirely excluded from consideration (some people certainly did refuse to go to the maximum treatment level), may play a less significant role in explaining such grim behaviour than do situational and wider contextual factors.

Similar interpretations emerge from an equally well-known study by Zimbardo and colleagues in the early 1970s.[30] In randomly assigning students to the social roles of either prison guard or prisoner in a realistic mock-prison setting, these researchers found that in a relatively short space of time, the 'prison guards' were acting in a cruel and aggressive fashion towards the prisoners. 'Prisoners' in turn rapidly became apathetic and manifested certain negative psychological symptoms. In this study, an explanation would clearly lay central emphasis upon social roles rather than intrapsychic factors. Furthermore, the fact that subjects in Zimbardo's experiment acquired the role sets so rapidly suggests the presence of deeply institutionalised role 'scripts' – that is, sets of role expectations. It suggests also that being a prison guard involves normative expectations of violent action towards prisoners.

An interview-based study of actual torturers indicates that while the above-mentioned research throws important light on some processes, the real situation involving the training of torturers comprises further aspects. After the fall of the Greek military dictatorship (1967-74), Haritos-Fatouros scrutinised official testimony records at the criminal trial of junta personnel and also interviewed former military police, some of whom had been torturers. It is apparent that systematic training and selection accounted for the behaviour of torturers in this case. The process of making a torturer included a number of recognisable steps.[31]

Firstly, trainees were selected at various stages: from initial recruitment to the military, then to the military police unit, subsequently to a special interrogation section, and finally as designated torturers within this section. Early selection paid particular attention to the political attitudes and beliefs of the recruit and his family, most notably their anti-communistic attitudes and actions. Selection for the interrogation office was based on close observation of recruits during basic training, with attention being given to the characteristics of obedience to orders, loyalty to the military regime, and physical hardiness.

Secondly, during the period of training and, later, of involvement as interrogation officials, a series of devices was directed towards emotionally binding the military policemen to the authority of violence. The whole period of training could be perceived as an initiation ritual or ceremony, aimed at creating a specialised subculture. It involved an extremely tough physical programme, ritualistic beatings, humiliation and degradation of recruits, ceremonies involving swearing allegiance to symbols of the junta authority, a stress on the hierarchical and unquestioned nature of this authority, crushing of any signs of resistance with the use of deprivation techniques among others, and a sharp focus on the important role of the military police in the protection of the new regime. Furthermore it was found that language played a significant role in the development of this subculture. A specific jargon was developed, and nicknames were used for colleagues to protect their identities. Nicknames were also employed for different methods of torture, for example a 'tea-party'. Anyone not belonging to this self-described 'elite' was referred to as of the 'outside world'.

Thirdly, the training period used systematic applications of learning principles directed at changing behaviour. Overlearning was used to teach obedience to authorities. Recruits were desensitised to the idea of torture by enduring harsh techniques of a similar kind as part of their 'normal' daily routine, and later by observation and gradual participation in the torture of others. Modelling was employed in the form of more experienced servicemen being used to beat and humiliate freshmen. Negative reinforcements included threats, intimidation, ridicule in the presence of others, and severe physical exercises as punishment, while positive reinforcement methods involved both material and social gains. Perhaps the most positive reward was membership in a high-status and highly feared military unit, particularly since most recruits came from fairly poorly educated, lower-status, country backgrounds.

The study concludes by saying: 'to believe that only sadists can perform such violent acts is a fallacy and a comfortable rationalisation to ease our liberal minds', and suggests for further investigation the hypothesis that 'if the proper learning procedures are applied under the right circumstances, any individual is a potential torturer'.[32]

Is it conceivable that one human being could inflict such awful treatment on another without any remorse or alteration of psychological states or values? Again, the evidence is not very clear, but most commentators would suggest the presence of psychological defence mechanisms which enable a plausible account to be given of torturers' extraordinary behaviour. For example, in presenting a heuristic model, Allodi suggests that torturers use some of the following defence mechanisms: rationalisations ('under orders', 'only a job', 'I didn't know', 'if I don't someone else will'); dissociations involving 'bureaucratic detachment and coldness', or amnesia, or automatisms; paranoid projection in perceiving victims as sick, verminous, sinful, personification of evil; use of intoxicants such as alcohol or drugs; splitting of roles, for example that of loving family man, husband, or father and that of torturer; acting out against depression, hopelessness, despair, fear and guilt; denial, involving euphemisms and the mendacious use of language.[33] The general upshot of these mechanisms is a mental transformation which brings about denial of the crime of torture, and a dehumanisation of the victim.

In reporting the torture situation in Greece in the early 1970s, Amnesty International suggested that torturers have to construct defences in order to carry out their work. At the Greek junta headquarters, for example, torturers were known to refer to themselves as 'doctors'. Amnesty further reported: 'the atmosphere surrounding the torture operation seems to rely on this kind of perverted irony, an *esprit de corps* which, like forced bravado in wartime, is necessary to sustain the belief that somewhere a higher authority will take responsibility for crimes committed in the name of the state'.[34]

Protection from anxieties engendered by this terrible work may not be complete however. Frantz Fanon for example, when a psychiatrist in Algeria in the 1950s, reported the case of a torturer who heard screams at night which prevented him from sleeping, and went to great lengths to stop the screams, by closing the windows, stopping his ears with cotton-wool, and turning on the radio or music in order not to hear this nocturnal uproar.[35] On the other hand interviews with the former Greek junta torturers suggested little sign of remorse for their devastating actions, which in at least one case crippled a man for life and left him with severe speech dysfunctions.

Although we do not have a full explanation for the torturer's attitude to the victim, one recent psychological approach may contribute towards an understanding. The 'just-world hypothesis' suggests that people justify the fate of innocent victims, and social injustices in general, by holding a belief that the world is after all a just one, therefore the victim must have in some or other way 'deserved' his suffering or negative fate. They 'want to believe that our world is so constructed that terrible things happen to people because they were "terrible" to others'.[36] As a mental operation, attempts are made to find the victims blameworthy either because of their actions or because of their personal attributes or characteristics.

In terms of this hypothesis, which has been supported by some research findings, the less deserving the victim, the greater the likelihood that he would be devalued. This involves a distortion of the image of the victim in order to maintain the belief that an injustice was not committed.

This belief in a 'just world' is of course an invention, a justification, a belief that this is the way the world 'should be'. It is backed up, according to Lerner, by the myth of the rational man, the myth of the good citizen. Although Lerner and his research associates have not specifically applied their hypothesis to the torture situation, and our use of this notion here is rather speculative, it does seem to offer some explanation in accounting for the torturer's derogation of his victim. Furthermore, it suggests a plausible explanation for the frequently observed response by the wider public, particularly those of the ruling classes, in demonstrating a distinct lack of sympathy when cases of torture, or even of ill-treatment of ordinary prisoners, are reported. A surprising number of public observers in such cases find, with some alacrity, 'just-world type' justifications for these atrocities.

Along with intrapsychic defences as described above, it is quite likely that social-psychological attributional biases constitute some part of the explanation for the otherwise inexplicable actions of torturers. Preliminary empirical evidence has been provided to support the hypothesis that 'commitment to the belief that they live in a just world can lead people to condemn victims, and invent functional myths about themselves, social causality, and others'.[37]

There is no real information about torturers in South Africa. As with other countries whose citizens are tortured, the activities of the security police in South Africa are shrouded in veils of secrecy. Legislation in terms of the Police Act and Prisons Act[38] largely precludes the possibility of publishing information about activities of police and prison personnel. One may comfortably assume that those who find their way into the security forces are carefully selected and thoroughly trained, but the precise criteria involved in selection and the methods of training remain largely unknown, and could not be reported even if they were known. It is further unknown whether anything approximating formal training in torture methods is conducted in South Africa. In this respect, Amnesty International at an earlier stage drew the following conclusion: 'Allegations of similar tortures have been made from so many centres and have involved so many local officers – in addition to certain interrogators who travel from Pretoria to other centres – that there is reason to believe that Security Branch Officers have been trained in these methods.'[39]

Evidence presented here points in precisely the same direction and we can only concur with the Amnesty conclusion. In certain respects it would not matter whether formal training in torture methods per se was received or not. There can be no doubt that security personnel are trained in *interrogational* methods, and that such methods would necessarily involve use of relatively subtle methods of psychological coercion (irrespective of whether formal psychological literature has been consulted). The torture methods themselves hardly need much additional formal training. What is far more at issue is whether the attitudinal preconditions for torturing are learned during training. There seems little doubt that this is the case in South Africa.

On torture

We live, in the latter half of the twentieth century, with a strange human paradox. Ours is a time when torture is entirely forbidden by international law[40] as well as in terms of domestic laws in many countries, but the practice of torture continues on a rampant scale[41] – usually accompanied by vehement denials by authorities. Since World War Two, awareness of and campaigns for human rights have reached unprecedented levels, yet the unmet needs for action have probably never been greater.

It is a tragic fact that torture seems to have been part of human history since the earliest recorded times. Yet it would be a fallacy to treat it as an unchanging and inevitable phenomenon. Rather, like all historical phenomena, the practice of torture has waxed and waned, changed in form, purpose, and legality. So too have the miserable victims of its persecutions been differently categorised over the centuries. Despite its periodic shifts, the history of torture is instructive in showing certain more-or-less invariant characteristics, the 'structure' of the torture situation – if such a term is useful.

Conspiracy theory: Drawing together the historical strands of its study, a recent major history of the subject characterises the torture situation as one rooted in a conspiracy theory or scenario. Torture 'survives to this day wherever governments believe themselves, or choose to believe themselves, to be beset by conspiracies and subversion'.[42] The conspiracy scenario, typified by an institutionalised paranoia, is often the response of a regime with a weak moral or social base. Dissent which emerges from contradictions in the social formation is interpreted as the product of the machinations of a secret or hidden enemy. An inquisitorial-type machinery, with the traditional features of secrecy, interrogation and torture, demands denunciations of those categorised as disloyal. It extracts statements, confessions and information in order to purge society of the apparently hidden enemy within. Ruthven sums up his study as follows:

> The Grand Conspiracy is a fantasy in the minds of the authorities, born of a paranoid response to the dissidence around them. . . . It is the reaction of the elite groups, especially in militarised societies, who stand to lose by social change. The Grand Conspiracy becomes a model of repression to be applied to every contingency. [It] takes on an increasingly ideological tone . . . [and] . . . 'foreign' ideas are seen as a source of the poison that is corrupting youth and destroying society.
> . . . The Grand Conspiracy is more than the freakish fantasy of deluded inquisitors, soldiers or policemen: it is the scenario according to which inquisitors and police or military terrorists achieve their own subversive aims of subjugating society and destroying the rule of Law in the name of Order. Torture which is invoked to defend the state in effect destroys it.[43]

Although nowhere in his study does Ruthven allude to contemporary South Africa, the above depiction captures almost exactly the social and political climate in which torture has developed as an institution in South African society.

The script of conspiracy has a considerable emotional appeal, particularly during times of economic and social stress. This is so, suggests Ruthven, for while conspiracies may be worrying they are also psychologically reassuring. Belief in a conspiracy provides coherence and a means of explanation for events that would otherwise seem incomprehensible. Furthermore, a conspiracy theory is especially attractive to the military or police in situations where they are faced with potentially hostile populations. The surface events of political unrest, usually disparate and with spontaneous roots, are recreated in the minds of the authorities into a single, coherent and necessarily organised movement. The assumption in such scenarios is that the population is being manipulated by hidden, omniscient leaders or agitators. Resistant action is not interpreted as a manifestation of grievances, but as the work of malignant forces, often under the sway of 'foreign' ideas or powers.

In South Africa over the past decade or more, state rhetoric has been exactly that of conspiracy theory – with its characteristic of explaining multicausal events in monocausal or cognitively simple terms.[44] Activities of the 'malignant forces' have been described in terms of a 'total onslaught', and the response of the authorities therefore 'logically' becomes one of 'total strategy'. Actions of reasonable critics and opponents are explained in terms of their being unwitting agents of masterminding organisations.

Such organisations do, of course, exist. They are created and produced in the first place by repressive forces of the regime. Major oppositional activity is banned, outlawed or driven underground where it of necessity has to operate in secretive fashion. In South Africa this has been the case since the 1950s onwards with the Communist Party, African nationalist organisations, trade unions, Black Consciousness groups, and most recently, affiliates of the United Democratic Front. Other church and student organisations have been closely scrutinised in government-commissioned 'witch-hunts'. There can be little doubt that part of the purpose of the most recent (1985-6) wave of emergency detentions was to seek out the hidden leaders and planners of disturbances. The inevitable conclusion of the conspiracy scenario is the treason charge; a number of such trials are, predictably, before South African courts at the time of writing.

Conspiracy rhetoric has been part of the South African state baggage for longer than the past decade. Since the mid-1970s, however, the economic and social crisis has deepened; so too has the discourse of conspiracy. This in turn becomes the justification for increased militarisation, security vigilance and repressive actions. The inevitable and escalating spiral of violence emerging out of the declining economy and increasing repression was tragically visible to all in the events of 1985. In times such as these it is usual to encounter arguments in defence of torture under emergency conditions. Such arguments need to be examined and challenged.

The logic of conspiracy theory attributes the cause of every disturbance and all violent acts to conscious planning. This leads to a strategy of seeking out the source of violence, and 'pressure for the introduction of torture becomes irresistible'.[45] Under such circumstances, arguments about the need to act quickly to save innocent lives are invariably used to justify the introduction of 'special interrogation techniques' for emergency conditions.

Such an argument has been put forward by Rudolph in his recent defence of interrogational torture.[46] The core of the defence is presented around a philosopher's imaginary situation, which in Rudolph's case appears roughly as follows. The police have arrested a man who has planted (or is strongly suspected of having planted) in the centre of a city, say Pretoria, a large explosive capable of killing dozens of people and injuring hundreds more. The question posed is how far it would be permissible for the police to go to extract information, not for subsequent prosecution, but for the sole purpose of preventing a disaster.

Rudolph claims that a moral defence of torture is permissible in such a case. He goes further however, and invoking the legal defence of necessity, argues that statutory provisions, with safeguards of course, should authorise police in such circumstances to 'use such force *as may be reasonably necessary* to obtain the information from the detainee'.[47] He concedes that it may be difficult to define in advance what may be deemed 'reasonably necessary'. It would depend on the circumstances in each case. If, says Rudolph, the issue turned on preventing an explosion of a nuclear device, 'it is difficult to contemplate on moral grounds any limits to the form of torture that could be warranted'.[48]

Before proceeding further the peculiarities of the imaginary situation upon which the case for interrogational torture rests should be noted. The case is a highly artificial example. The police have apprehended the actual (or strongly suspected) perpetrator – not the more likely situation of having someone who may, perhaps, know something of the case. The situation is couched in emotionally irresistible terms: the killing of dozens and injuring of hundreds, cast within the language of 'saving the lives of many innocent people'.[49] The explosive is naturally taken to be a real one, that actually will work, and will be successfully destructive as claimed. Moreover, the ensuing interrogational torture takes place in an acceptably clinical environment, under the control of senior officers; safeguards are adhered to, torture ceases upon the disclosure of relevant information, the police impeccably discharge their burden of proof demonstrating that the situation was a real emergency (or that they held a reasonable belief of an emergency!), and when the whole business is over the information obtained is not used for any subsequent criminal action.

The situation is highly artificial, as is the set of remedial actions. Shue deals with such an issue, as follows:

there is a saying in jurisprudence that hard cases make bad law, and there might well be one in philosophy that artificial cases make bad ethics. If the example is made sufficiently extraordinary, the conclusion that the torture is permissible is secure. But one cannot easily draw conclusions for ordinary cases from extraordinary ones, and as the situations described become more likely, the conclusion that the torture is permissible becomes more debatable.[50]

There are further assumptions made in such artificial cases as that used by Rudolph. One is that under torture the information will be given at all; another is that the information will be accurate and true; a third is that information could be obtained in sufficient time to counter the threats.

One could note further that when cases like this are raised, no empirical evidence of actual existing practices of torture is mentioned. Defenders of torture, as Rudolph here, are also usually too squeamish to raise the issue of the precise 'clinical' methods of torture to be used, or of precisely how any 'safeguard committee' is to supervise the situation to ensure that the 'reasonably necessary' limits are not exceeded.

This stock case of defence is invariably based on Jeremy Bentham's utilitarian philosophy, although often enough, as Rudolph shows, Bentham's own arguments are not closely heeded.[51] The core of Bentham's defence of torture is as follows. Ordinarily the amount of proof needed to justify torture would be the same as that normally required for punishment. However, where this proof is less than certain, torture should only be allowed if the public interest in what could be revealed was greater than the danger of an innocent man suffering, or 'where the safety of the whole state may be endangered'.[52]

Recognising the dangers of torture, however, and the possibility that magistrates might use these powers in the establishment of tyranny, Bentham proposed that torture should only be allowed in cases of individual and not political crimes. Why? He argued that the hand of government might be too strong against those who 'under the names of rebels, libellers, or sowers of sedition, may in fact be the best friends and defenders of the people'.[53] Since Rudolph's imaginary South African situation would almost certainly fall within a political context, use of Bentham's utilitarianism is invalid.

The utilitarian argument in whatever form rests centrally on the highly questionable assumption that torture produces accurate information. In the strong abolitionist case put by Beccaria (1764), torture was regarded as a poor method of obtaining the truth. Much earlier Roman jurists, hardly the souls most concerned about torture of slaves, had been cautious about the value of evidence obtained from torture.[54] Bentham, while disagreeing with Beccaria, gave no further grounds for claiming that torture yielded valid information. If no argument can be made in favour of its validity, then no case exists for the utility of information obtained in this manner.

In concluding this section, we argue that no justification on any grounds whatsoever can be found for the practice of torture. Rather, our goal should be the complete eradication of this blight. It would appear that we have some way to go yet towards that achievement. The recommendations in the following section, applying specifically to the South African situation, are offered in the spirit of contributing towards a world free of the fear and horror of torture.

Recommendations[55]

(1) Since torture as practised in South Africa contravenes the widely accepted international conventions of human rights as well as medical, legal and psychological ethics, and since safeguards both in South Africa and elsewhere have usually proved ineffective in protecting detainees from physical and psychological abuses, it is recommended that the whole system of detention in terms of the security laws should be abolished forthwith and that South Africa revert to the ordinary principles of criminal justice.

Our study of the use of security legislation over the past 25 years affords no optimism for concluding that the present South African government would respond sympathetically to this recommendation. Since the introduction of the 90-day detention clause in 1963, the use of such security legislation has been a vital component of government policy. This legislation is particularly important to the government at the present time, given its refusal to negotiate with any organisation that is not prepared to accept its prescribed agenda for 'reform'. As the present government's reform proposals are inextricably linked to the repression of a whole range of organisations, it is extremely unlikely that such legislation will be abolished; rather it will be brought into increasing use. The reaction of the Minister of Law and Order to the publication of the preliminary Report of the findings contained in this work provides no reason for any optimism about the possible relaxation of the detention provisions. Minister Le Grange refused to concede that there were any major inadequacies with the present system of detention; he did not offer one word of concern that 13,7 per cent of all Section 29 detainees have complained officially of their treatment – indeed he cited this figure somewhat triumphantly to show that our finding that 83 per cent of 176 respondents' alleged physical torture was incorrect; and he referred once again to the Rabie Commission to justify the need for 'this type of security legislation'.[56] Given this attitude, there is a need for detailed legislation that can offer minimal safeguards against further abuse of detainees. Our proposals are drawn heavily from the legislative positions in Northern Ireland and Israel in addition to the recommendations of the Bennett Report[57] and the Royal Commission on Criminal Procedure of 1981.[58]

During the 1986 parliamentary debate on the Law and Order vote, the Minister of Law and Order told parliament that had we carefully examined the ministerial Directions concerning conditions under which detainees must be held, we would have found that the majority of our proposals were already contained therein. Indeed, we have examined the ministerial Directions carefully. On account of the escape clauses contained there,[59] the police are effectively left to police themselves.[60]

(2) The basis of our proposals is that the rights of detained persons, as well as the duties and limitations of state officials such as police, security police and prison personnel, should be laid down by parliament in the form of easily accessible legislation which grants clearly enforceable rights to detainees.

Provisions must be made for the following:

– A clear operational definition of torture, which should include at least all those actions, both physical and psychological in form, as listed in Tables 10 and 11 in Chapter 5 of this book.

– A clear statement forbidding the practice of torture as defined above, together with severe penalties for offenders of such prohi-

178 Conclusion and recommendations

bitions.

- Clarity with respect to routine investigative procedures among police and prison personnel to ensure that torture and abuse of detainees are discontinued.

- The establishment of an independent body to which police and prison officials are responsible in respect of the previous point. Such a body should comprise representatives, acceptable to all sections of the community, of legal, medical and psychological professions, as well as of detainee support groups and churches. Members of this independent body should have full right of access to detainees and detention facilities at any time.

- All information with respect to detention of persons under security legislation must be treated as public information. Full statistical details regarding detainees should be required as an annual report to parliament.

- The provision for an operationally defined code of conduct for interrogation practices including: the specific prohibition against (i) any order or action requiring a prisoner to strip or expose himself or herself; (ii) any order or action requiring a prisoner to carry out any physically exhausting or demanding action or to adopt or maintain any such stance (for example, forced standing); (iii) the use of obscenities, insults or insulting language concerning the prisoner's friends, families or associates, his political beliefs, religion or race; (iv) use or threats of physical force; (v) use or threats of sexual assault.

- There must be no more than two interrogators present during the interrogation at any one time, as well as a limitation on the number of interrogation 'teams' interviewing one detainee.

- Provision must be made for the interruption of interviews for refreshments and meals after specified times as well as provision for adequate sleep and exercise.

- Interrogators must identify themselves to detainees by name and number.

- All interrogation sessions should be monitored by means of videotape recordings, access to which is granted to the independent monitoring body proposed above. However, videotape recorders should not be utilised for purposes of monitoring detainee cells. It is important to emphasise that no police questioning of a detainee should be allowed unless videotaped.

- The right of access by detainees to independent medical practitioners of their own choice.

- The right of access of detainees to independent lawyers of their own choice.

- The right of detainees to receive visitors, including family members, friends and members of support groups.

- The abolition of solitary confinement and any other form of prescribed social isolation as conditions for holding detainees.

– The provision of sound and adequate facilities for health care, nutrition, washing, exercise, light and air, and clothing change.
– The right of detainees to have reading and writing materials of their own choice.
– Currently established detainee support groups must be consulted fully in drawing up legislation as proposed here.

(3) It is recommended further that courts of law be provided with the necessary powers and machinery to intervene in the case of an alleged failure to subscribe fully to the legislated provisions as recommended above, including the right of the detainee or his family to approach the court to enforce any of the rights to be accorded to a detainee, and the unfettered right of the court to demand that the detainee appear in person before the court.

Complete jurisdiction must be restored to courts of law to pronounce upon the validity of any action taken by the State President, or Minister of State, or official acting under their authority with respect to detention in terms of security legislation, and to order the release of any person detained if satisfied that inadequate grounds exist for further detention.

(4) It is recommended that the current position whereby a confession placed in writing before a magistrate is deemed to be made freely and voluntarily unless the accused can prove otherwise, be abolished as far as any accused who has been detained in terms of security legislation or emergency regulations is concerned. Such evidence should not be admissible unless the state can prove that all the procedural safeguards outlined above have been complied with.

(5) There should be no restrictive prescription period regarding either commencement or completion of proceedings instituted against the state for alleged physical or psychological abuse of detainees.

(6) In the light of evidence presented in this report, it is recommended that psychological coercion, apart from physical coercion, be regarded by courts of law as sufficient grounds upon which to challenge admissibility of confessions or admissions, and to challenge the reliability of evidence by witnesses subjected to such coercion.

(7) A definition of psychological coercion as in (6) above should include the following classes of actions: (a) mental weakening devices, including blindfolding, hooding, solitary or isolated confinement, prolonged interrogation, drug administration; (b) communication devices on the part of interrogators that distort, confuse, threaten or humiliate and degrade; (c) mental terror devices, including mock executions, threats of violence to persons or their families and friends, and witness of torture of others; (d) humiliation devices, including verbal abuse, ridicule, nakedness, sexual harassment, and excrement abuse; and (e) threats of indefinite, continued or renewed detention.

(8) In the light of the results of the present report as well as of recommendations (6) and (7) above, it is further recommended that

Conclusion and recommendations

until provision is made for adequate safeguards, South African courts of law should disregard all evidence, admissions or confessions made by detainees who remain within the closed system of detention. Our findings, together with other psychological research, allow us to conclude that there can be no guarantee of the reliability of such evidence.

(9) In recognising that provisions for detention under emergency regulations are considerably more severe than those under permanent detention statutes, it is urged that recommendations (2) to (8) should apply to detention under emergency conditions as well.

(10) It is noted that certain professional bodies, for example the Psychological Association of South Africa and the Society of Psychiatrists of South Africa, have failed to make even minimal statements condemning the present system of detention, and that the record of other bodies representing law, medicine and related professions in South Africa has been less than adequate in attempting to combat the practice of torture. It is therefore recommended that professional bodies, such as those representing the institutions of law, medicine, mental health, education and religion, appoint permanent committees with a brief to monitor, challenge, eradicate and outlaw torture and abuse of security detainees in South Africa.

We would further warn that if the South African courts do not intervene to protect detainees who are being treated in flagrant violation of even the inadequate ministerial directives of 1982 (clause 15 of which provides that a detainee shall at all times be treated in humane manner); and to render detainees' admissions and confessions inadmissible – the confidence of much of the population in the courts and hence in the criminal justice system will be irreparably destroyed.

In conclusion it may be noted that justice is hardly to be expected in a fundamentally unjust society. It is recognised that the origin of torture in South Africa is located in the procedures and institutions designed to maintain the oppressive and exploitative social order. Until these injustices are removed, until the oppressive social order is changed, grave fears are expressed about future protection against torture in South Africa.

Postscript

After most of the empirical work for this study – but not yet the extensive writing – was completed, three sets of events occurred that are worth reporting, even if only in outline. One was the declaration of a state of emergency in July 1985, another was the response to a preliminary version of the main empirical findings of the present work which was released in September 1985. Finally, at the end of the chapter we comment briefly on the 1986 emergency.

State of emergency

A state of emergency was declared on 21 July 1985 in 36 magisterial districts, largely in the Transvaal and Eastern Cape, in terms of the Public Safety Act of 1953. This measure constituted the state's response to increasing evidence of a major political crisis. The crisis, rooted in the politics of the previous decade, began on 3 September 1984 when South African Defence Force troops entered townships in the Vaal triangle to control and suppress stayaway protests against rent increases. Fuelled by the presence of security forces, the cycle of resistance and repression quickly escalated and spread geographically to other parts of the Transvaal and later to the Eastern Cape. The death toll mounted alarmingly; black collaborators were killed by protesters, but the majority of victims were those killed in clashes with security forces.

In late 1984 and early 1985 resistance in Transvaal and Eastern Cape townships strengthened and deepened in the form of stayaways, school boycotts, rent protests, attacks on state property and on the houses, property or persons of those suspected of collaborating with apartheid (police, councillors, informers), and in a general mood of increased militancy. Security forces responded with sjambok and baton attacks, and with teargas, rubber bullets, birdshot, buckshot and, of course, live ammunition. On the 25th anniversary of the Sharpeville killings, police opened fire on a funeral procession at Langa, near Uitenhage, killing 20 people. Townships were sealed off, and house-to-house searches conducted while arrests, detentions and the banning of meetings increased in frequency. Funerals more and more took the form of large-scale political protests, since other forms of indoor or outdoor meetings were either heavily restricted or banned. On the very day of the emergency declaration a mass funeral, attended by an estimated 30 000 people, was held in Cradock for four community leaders and United Democratic Front activists who had been killed under mysterious circumstances.

Two commissions of inquiry were appointed to investigate the unrest. The Kannemeyer Commission (RP 74/85) reported on the Langa massacre of 21 March 1985. It found that the security police had contributed to the frustrations and resentment of the inhabitants of the Langa township, that the police were poorly equipped to deal with a riot situation, and that police policy in respect of riot control was hopelessly inappropriate.

The Van der Walt Commission (RP 88/85) examined the education problems which had contributed to the disturbances in the Vaal triangle in September 1984. The Commission found, inter alia, that 'the people's confidence in the police was seriously shaken. . . . The presence of the police . . . increasingly had an irritating effect. . . . The general feeling about the police is also basically the attitude to the Defence Force.'

Emergency regulations gave almost unfettered powers to the security forces (the police, the defence force, and railway police). A member of the security forces of any rank could arrest without warrant and detain for a period of 14 days without charge. The 14-day period could be extended on the authority of the Minister of Law and Order, for a potentially unlimited period. Emergency regulations indemnified members of the security forces against prosecution, on condition that they had acted in 'good faith'. Furthermore, additional orders could be issued by the Commissioner of the South African Police that detailed further specific restrictions in demarcated areas. By the end of the second month of the emergency, more than ten such orders had been promulgated. These gave specific controls over movement of persons, non-residents in particular areas, school boycotts, and possession of petrol, and included restrictions on funerals, meetings, concerts and commemorative gatherings.

Rules controlling detainees under emergency regulations may be regarded in certain aspects as more severe than those governing detention under the Internal Security Act. Emergency detainees could be held indefinitely. Emergency detainees could also be subjected to various punishments for a wide range of 'disciplinary contraventions'. Included in the lengthy list of contraventions were: replying falsely to the detaining staff; disobeying a lawful command; being insolent or disrespectful towards an official; singing, whistling or making unnecessary noise; being a nuisance; or making false, frivolous or malicious complaints. Punishments included corporal punishment of up to six strokes, or solitary confinement of up to 30 days on spare or reduced diet.

During the $7\frac{1}{2}$ months of the emergency (it was finally lifted on 7 March 1986, after having been extended on 26 October 1985 to include eight further magisterial districts in the Western Cape and Boland regions) a total of 7 992 people were detained under emergency regulations. While the majority were held under the 14-day clause, many were detained for much longer periods, some for four or five months. This was the case particularly for those arrested during the first week or ten days. Some 25 per cent of those arrested within the first ten days of the emergency were still being held at the end of October 1985, a period of nearly 3½ months.

The overall pattern of emergency detentions may be summarised as follows. In terms of regions, most detentions occurred in the Transvaal (43 per cent) and Eastern Cape (41 per cent). The Western Cape accounted for 16 per cent. The majority of detainees (probably more than 90 per cent) were black males. It is likely that many of them would have been young, under 25, although no formal figures in this regard are available. As regards detention of children, the Ministry of Law and Order eventually admitted that 2 016 detainees were children under the age of 16. This admission came after repeated denials during 1985 that children were being held.

The major targets of emergency detention included a wide range of organisations: civic, student, religious, community, and women's groups, as well as trade unions. Clearly the most serious affected was the United Democratic Front (UDF) and its affiliate organisations. During earlier phases of emergency roughly one detainee in five was a member of the Congress of South African Students (COSAS), one of the leading UDF affiliates.

Banning of organisations and persons constituted a further part of the pattern of the emergency. Most notably, COSAS was banned on 28 August 1985. Since 1979, it had become the leading body representing black students' demands for change in education policy, and as a result had frequently felt the wrath of the state. Banning of individuals also occurred. By the end of February 1986 a total of 68 persons, 61 in the Western Cape, had been subjected to banning. Under these orders, individuals were severely restricted, after release from detention, for the remaining duration of the emergency period, in terms of movement, attendance of meetings, and entrance to certain buildings, and were precluded from publishing any material. In a few other cases, bannings of individuals under the Internal Security Act were imposed for a period of five years.[1] In addition, as already mentioned, numerous meetings and gatherings were banned, either under emergency regulations or under the Internal Security Act. In the Western Cape, meetings of 102 separate organisations were banned for the duration of the emergency. Other gatherings banned included concerts, candlelight vigils and 'fun-runs', all regarded by the authorities as less than entirely innocuous. Restrictions on funerals became progressively tighter.

Throughout the emergency period there were frequent reports and allegations of abuse and torture of emergency detainees, including children. A number of temporary interdicts were granted by the courts, restraining the police and security police in particular from assaulting detainees. In the most notable of these cases, Dr Wendy Orr, a district surgeon, and 43 other applicants were granted an interim interdict on 25 September 1985, restraining the police from assaulting all present and future detainees in the Port Elizabeth and Uitenhage districts. Dr Orr presented medical evidence consistent with claims of severe physical torture.

This brief and rather bland summary of statistics captures nothing of the heightened tension and violent emotions and actions that characterised this period. There is little evidence that emergency regulations brought about a reduction in the death toll. By early 1986, over one thousand deaths had occurred since September 1984.

Other forms of repression

Large-scale use of emergency detention provisions did not mean a decrease in security law detentions. On the contrary, security detentions increased substantially. During 1985, a total of 1 684 persons were detained under security legislation in South Africa and a further 1 953 under similar laws in the 'independent states', most of them in Transkei. By contrast, in 1984 some 1 149 people were detained, 617 in South Africa and 532 in the 'homelands'.

Most people detained in South Africa were held under Section 50 of the Internal Security Act. Section 50 was used in non-emergency areas, enabling authorities to assume emergency-type powers without having to declare an emergency in these areas. However, a large number (406 persons) were detained under Section 29 as well. This contrasts with the DPSC figure of 280 Section 29 detainees in 1984. It is worth noting that the figure of 280 known to the DPSC has been superseded by a figure of 426 as reported for 1984 by the Minister of Law and Order on 12 December 1985. The secrecy surrounding security detentions makes it inevitable that figures are not always accurate. Unofficial figures are invariably lower than those given at later dates by the authorities.

An analysis of known detainees other than in Transkei shows the following breakdown for target groups during 1985: scholars, students, teachers (27 per cent); community and political workers (28 per cent); trade unionists (4 per cent); clergy and church workers (1 per cent); journalists (2 per cent); others, or unidentified activity (38 per cent). In contrast to 1984, the scholars and students were down from 51 to 27 per cent, while detainees in other categories increased; community and political workers from 20 to 18 per cent, and the 'other' category from 24 to 38 per cent.

Consistent with the pattern of previous years, the majority of security detainees (nearly 60 per cent) were released without charge. Only 14,7 per cent were brought before a court and only 1,8 per cent were convicted. Since a remaining 25 per cent were still in detention at the year end, the figures of those released without charge may be expected to rise. The conviction rate of security detainees in 1984 was 1,4 per cent and in 1983 was 6,7 per cent.

The death of one security detainee occurred during 1985, that of trade unionist Andries Raditsela, a member of the executive council of the Federation of South African Trade Unions (Fosatu). Raditsela died on 6 May, two days after being detained by security police. He apparently sustained head injuries, following an alleged assault by the police. The inquest arising from his death has not yet been completed at the time of writing. Apart from Raditsela, more than ten persons died in police custody, after their arrest under circumstances that appear to be politically related, though they were not actually being held under detention laws at the time of their death. Three of those who died in custody were under the age of 18. One may note that the distinction between deaths in detention and those in police custody for politically related matters is rather fine and tenuous.

In addition to emergency and security detentions, thousands of other people were arrested during the course of 1985 on charges related to security or political matters. The greater number of these arrests were related to the 'unrest' and to malicious damage to property. Increased use was made in particular of the charge of public violence, and severe sentences were fairly standard for those convicted: lengthy prison sentences for first offenders, and corporal punishment for juvenile males. In this respect one may note that early in 1986 the state initiated moves to extend the range of offences punishable by whipping, in order to include further political or unrest-related offences.

One feature of court trials in 1985 was the high number of persons on charges of attending unlawful gatherings and demonstrations. Most forms of peaceful protest in South Africa are criminal offences in terms of the law. Perhaps the courts took this factor into consideration, since (according to DPSC figures) only 10 per cent of the charges relating to unlawful gatherings reached convictions.

During the course of 1985, a total of 56 persons faced charges of treason in eight different trials. Of these, four trials were completed, 8 persons being convicted and 16 acquitted. In the most dramatic of these acquittals, 12 UDF leaders in the Pietermaritzburg trial had charges against them dropped on 9 December 1985. As with other forms of repression, the UDF has been most affected by treason trials; a number of these trials continued into 1986.

With the substantial increase of almost daily incidents of 'repression in the streets', along with the sealing off of townships, house-to-house searches, and general police harassment, there can be no doubt that 1985 was one of the most bitter years of repression in the recent history of South Africa.

Responses to the 'Torture Report'
The preliminary report of the main empirical findings of this study

was released on 11 September 1985. On the following days it was fairly extensively covered in the South African press, most thoroughly by the *Cape Times* on 12 September, and to some extent by the foreign press. There was also apparently some coverage by foreign radio and television. Not surprisingly, the government-controlled South African radio and television did not deem it sufficiently newsworthy for coverage. The Afrikaans-language press were notably silent on the first day, although the information was available. The Cape-based mouthpiece of the National Party, *Die Burger*, gave limited coverage to the findings on 13 September under the heading, 'Police React to the Report'. It was not surprising to find that the police reaction was one of vehement denial. The relevant government department of Law and Order was not to respond officially for a further three months.

Over the following few weeks the English-language press made occasional references to the Report's findings, particularly in relation to growing concern about the safety of mounting numbers of emergency and security detainees, and in commentary on a case being heard in the Port Elizabeth Supreme Court in which Dr Wendy Orr submitted medical evidence that substantially corroborated the findings of the preliminary Report. Throughout this time there was widespread concern about abuses and excesses by security forces throughout the country, and the media presented coverage of violent breakups by police of peaceful protests; insistent demands were also made for lifting the state of emergency and releasing detainees and other political prisoners.

The press 'campaign' against the Report in *Die Burger* began on 29 October 1985 and lasted for nearly four weeks. This took the form of letters, by academics and others from various parts of the country, which were severely critical of the Report. There can be little doubt that this was an orchestrated attempt by the pro-government press to discredit the findings, and thereby reassure government supporters that such practices did not occur in South Africa. It may be noted in passing that few of the critics could be regarded as in any way expert in empirical social science methods.

Amongst the arguments made in the letters to *Die Burger* was that the study was unscientific because the identities of respondents and interviewers were not furnished, or the questionnaire was not included, or that since the researchers were not medical or legal experts or policemen they were not qualified to conduct such research. The most persistent cry concerned the lack of identities of respondents, with the veiled, if not explicit, suggestion that the researchers fabricated the data and findings; or that, as identities were not presented, the research claims could not be tested in a court of law – a suggestion that only legal tests, and not the methods of social science, could constitute adequate evidence.

A more serious criticism raised, with greater justification, questions of research methodology. Critics claimed that the study was unscientific because respondents were not randomly sampled, instruments were not reliable or valid, and the interview and questionnaire methods would necessarily exaggerate prevalence data. Finally it was asserted that the study could not be scientific on the grounds that it was politically motivated and therefore biased. To the credit of *Die Burger* it should be mentioned that a number of letters supportive of the Report were also included in this period of correspondence.

In early November, soon after this press campaign began, the Minister of Law and Order issued the first official response. He said that although he was still busy studying the Report, he could already say that it was a wholly unscientific and politically biased piece of work. It was another six weeks though before his formal response was issued!

On 12 December 1985, exactly three months after the release of the preliminary Report, the formal reply from the Minister of Law and Order appeared, with front-page headlines and a full-page spread opposite the leader page, in *Die Burger*. The reply took the form of a scathing attack on the Report, largely repeating the criticisms made by the earlier letter campaign. In addition new figures were reported, claiming that only 13,7 per cent of Section 29 detainees between 1982 and 1985 had reported complaints or laid charges of assault. Therefore, he concluded, the figures of the Torture Report must be wrong. Furthermore, in none of these cases of alleged assault had the allegations been proved in a court of law. The Minister also gave figures which claimed that virtually all detainees had been visited by inspectors of detainees whereas the Report had found that only 34 per cent of post-1982 detainees had acknowledged such visits. The Minister also stated that the report was incorrect in exaggerating the figures of those who had died in detention by including cases from Venda and Transkei.

In the front-page headlined article in *Die Burger* on the same day, a number of extraordinary additional allegations were made which give credence to the view that *Die Burger* was attempting to manufacture a scandal to discredit the study further. *Die Burger* coined the term 'Fostergate' to indicate that the Report was scandalous in two respects, misinformation and misuse of taxpayers' money.

Misuse of taxpayers' money was alleged because the University of Cape Town receives a government subsidy, and in the eyes of *Die Burger*, a study of this sort could not be regarded as legitimate research activity. In fact, the study was entirely financed by the Ford Foundation of the USA.

Although it was never quite clear what the allegation of 'misinformation' referred to, one may assume that because the findings were regarded (by a few critics and *Die Burger*) as wrong, the Report as a whole was considered guilty of misinformation. This is of course a ludicrous claim.

Die Burger also reported that there was mounting tension between the government and the University of Cape Town over the matter of the

Torture Report. Dr Saunders, principal and vice-chancellor of the University, denied such suggestions. A further statement in *Die Burger* claimed that the principal researcher (Don Foster) had declared in lectures to students that he was making a major South African film in which gruesome scenes of torture would be included. This statement is absolutely without foundation, and *Die Burger* made no attempts to verify this allegation with the principal researcher.

The next day, 13 December, *Die Burger* again ran a front-page article in which a second member of the cabinet, the Minister of Justice, apparently demanded that the University of Cape Town 'distance itself' from the Torture Report. Veiled threats were given of severe consequences if this did not occur, but no action was taken. On 14 December, *Die Burger* carried a report in which the Chancellor of the University of Cape Town was said to have made some positive comments about the government's reform programme. Comment about the Torture Report was suddenly dropped. Only in the New Year did a third cabinet member, Mr Louis Nel of the newly formed Information Department, join in the chorus of condemnation by coupling the 'Torture Report' with a planned film on the life of Steve Biko by Sir Richard Attenborough, and suggesting that these were two of the most important manifestations of anti-government propaganda. In late April and early May 1986, the Report was again castigated, this time in parliament, by the Minister of Law and Order, who labelled it as 'thoroughly subjective and politically biased', its sole purpose being to 'bring into disrepute and under suspicion the government, the security police and the system of security legislation'.

The Minister thanked Mr Freek Swart of *Die Burger* for his coverage of the Report and suggested that Mr Swart 'had rendered an outstanding service to South Africa by describing and analysing the report in such a manner'. The Minister's speech repeated the major conclusions made in the earlier departmental reply to the Report and he ended by declaring that the Report was 'not worth more than the paper on which it had been written'.

During this period no positive change whatsoever was effected in respect of security legislation. No consideration was given to the inhumane legislation, to the investigation of excesses by police or security forces, or to the lack of safeguards in security laws against the possible abuse and torture of detainees. The only minor change occurred when the government agreed in principle in December 1985 to allow detainees to select doctors from a list compiled by the Medical Association of South Africa. However, this provision still falls well short of the ethical principles of the World Medical Association's Tokyo Declaration, and of the demands from many quarters for access to independent medical practitioners. In the light of the overwhelming evidence of abuse and torture of detainees, the lack of positive response on the part of the authorities must be regarded in the most dismal light.

The Minister's criticisms of the Torture Report, referred to above, can be reduced to the following charges.

(a) Minister Le Grange claims that official figures from the Directorate of Security Legislation refute the findings of the Report as the Report does not reflect 'the true state of affairs contained in the records of the Directorate for Security Legislation' (*Die Burger*, 12 December 1985).

However, the Directorate's figures of 13,7 per cent (138 cases from a total of 1 007 reported complaints of assault by Section 29 detainees between 1982 and 1985) do not prove that the real number of assaults was only 13,7 per cent. In fact, it is well known that reported figures in all areas of crime are considerably lower than actual occurrences of particular crimes. Former detainees may not report assaults for any one of the following reasons: fear of further victimisation by the authorities; lack of confidence in the legitimacy of the legal process; a sense of futility in relation to the legal process; the problem of prescription, in that assault charges lodged 6 months after the event occurred will not be enforced. In this regard the Torture Report found the average period in detention to be over 4 months; indeed, many detainees have been held for periods longer than 4 months, and would not be legally permitted to lodge assault claims.

In this connection we refer the Minister to the Law Society's own Le Roux Commission,[2] in which it was found that detainees' complaints of assaults were not investigated speedily, with sufficient care, or independently. The Commission cited a number of examples where complaints of assault were attended to by the authorities after an unreasonably long period.

Similar evidence was given by an inspector of detainees in the Aggett inquest. He told the inquest court that detainees were frightened of lodging complaints of assault for fear of further police harassment. Notwithstanding such evidence, 138 detainees have reported assaults during detention over the past four years, a figure which in itself constitutes damning evidence and which in Western countries would constitute sufficient grounds for a major commission of inquiry.

(b) Minister Le Grange claims that the Directions regarding the detention of persons (1982) are legally binding. This is open to doubt, one legal view being that they are simply internal departmental guidelines which will not be enforced by the courts. Yet even if the courts are prepared to enforce the Directions, the numerous ouster clauses which they contain afford negligible legal protection for a detainee. The Minister has attacked our suggestion that torture should be statistically defined and has referred to the absence of such a definition in the European Convention of Human Rights. However, the Convention is 'policed' by a court which has developed its own concept of torture.

The major problem with the Directions as presently defined is that there is no independent body to monitor the police. Furthermore,

South African detainees are completely isolated from the outside world, without right of access to a lawyer. In such circumstances how are they to enforce any right that they might have under the common law?

Minister Le Grange claims that some of our recommendations are included in the Directions. Which ones? Unfortunately, the Minister gives no details, for it is clear that none of the recommendations of the Report, which provide for *minimal* safeguards for all security detainees (not only for Section 29 detainees, which is the only section covered by the Directions), are contained in the published Directions.

The recommended establishment of an independent body with rights of access to detainees is considered by the Minister (apparently with reference to the Bennett Commission in the United Kingdom) as 'not practical'. We submit that the Minister should provide an alternative suggestion for a 'practical' body which would be agreed upon by all sections of the South African community as a satisfactory monitoring body.

We are pleased that the Minister regards the Bennett Commission as providing a comparative criterion with respect to safeguards for detainees. Had he consulted Chapter 7 of the Bennett Report he would have discovered the recommendation that a detainee should have access to his own medical practitioner, while Chapter 14 presents the well-argued recommendations of the Commission that every detainee should have access to a solicitor after 48 hours in detention.

(c) Official departmental figures and statistics *do not* constitute scientific data. Therefore any attempt to discredit the findings of the Report by the presentation of official statistics must fail on the grounds of incomparability of data. The appropriate challenge to findings of the Report would be to conduct another similar scientific survey, improving (if possible) the scientific methods utilised.

The repeated attack on the Report for not providing names of interviewers and respondents, amounts to precisely nothing. It is never the standard practice of psychological, medical or social scientific research to furnish such identities. On the contrary, it is standard ethical practice in social science to guarantee confidentiality of respondents. We challenge the Minister and other critics to demonstrate where it is regarded as standard practice to give identities of respondents in psychological, medical or social scientific research, and in particular with regard to police and prison studies.

A further repeated criticism is that our findings cannot be tested in a court of law since the identities of respondents are not provided. This misses the point entirely. The nature of evidence before a court of law and that of evidence in social science research are not the same. We submit that our study produces sound scientific evidence of torture. The value of such evidence may be tested by replicating the study using similar methods. Replication should employ a different sample, and the identity of the sample is no obstacle to replication.

Minister Le Grange says that the findings are based on a small number of detainees. However, in social scientific terms (as well as common sense terms), 176 cases of detention is not a small sample.

The Minister claims that the research is guilty of inadequate generalisation of results. Unfortunately the Minister, along with other critics, fails to mention that the Torture Report provides full details of the representative nature of the sample in terms of gender, 'population group', area of work and other characteristics, and that the sample was drawn on a national basis. In other words, generalisation of findings is fully warranted on scientific grounds.

The Minister, as well as other critics, simply fails to mention many other aspects of the research findings which support the validity of the study:

(i) Highly similar patterns of abuse were reported from all parts of the country.

(ii) Variations in regional areas accord with what is well known about treatment of detainees, and accord generally with patterns of deaths in detention.

(iii) The pattern of psychological and health symptoms reported by detainees (and passed over in silence by most critics) accords well with recent research findings of torture victims in Western countries. Since most detainees are not medically trained and therefore would be unaware of symptomatology patterns, these findings in particular provide powerful validity checks of the severe nature of treatment meted out to detainees.

(iv) Many additional findings, such as the mean period of detention, the length of the interrogation sessions, the patterns of physical transfer of detainees, repeated detentions, the number of interrogators used, as well as the breakdown of results in terms of gender and 'population group', are all passed over in silence by the Minister and other critics.

No research findings stand entirely on their own. In this respect it is notable that neither Minister Le Grange nor other critics have mentioned that the general thrust of the Torture Report is supported by other work. In 1982 the Detainees' Parents Support Committee (DPSC) submitted to the Minister of Law and Order a memorandum of more than 70 affidavits from former security detainees. The reported patterns of assault are remarkably similar to those of the Torture Report. In 1973 the United Nations also found substantial evidence of torture of detainees in South Africa. Findings of the MASA Report on Detainees in 1983 point in the same direction, and confirm that conditions of detention constitute a 'health hazard' beyond that of convicted prisoners. The medical evidence of Dr Wendy Orr already referred to provides substantial additional data of a very similar nature.

In summary it may be added that the purpose of the Report was not to discredit the authorities but on the contrary to investigate whether failures in the system of safeguards for security detainees may occur, and to that extent to suggest legal and other principles which would prevent the possibility of any abuse, physical or psychological, of security detainees. The South African system of safeguards in detention falls far short of those provided for in Northern Ireland and Israel, two countries which have found it necessary to use security legislation.

We therefore call again on the Minister to consider the shortcomings of the system and as a matter of urgency to provide the necessary changes that would eradicate entirely the possibility of torture in all forms of security and emergency detention.

We now turn to matters of principle.

The Minister has criticised our claim that detention is used for political purposes. We are not the first to voice such criticism. For example, in 1984 the Association of Law Societies said that the large number of persons detained could be considered as evidence that detention was used as the first resort rather than as an exception, which at most should be its purpose.[3]

The collapse of the state's case in the 1985 Pietermaritzburg treason trial offers clear evidence of the use made of detention in this country. Most detainees are not charged, so that when a case does arise from the detention of a number of people, it is interesting to examine the basis upon which the detentions were made. (According to the DPSC's November 1985 Report only 111 out of 605 detainees released from detention in 1985 were charged in a court.) After all, as the Minister points out in his statement, Section 29 covers only two categories, namely the 'terrorist' and the person who possesses information about a person who has or is about to commit 'terrorism'. When a detainee is brought to trial the reasons for the detention can be analysed with the assistance of the state case. In the Pietermaritzburg treason trial the government detained the accused, in circumstances which placed the country's relationship with the United Kingdom at risk, charged the detainees with the grave crime of treason, and then produced the flimsiest of evidence built upon far-fetched and unsubstantiated inferences. If ever the allegation of detention as a political tool (in this case against an organisation with which the government refuses to negotiate) was proved, it was in this treason trial.

In conclusion we wish to argue that the substance of the findings in the earlier preliminary Report, and in the present volume, cannot be dismissed on scientific, political or any other grounds. Detention as it presently exists on South African statute books, and torture, here and in any country, remain thoroughly uncivilised practices. It is the responsibility of all relevant authorities to address themselves to framing legislation and additional supporting practices which would unequivocally prevent any possibility of abuse of all security law and emergency detainees, and for that matter, of each and every citizen.

The 1986 state of emergency

It seems somewhat unusual to write a postscript to a postscript, but the declaration of another state of emergency scarcely four months after the 1985 emergency was lifted illustrates the difficulty of presenting an accurate contemporary account of South Africa and the system of political repression employed.

On 12 June 1986 the State President declared a state of emergency which, unlike the limited 1985 version, applied throughout South Africa.

The emergency regulations which were issued in terms of the Public Safety Act[4] were designed to crush the extra-parliamentary opposition, 'to create a situation of relative normality . . . so that it is possible to proceed with the reform programme'.[5]

These regulations were more draconian than those which operated in 1985. The two main features of the regulations were the extensive powers of arrest and detention granted to all members of the security forces, and a series of provisions which were designed to censor the press and curb its ability to report on political unrest in the country.

The regulations have been effective in restricting the flow of information. Editions of two newspapers have been confiscated by police and the widely drafted regulations have made it difficult for editors to produce newspapers without extensive legal assistance.[6]

The number of people detained during the present emergency has been far higher than was the case in 1985. The government released the names of 9 337 persons who had been detained for more than 30 days by 31 August 1986 but the PFP missing persons' bureau estimates that almost 15 000 have been detained since 12 June.[7] By the end of 1986 the Detainees' Parents Support Committee estimated that roughly 25 000 people had been detained under emergency regulations, and a further 3 000 approximately under security legislation. Once again, many of those held were children. Allegations of abuses continued on a widespread basis.

Another difference between the two emergencies concerns the role of the courts. In the present emergency a number of judgments curtailing executive power have been handed down.[8] Whether this is the beginning of a new, more liberal approach on the part of the South African judiciary remains to be seen.

However, the extent of the present repression and the scale of detentions make it all the more important for the courts to restrict executive power. As UDF member Lechasa Tsenoli put it after being released from detention following a court order, 'We are all concerned to defend whatever legal space we have left after the state's erasing of the law. That space does not come about because of the state's benevolence but through struggles in various fields including the legal field. The more we can stop the state from acting in excess to the detriment of the community the better.'[9]

Postscript

Although the findings published in this book relate to events prior to the 1985 and 1986 states of emergency, there is little reason to believe that the situation of detainees has improved to render our conclusions an inaccurate picture of present day conditions. For this reason, the implementation of our recommendations concerning detention has become perhaps more important than when they were originally drafted.

Appendices

APPENDIX A: Composition of the sample cases (raw data)

Gender	
Male	145
Female	31

'Race'	
African	127
Coloured	18
Indian	18
White	13

Age detained	
Below 16	4
16–20	54
21–25	54
26–30	28
31–35	14
36–40	9
Over 40	10
Missing	3

Area of work	
Student	92
Unions	25
Community	21
Political organisation	15
No organisation	8
Youth	7
Other work	5
Missing	3

Religion	
Christian	93
Moslem	11
Hindu	5
Atheist	2
Jewish	1
Other	3
Missing	61

Education	Pre-detention	Post-detention
High school	110	106
University	54	60
Primary school	6	2
Technical	2	2
Other	1	3
Missing	3	3

Employment	Pre-detention	Post-detention
Student	99	51
Skilled work	18	11
Professional	14	23
Clerical	8	5
Unemployed	7	46
Organisation worker	6	10
Trade union	5	11
Unskilled	5	1
Other	11	16
Missing	3	2

Marital status	Pre-detention	Post detention
Single	120	111
Married	27	35
Steady relation	22	20
Children	5	7
Separated/divorced	–	1
Missing	2	2

Year detained	
1974	2
1975	1
1976	20
1977	25
1978	7
1979	8
1980	31
1981	37
1982	7
1983	34
1984	4

Living arrangements	Pre-detention	Post detention
Family	148	141
Friends	13	13
One another	4	8
Alone	4	10
Other	5	2
Missing	2	2

Geographical city	Person's origins	Place where detained	Place where held
Johannesburg	49	52	52
Port Elizabeth	46	29	40
East London	31	32	33
Durban	22	21	21
Cape Town	24	21	20
Other	2	20	8
Missing	2	1	2

Geographical region	Person's origins	Region where detained	Region where held
Transvaal	50	52	54
Eastern Cape	47	37	43
Border	32	38	34
Natal	22	22	24
Western Cape	24	23	20
Missing	1	4	1

APPENDIX B: Pre-detention aspects

Harassment type (19 missing cases Total N = 157)	Gender Male (131)	Gender Female (26)	African (112)	Coloured (15)	Indian (17)	White (13)	Row total (157)
No harassment	40,5	46,2	41,1	26,7	47,1	53,8	41,4
Raids/visits	28,2	34,6	30,4	33,3	29,4	15,4	29,3
Tailing/following	26,0	15,4	20,5	46,7	23,5	30,8	24,2
Short term detention	11,5	7,7	10,7	13,3	17,6	–	10,8
Intimidation of family	9,2	3,8	7,1	20,0	5,9	7,7	8,3
Phoned to call in to Security Police	4,6	–	2,7	6,7	11,8	–	3,8
Phone calls	2,3	3,8	2,7	–	–	7,7	2,5
Phone tapping	1,5	–	0,9	–	–	7,7	1,3
Attacked	0,8	–	–	–	5,9	–	0,6
Damage to property	0,8	–	–	–	5,9	–	0,6
Other harassment	10,7	7,7	8,0	13,3	11,8	15,4	10,2

Percentages based on total number of respondents in each column

Harassment type (20 missing cases Total N = 156)	W. Cape (17)	E. Cape (38)	Border (29)	Natal (24)	Tvl (48)	Row total (156)
No harassment	47,1	28,9	37,9	58,3	43,8	41,7
Raids/visits	17,6	42,1	34,5	29,2	18,8	28,8
Tailing/following	35,3	23,7	27,6	20,8	18,8	23,7
Short-term detention	5,9	15,8	19,3	4,2	12,5	10,9
Intimidation of family	5,9	5,3	3,4	4,2	16,7	8,3
Phoned to call in in Security Police	–	5,3	–	–	8,3	3,8
Phone calls	5,9	2,6	3,4	–	2,1	2,6
Phone tapping	5,9	–	–	–	–	1,3
Attacked	–	–	–	–	–	0,6
Damage to property	–	–	–	–	2,1	0,6

Expectation of detention	n	%
Yes	89	54,9
No	73	45,1
Total	162	
Missing:	14	

Knowledge of law	n	%
Very good	4	2,7
Quite good	12	8,0
Reasonable	47	31,8
Poor	32	20,6
Very poor	56	37,3
Total	150	99,9
Missing:	26	

Harassment type (22 missing cases Total N = 154)	Age groups							Row total (154)
	−20 (51)	21–25 (48)	26–30 (25)	31–35 (12)	36–40 (9)	Over 40 (9)	
No harassment	31,4	50,0	44,0	33,3	55,6	44,9	41,6
Raids/visits	33,3	29,2	20,0	33,3	33,3	11,1	28,6
Tailing/following	17,6	29,2	32,0	33,3	11,1	11,1	24,0
Short term detention	11,8	12,5	8,0	–	11,1	22,2	11,0
Intimidation of family	11,8	6,3	12,0	8,3	–	–	8,4
Phoned to call in to Security Police	2,0	2,1	12,0	–	11,1	–	3,9
Phone calls	2,0	2,1	–	16,7	–	–	2,6
Phone tapping	2,0	2,1	–	–	–	–	1,3
Attacked	–	–	–	–	11,1	–	0,6
Damage to property	–	–	–	–	11,1	–	0,6
Other harassment	7,8	–	24,0	25,0	–	33,3	10,4

Preparation forms	n	%
None	41	26,6
Hearing general information	90	58,4
Speaking to ex-detainees	53	34,4
Thinking about detention	35	24,7
Reading information	14	9,1
Legal consultation	10	6,5
Physical preparation	5	3,2
Medical	1	0,6
Other	35	22,7

Multiple answers possible. 22 cases missing; percentages based on 154 cases.

APPENDIX C: Patterns of arrest

Place of arrest	n	%
Home	94	53,3
Work	10	5,9
Other home	12	7,1
Other	54	31,8
Total	170	100,0

Missing cases: 6

Number of police	n	%
1–5	85	54,1
6–10	35	22,3
11–20	24	15,3
20–100	13	8,3
Total	157	100,0

Missing cases: 19

Time of arrest	n	%
00–03 hrs	30	18,2
03–06 hrs	42	25,5
06–09 hrs	18	10,9
09–12 hrs	33	20,0
12–15 hrs	12	7,3
15–18 hrs	9	5,5
18–21 hrs	11	6,7
21–24 hrs	10	6,1
Total	165	100,1

Missing cases: 11

Vehicle used	n	%
Car	119	81,5
Police van	17	11,6
Truck	3	2,1
Combi	2	1,4
Other	5	3,4
Total	146	100,0

Missing cases: 30

Others present	n	%
Yes	156	95,1
No	8	4,9
Total	164	

Missing: 12

Relatives informed	n	%
Yes	137	53,3
No	18	11,6
Total	155	

Missing: 21

Taken to	n	%
Police station	90	53,3
Security	76	44,9
House	1	0,6
Other	2	1,2
Total	169	100,0

Missing cases: 7

Manner of arrest	n	%
Violent	11	6,5
Rough	26	15,5
Aggressive	76	45,2
Calm	54	32,1
Unclear	1	0,6
Total	168	99,9

Missing cases: 8

APPENDIX D: General patterns of detention

Section detained under		First n	First %	Second n	Second %	Third n	Third %
Interrogation	s6	46	26,7	52	67,5	1	14,3
	s29	29	16,9	2	2,6	–	–
Preventive	s10	2	1,2	18	23,4	2	28,6
	s28	10	5,8	–	–	–	–
Short-term	s22	83	48,3	2	2,6	–	–
	s50	2	1,2	–	–	–	–
Witness	s12	–	–	1	1,3	3	42,9
	s31	–	–	2	2,6	1	14,3
Total		172	100,0	77	100,0	7	100,1
Missing		4		99		169	

Period detained	n	%
00–30 days	23	13,1
31–60 days	21	11,9
61–90 days	21	11,9
91–120 days	31	17,6
121–150 days	27	15,3
151–180 days	18	10,2
181–270 days	22	12,5
271–360 days	4	2,3
561 or more days	9	5,1
Total	176	100,0

Multiple detentions	n	%
Yes	89	50,9
No	86	49,1
Total	175	

Missing: 1

Number of times detained	n	%
Twice	37	43,0
Three times	23	26,7
Four times	17	19,8
Five times	7	8,1
Six times	1	1,2
Seven times	1	1,2
Total	86	100,0

Missing: 3
89 claimed multiple detention

Number of times transferred	n	%
Once	27	16,8
Twice	66	41,0
Three times	41	25,5
Four times	20	12,4
Five times	5	3,1
Six times	–	–
Seven times	1	0,6
Eight times	1	0,6
Total	161	100,0

Missing: 15

APPENDIX E: Physical conditions of detention

Access to external light		
Yes	67	61,5%
No	42	38,5%
Total	109	
Missing	67	

Access to cell light-switch		
Yes	7	5,5%
No	120	94,5%
Total	127	
Missing	49	

Clean clothes received		
Regular	37	24,7%
Irregular	49	32,7%
None	64	42,7%
Total	150	
Missing	26	

Access to writing material		
Yes	15	9,4%
No	145	90,6%
Total	160	
Missing	16	

Sleeping conditions		
Poor	128	74,4%
Medium	43	25,0%
Good	1	0,6%
Total	172	
Missing	4	

Dental treatment received		
Sound	15	9,8%
Poor	5	3,3%
None	133	86,9%
Total	153	
Missing	23	

Exercise opportunity		
Regular	55	36,4%
Irregular	38	25,2%
No exercise	58	38,4%
Total	151	
Missing	14	

Access to reading material		
Yes	81	50,0%
No	81	50,0%
Total	162	
Missing	14	

Exercise time		
Under 30 mins	24	35,8%
30–60 mins	40	59,7%
Over 60 mins	3	4,5%
Total	67	
Missing	109	

Medical treatment received		
Sound	48	30,4%
Poor	70	44,3%
None	40	25,3%
Total	158	
Missing	23	

Food parcels received		
Regular	28	18,2%
Irregular	36	23,4%
None	90	58,4%
Total	154	
Missing	22	

APPENDIX F: Conditions of interrogation

Teams used	n	%
Yes	27	16,7
No	135	83,3
Total	162	
Missing	14	

Statement made	n	%
Yes	105	67,3
No	51	32,7
Total	156	
Missing	20	

Approximate average length of interrogation sessions	n	%
One hour	9	5,9
Two hours	19	12,4
Three hours	4	2,6
Four hours	19	11,4
Five hours	6	3,9
Six hours	26	17,0
Seven hours	17	11,1
Eight hours	24	15,7
Nine hours	8	5,2
Ten hours	7	4,6
Twelve hours	5	3,3
Sixteen hours	6	3,9
24 hours	3	2,0
Total	*153*	*100,0*
Missing	23	

Average number of interrogation sessions	n	%
One	16	10,3
Two	47	20,3
Three	36	23,2
Four	21	13,6
Five	13	8,4
Six	11	7,1
Seven	4	2,6
Eight	2	1,3
Nine	1	0,7
Ten	3	1,9
More than ten	1	0,7
Total	*155*	*100,1*
Missing	21	

Average number of interrogation sessions	n	%
0–5 sessions	62	40,0
6–10 sessions	37	23,9
11 or more sessions	56	36,1
Total	*155*	*100,0*
Missing cases	21	

APPENDIX G: Interpersonal contact during detention

Contact with authorities (3 missing cases N = 173)	Male (143)	Female (30)	African (124)	Coloured (18)	Indian (18)	White (13)	Row total (173)
Security police	99,3	96,7	98,4	100,0	100,0	100,0	98,8
Magistrate	62,2	83,3	70,2	66,7	33,3	69,2	65,9
Medical	62,2	73,3	66,1	55,6	55,6	69,2	69,2
Police	57,3	66,7	57,3	55,6	72,2	61,5	59,0
Warders	42,7	60,0	41,1	61,1	44,4	69,2	45,7
Inspector	15,4	26,7	16,7	22,2	22,2	15,4	17,5

Contact with authorities (6 missing cases N = 170)	Age groups						Row total
	−20	21–25	26–30	31–35	36–40	Over 40	
	(56)	(54)	(28)	(14)	(8)	(10)	(170)
Security police	100,0	98,1	100,0	100,0	100,0	90,0	98,8
Magistrate	58,9	61,1	71,4	78,6	62,5	90,0	65,3
Medical	53,6	68,5	64,3	85,7	75,0	60,0	64,1
Police	64,3	66,7	46,4	57,1	50,0	40,0	59,4
Warders	44,6	40,7	50,0	57,1	37,5	60,0	45,9
Inspector	7,1	22,2	14,3	14,3	50,0	30,0	17,1

Contact with authorities (4 missing cases N = 172)	Geographical region					Row total
	W. Cape	E. Cape	Border	Natal	Tvl	
	(20)	(43)	(34)	(24)	(51)	(172)
Security Police	100,0	100,0	97,1	100,0	98,0	98,8
Magistrate	50,0	48,8	79,4	66,7	76,5	65,7
Medical	60,0	48,8	79,4	70,8	64,7	64,0
Police	60,0	69,8	35,3	79,2	56,9	59,3
Warders	60,0	30,2	26,5	41,7	68,6	45,9
Inspector	20,0	7,0	–	29,2	31,4	17,9

Contact with non-authorities (3 missing cases N = 170)	Male	Female	African	Col-oured	Indian	White	Row total
	(140)	(30)	(122)	(18)	(18)	(12)	(170)
No contact	21,4	30,0	24,6	11,1	33,3	8,3	22,9
Other detainees	55,7	43,3	52,5	72,2	44,4	50,0	53,5
Common criminals	35,0	43,3	35,2	50,0	16,7	58,3	36,5
Family & friends	25,0	30,0	18,9	38,9	38,9	58,3	25,9
Legal persons	2,1	10,0	0,8	16,7	5,6	8,3	3,5

Contact with non-authorities (8 missing cases N = 168)	Age groups						Row total
	−20	21–25	26–30	31–35	36–40	Over 40	
	(56)	(53)	(27)	(14)	(8)	(10)	(168)
No contact	19,6	26,4	14,8	14,3	62,5	30,0	23,2
Other detainees	57,1	54,7	55,6	64,3	25,0	40,0	54,2
Common criminals	37,5	35,8	48,1	28,6	12,5	20,0	35,7
Family & friends	21,4	28,3	25,9	42,9	–	30,0	25,6
Legal persons	–	3,8	3,7	21,4	–	–	3,6

Contact with non-authorities (6 missing cases N = 168)	Geographical region					Row total
	W. Cape (20)	E. Cape (42)	Border (33)	Natal (24)	Tvl (51)	(170)
No contact	10,0	23,8	30,3	20,8	23,5	22,9
Other detainees	70,0	54,8	48,5	45,8	52,9	53,5
Common criminals	50,0	42,9	27,3	25,0	37,3	37,3
Family & friends	40,0	4,8	3,0	45,8	43,1	25,9
Legal persons	20,0	–	3,0	4,2	–	3,5

APPENDIX H

Forms of physical torture by demographic factors

Forms of physical torture	Age groups						Row total
	–20 (58)	21–25 (53)	26–30 (28)	31–35 (14)	36–40 (9)	Over 40 (10)	(172)
No physical torture	6,9	17,0	21,4	50,0	11,1	30,0	17,4
Beatings	86,2	85,5	67,9	50,0	77,8	50,0	74,4
Forced standing	53,4	50,9	46,4	50,0	55,6	20,0	49,4
Maintain abnormal body position	29,3	28,3	53,6	42,9	33,3	10,0	33,1
Forced gym exercise	24,1	24,5	42,9	35,7	33,3	10,0	27,9
Bag over head	25,8	20,8	28,6	28,6	33,3	–	23,8
Electric shocks	25,8	15,1	39,3	21,4	33,3	20,0	24,4
Food deprivation	20,7	20,8	17,9	35,7	22,2	20,0	21,5
Strangulation	17,2	17,0	28,6	7,1	11,1	10,0	17,4
Suspension	6,9	13,2	25,0	7,1	33,3	10,0	13,4
Cold water	6,9	11,3	14,3	28,6	11,1	10,0	11,6
Water deprivation	5,1	7,5	3,6	21,4	11,1	30,0	8,7
Application of cigarettes/ chemicals	8,6	3,8	14,3	7,1	–	–	7,0
Bright light	3,4	3,8	3,6	–	–	10,0	3,5
Excess cold	5,1	3,8	3,6	–	11,1	–	4,1
Excess heat	–	1,9	3,6	8,1	–	–	1,7
Walk barefoot over glass/stones	–	–	3,6	–	–	–	1,6
Other torture	25,9	28,3	32,1	28,6	33,3	–	26,7

Forms of physical torture	W. Cape (20)	E. Cape (43)	Border (34)	Natal (24)	Tvl (53)	Row total (174)
No physical torture	55,5	4,7	8,8	16,7	18,9	17,2
Beatings	35,0	93,0	91,2	62,5	69,8	74,7
Forced standing	20,0	65,1	50,0	54,2	45,3	49,4
Maintain abnormal body position	10,0	37,2	44,1	37,5	30,2	33,3
Forced gym exercise	–	27,9	67,6	29,2	11,3	27,6
Bag over head	–	30,2	44,1	12,5	20,8	24,1
Electric shocks	–	34,9	38,2	12,5	20,8	24,1
Food deprivation	5,0	27,9	11,8	37,5	20,8	21,3
Strangulation	–	14,0	44,1	8,3	15,1	17,8
Suspension	5,0	9,3	44,1	4,2	3,8	13,2
Cold water	–	7,0	23,5	8,3	13,2	11,5
Water deprivation	–	11,6	8,8	8,3	9,4	8,6
Application of cigarettes/chemicals	–	4,7	26,5	4,2	1,9	7,5
Bright light	–	2,3	2,9	8,3	5,7	4,0
Excess cold	–	11,6	2,9	–	1,9	4,0
Excess heat	–	–	–	–	5,7	1,7
Walk barefoot over glass/stones	–	–	2,9	–	–	,6
Other torture	5,0	37,2	44,1	16,7	20,8	27,0

Geographical region

Comparison of distributions reported in four different studies: percentages

Rasmussen & Lunde (1980)

Beatings	93
Trauma to head	62
Electric torture	42
Trauma to genitals	33
Falanga	30
Suspension	27
Food/drink deprivation	21
Water torture	19
Physical exhaustion	17
Burning (eg cigarettes)	8
Bright light	7
Pharmacological	7
Tooth torture	7
Other physical forms	27

1. N=135
2. Sample: torture victims from Chile 42, Greece 35, Spain 32, Argentina 13, N. Ireland 5, other 8. Refugees in Denmark.
3. Method: examined by members of the Danish Medical Group, 1975-80.

Present study

Beatings	75
Forced standing	50
Abnormal body position	34
Forced exercise	28
Bag over head	25
Electric	25
Food deprivation	21
Strangulation	18
Manacles	15
Suspension	14
Cold water	12
Water deprivation	9
Application of cigarettes, chemicals	8
Pulling hair/beard	5
Bright light	4
Excess cold	4
Genital abuse	3
Falanga	3
Excess heat	2

1. N=175
2. Sample: security law detainees in South Africa. No a priori selection for victims of physical torture.
3. Method: tape-recorded field interviews with aid of a semi-structured questionnaire, 1983-4.

Allodi & Cowgill (1982)

Beatings	98
Slaps, kicks, punches	98
Rifle butt	78
Whip, baton, stick	61
Electric torture	66
Starvation	39
Minimal food (2 days)	29
Water deprived (2 days)	37
Cold-water torture	37
Sexual molestation	34
Broken bones	27
Rape	15
Applications of cigarettes, chemicals, hot water	29
Other forms of torture (bag, bright light, nails removal, hanging by fingers)	29

1. N=175
2. Sample: refugees from 3 Latin American countries who alleged being tortured. Refugees in Canada.
3. Method: interviewed by a psychiatrist, 1977-81.

Randall et al (1983)

Beatings	86
Electric torture	66
Food deprivation	65
Water deprivation	62
Restricted movement	46
Extreme heat/cold	38
Submarine	27
Loud noise/music	24
Suspension	20
Burns	20
Forced standing	18
Bright lights	16
Telephone	16
Sexual abuse	11
Asphyxiation (bag)	11
Stretching	11

1. N=44
2. Sample: torture victims from 6 Latin American countries, mainly Chile 25, and Argentina, 10. Refugees in USA.
3. Method: interviewed by medical teams, completion of research questionnaires, and examination, 1978-82.

APPENDIX I

Forms of psychological torture by demographic factors

Forms of psychological torture	−20 (56)	21–25 (54)	26–30 (28)	31–35 (14)	36–40 (9)	Over 40 (19)	Row total (172)
No psychological torture	–	–	–	–	–	–	-
False accusations	86,0	87,0	78,6	64,3	77,8	80,0	82,6
Solitary confinement	68,4	83,3	82,1	92,9	88,9	80,0	79,1
Verbal abuse	63,2	83,3	75,0	78,6	44,4	60,0	71,5
Threatened violence	59,7	72,2	60,7	57,1	66,7	80,0	65,1
Good/bad interrogators	42,1	66,7	75,0	42,9	55,6	50,0	56,4
Given misleading information	47,4	59,3	53,6	50,0	11,1	60,0	51,2
Witness or knowledge of others' torture	52,6	42,6	42,9	35,7	33,3	40,0	44,0
Threatened with execution of self or family	40,4	46,3	39,3	42,9	33,3	30,0	41,3
Offering rewards	28,0	37,0	35,7	35,7	33,3	40,0	33,7
Forced to undress Constant interrogation	22,8	22,2	14,3	35,7	22,2	50,0	23,8
Blindfolded	12,3	14,8	21,4	14,3	–	30,0	15,1
Sleep deprivation	14,0	14,8	14,3	35,7	11,1	10,0	15,7
Threatened with prolonged detention	15,8	5,6	7,1	7,1	–	–	8,7
Knowledge of abuse of friends or family	5,3	5,6	3,6	7,1	11,1	10,0	5,8
Sham executions	1,8	3,7	7,1	–	–	–	2,9
Administration of drugs	3,5	1,9	–	–	11,1	10,0	2,9
Excrement abuse	–	1,9	1,3	7,1	–	–	1,7
Use of animals	5,3	–	–	–	–	–	1,7
Other psychological torture	10,5	14,8	10,7	14,3	–	10,0	11,6

Forms of psychological torture	W. Cape (20)	E. Cape (43)	Border (34)	Natal (24)	Tvl (53)	Row total (174)
No psychological torture	–	–	–	–	–	–
False accusations	63,0	90,5	73,5	95,8	83,8	82,8
Solitary confinement	85,0	69,0	61,8	95,8	87,0	78,7
Verbal abuse	65,0	71,4	64,7	75,0	75,9	71,3
Threatened violence	55,0	64,3	47,1	91,7	66,7	64,4
Good/bad interrogators	40,0	50,0	58,8	87,5	53,7	56,9
Given misleading information	40,0	50,5	44,1	83,3	53,7	51,1
Witness or knowledge of others' torture	10,0	59,5	55,9	41,7	40,7	44,8
Threatened with execution of self or family	10,0	52,4	55,9	62,5	24,1	40,8
Offering rewards	5,0	21,4	52,9	54,2	33,3	33,9
Forced to undress	5,0	33,3	50,0	20,8	16,7	26,4
Constant interrogation	20,0	16,7	11,8	62,5	20,4	23,6
Blindfolded	–	9,5	14,7	12,5	27,8	15,5
Sleep deprivation	10,0	16,7	8,8	25,0	16,7	15,5
Threatened with prolonged detention	10,0	9,5	–	12,5	11,1	8,6
Knowledge of abuse of friends or family	–	2,4	–	12,5	11,1	5,7
Sham executions	–	–	8,8	4,2	1,9	2,9
Administration of drugs	–	2,4	–	–	7,4	2,9
Excrement abuse	–	2,4	–	4,2	1,9	1,7
Use of animals	–	–	–	–	5,6	1,8
Other psychological torture	20,0	11,9	–	8,3	16,7	11,5

Comparison of distributions reported in four different studies: percentages*

Rasmussen & Lunde (1980)	
Sexual abuse	59
Isolation (solitary)	37
Sham executions	36
Forced to hear/watch others' torture	34
Threats of harm to family members	33
Sleep deprivation	30
Other forms of mental torture (threats, humiliations, mental exhaustion)	27

Allodi & Cowgill (1982)	
False accusations	85
Verbal abuse	78
Threats of execution	76
Sham executions	29
Other forms of mental torture	29

Randall *et al* (1983)	
Verbal abuse	100
Denial of privacy	100
Personal hygiene prevented	100
Blindfolding	92
Nakedness	73
Isolation (solitary)	68
Witness torture	65
Threats of death	62
Sleep deprived	54
Sham executions	46
Overcrowding	32
Threats of torture	24
Pharmacological abuse	24
Threats against family	22
Fluctuation of interrogators' attitude	19
Infected environment (lice)	13
Excrement in food	8
Hypnosis	3

Present study	
False accusations	83
Solitary confinement	79
Verbal abuse	71
Threats of violence	64
Good/bad interrogators	57
Misleading information	51
Witness or knowledge of others' torture	45
Threats of execution to self/family	41
Offered rewards	34
Forced to undress	27
Constant interrogation	23
Blindfolded	15
Sleep deprived	15
Threats of prolonged detention	9
Knowledge of abuse of family or friends	6
Sham executions	3
Drugs administered	3
Excrement abuse	2
Animals	2
Other forms	11

* Samples as reported for types of physical torture in Appendix H

APPENDIX J: Health problems during detention

Health problems* (11 missing cases; 165 valid)	−20 (53)	21–25 (52)	26–30 (28)	31–35 (13)	36–40 (9)	Over 40 (10)	Row total (165)
No health problems	5,6	1,9	–	7,7	11,1	–	3,6
Difficulty sleeping	60,4	63,5	57,1	53,8	66,7	70,0	58,8
Headaches	43,4	55,8	57,1	61,5	66,7	70,0	53,9
Weight loss	45,3	44,2	50,0	61,5	22,2	50,0	44,8
Appetite loss	37,7	46,2	53,6	30,8	33,3	60,0	43,6
Nightmares	34,0	44,2	42,9	23,1	44,4	50,0	39,4
Difficulty concentrating	32,1	51,9	50,0	46,2	44,4	50,0	44,2
Tiredness	30,2	32,7	42,9	46,2	44,4	50,0	36,4
Difficulty with memory	24,5	30,8	53,6	46,2	11,1	70,0	34,5
Stomach pains	26,4	26,9	32,1	30,8	22,2	40,0	28,5
Restlessness	26,4	32,7	32,1	7,7	–	50,0	27,9
Depression	18,9	36,5	28,6	30,8	11,1	30,0	27,3
Constipation	20,8	23,1	39,3	23,1	22,2	30,0	25,5
Shivering	18,9	25,0	28,6	23,1	33,3	30,0	24,2
Crying	22,6	26,9	28,9	7,7	33,3	20,0	24,2
Rapid heart beat	9,4	15,4	14,3	15,4	33,0	30,0	15,2
Nausea	9,4	17,3	17,9	23,1	22,2	20,0	18,2
Sweating	13,2	21,2	14,3	7,7	33,3	30,0	17,6
Trembling	5,6	23,1	7,1	7,7	11,1	10,0	12,1
Diarrhoea	9,4	15,4	14,3	7,7	11,1	10,0	12,1
Uncontrollable laugh	11,3	7,7	14,3	–	–	–	8,5
Hyperactive	5,6	7,7	14,3	–	–	10,0	6,1
Other problems	75,5	75,0	75,0	92,3	77,8	100,0	78,2

* 'Excessive fantasy' is here included under 'other health problems' in contrast with Table 12 in the text of the study; thus 'other' percentage here is greater.

Health problems★ (9 missing cases; 165 valid)	W. Cape (19)	E. Cape (41)	Border (34)	Natal (24)	Tvl (49)	Row total (167)
No health problems	5,3	2,4	–	8,3	4,1	3,6
Difficulty sleeping	52,6	53,7	58,8	66,7	63,3	59,3
Headaches	42,1	39,0	70,6	58,3	55,1	53,3
Weight loss	36,0	53,7	47,1	37,5	42,9	44,9
Appetite loss	10,5	43,9	44,1	45,8	55,1	43,7
Nightmares	10,5	41,5	55,9	25,0	46,9	40,1
Difficulty concentrating	31,6	36,6	61,8	45,8	42,9	44,3
Tiredness	21,1	19,5	52,9	37,5	44,9	36,5
Difficulty with memory	5,3	29,3	55,9	29,2	36,7	34,1
Stomach pains	5,3	34,1	32,4	16,7	34,7	28,1
Restlessness	10,5	24,4	14,7	29,2	44,9	27,5
Depression	47,4	14,6	14,7	29,2	36,7	26,9
Constipation	21,1	22,0	20,6	16,7	36,7	25,1
Shivering	–	17,1	29,4	29,2	34,7	24,6
Crying	15,8	17,1	17,6	20,8	38,8	24,0
Rapid heart beat	–	7,3	14,7	29,2	22,4	15,6
Nausea	10,5	29,3	14,7	4,2	20,4	18,0
Sweating	–	9,8	20,6	16,7	28,6	17,4
Trembling	–	7,3	8,8	29,2	16,3	12,6
Diarrhoea	10,5	7,3	17,6	12,5	12,2	12,0
Uncontrollable laugh	–	12,2	11,8	4,2	8,2	8,4
Hyperactive	–	4,9	5,9	4,2	10,2	6,0
Other problems	84,2	70,7	82,4	70,8	81,6	77,8

★ 'Excessive fantasy' is here included under 'other health problems' in contrast with Table 11 in body of study; thus 'other' percentage here is greater.

Details of responses coded as 'other' problems	n	%
Psychological symptoms:	18	10,7
cognitive, e.g. hallucination, confusion, depressive thoughts (7);		
depressive, e.g. submissive, demoralised (4);		
anxiety, e.g. phobias, fears (4);		
mood, e.g. elated, frustrated (3)		
Body pains, specific or diffuse	14	8,3
Ear problems	11	6,6
Skin problems:	11	6,6
skin rash (5);		
other (pimples, itches) (6)		
Weight increase (9) or fluctuation (1)	10	6,0
Eyes weakened (6) or sore (4)	10	6,0
Back problems	9	6,5
Nervousness, more than usual	8	4,8
Chest constriction	7	4,2
Excess (5) or burning (2) urine	7	4,2
Slept more than usual	6	3,6
Tension symptoms:	6	3,6
eye twitch, uncontrolled screaming, asthma, etc.		
Vomiting	5	3,0
Hair falling out	3	1,8
Total	125	

Percentages: expressed as percentage of total sample size for health problems during detention, N = 168.

APPENDIX K: Problems on release from detention

Release problems* (19 missing cases; N = 157)	−20 (50)	21–25 (50)	26–30 (27)	31–35 (13)	36–40 (7)	Over 40 (10)	Row total (157)
No release problems	6,0	–	–	–	14,3	10,0	3,2
Easily tired	46,0	38,0	51,9	38,5	28,6	80,0	45,2
Relating to friends	42,0	38,0	37,0	53,8	28,6	30,0	39,5
Change in eating habits	30,0	28,0	40,7	46,2	42,9	60,0	35,0
Relating to family	34,0	34,0	37,0	53,8	28,6	20,0	35,0
Getting to sleep	36,0	36,0	25,9	38,5	42,9	30,0	34,4
Nightmares	32,0	34,0	37,0	15,4	42,9	50,0	33,8
Irritability	22,0	44,0	22,2	38,5	14,3	20,0	29,9
Depression	18,0	24,0	22,2	30,8	42,9	30,0	23,6
Scars left on body	30,0	10,0	29,6	7,7	28,6	–	19,7
Relating to other people	18,0	16,0	14,8	23,1	14,3	30,0	17,8
Change in tobacco consumption	14,0	26,0	14,8	23,1	–	–	17,2
Fear/nervousness	8,0	20,0	11,1	7,7	–	20,0	12,7
Change in alcohol consumption	10,0	8,0	18,5	23,1	–	10,0	11,5
Headache	12,0	2,0	18,5	7,7	14,3	30,0	10,8
Easily woken up	6,0	12,0	11,1	15,4	–	20,0	10,2
Fear of redetention	6,0	10,0	11,1	15,4	14,3	–	8,9
Anxiety	10,0	8,0	7,4	–	–	10,0	7,6
Physical disability	8,0	6,0	3,7	7,7	14,3	10,0	7,0
Interrupted sleep	6,0	4,0	11,1	7,7	–	10,0	6,4
Hyperactivity	6,0	6,0	11,1	7,7	–	–	6,4
Passivity	6,0	4,0	–	–	–	10,0	3,8
Reduced hearing	–	–	11,1	–	14,3	20,0	3,8
Relating to authority	2,0	4,0	–	–	–	–	1,9
Other release problems*	44,0	56,0	74,1	69,2	42,9	70,0	56,7

* The following problems are included here under 'other release problems': problems with concentration, memory and wanting to be alone. Contrast with Table 12 in body of this study.

Release problems (17 missing cases; N = 159)	W. Cape (17)	E. Cape (35)	Border (33)	Natal (24)	Tvl (50)	Row total (159)
No release problems	11,8	–	–	4,2	4,0	3,1
Easily tired	17,6	48,6	90,9	39,3	30,0	45,9
Relating to friends	29,4	22,9	36,4	41,7	54,0	39,0
Change in eating habits	23,5	31,4	72,7	29,2	20,0	35,2
Relating to family	35,3	17,1	39,4	41,7	42,0	35,0
Getting to sleep	47,1	40,0	36,4	29,2	28,0	34,6
Nightmares	17,6	51,4	33,3	8,3	38,0	33,3
Irritability	41,2	31,4	39,4	25,0	24,0	30,8
Depression	29,4	5,7	15,2	29,4	38,0	23,9
Scars left on body	–	28,6	33,3	4,2	18,0	19,3
Relating to other people	17,6	8,6	3,8	20,8	32,0	17,6
Change in tobacco consumption	29,4	17,1	30,3	16,7	8,0	18,2
Fear/nervousness	11,8	8,6	12,1	25,0	10,0	12,6
Change in alcohol consumption	17,6	8,6	33,3	–	4,0	11,9
Headache	11,8	2,9	18,2	8,3	12,0	10,7
Easily woken up	5,9	2,9	18,2	8,3	12,0	10,1
Fear of redetention	23,5	–	3,0	4,2	16,0	8,8
Anxiety	–	2,9	–	12,5	16,0	7,5
Physical disability	–	11,4	12,1	4,2	4,0	6,9
Interrupted sleep	11,8	2,9	6,1	–	10,0	6,3
Hyperactivity	5,9	8,6	–	–	12,0	6,3
Passivity	5,9	5,7	–	–	6,0	3,8
Reduced hearing	–	2,9	12,1	–	2,0	3,8
Relating to authority	–	2,9	–	4,2	2,0	1,9
Other release problems*	64,7	48,6	60,6	37,5	66,0	56,6

* The following problems are included here under 'other release problems': problems with concentration, memory and wanting to be alone. Contrast with Table 12 in body of this study.

Details of responses coded as 'other' problems	n	%
Other psychological problems:	22	13,8
psychosomatic: nausea (2), sweating (2), sexual (2), breast pains (2), enuresis (1);		
anxiety: rapid heartbeat (2), uncontrolled laughter (1), fear assassination (1), emotional (1);		
depressive: loss confidence (2), crying (1), slept more (1);		
cognitive: intrusive thoughts (1), fantasy (2);		
social: intolerant (1)		
Aggressiveness	12	7,5
Other physical problems	10	6,3
Stomach pains	8	5,0
Tense	5	3,1
Excessive talking	5	3,1
Constipation	5	3,1
Shaking	5	3,1
Greying hair	5	3,1
Feel alone in a group	5	3,1
Insecure	3	1,9
Less trust in people	3	1,9
Emotionless	3	1,9
High blood pressure	3	1,9
Easily bored	3	1,9
Noise in ears	3	1,9
Total	*100*	

Percentages: expressed as percentage of total sample for release problems, N = 160.

APPENDIX L

South African detention numbers 1974–1985: official and unofficial

Official		Unofficial	
1974	—	January 1974– 30 June 1976	217 (Terrorism Act only)
1975	—	1976	433
June 1976– August 1978	2430	1977	714 (at 30 November)
July 1977– June 1978	501	1978	261 (at 30 November)
July 1978– June 1979	113	1979	334 (at 30 November)
1980	1243	1980	768 (at 30 November plus 227 in 'homelands')
1981	974	1981	772 (includes 'homelands')
1982	210	1982	181 (at 30 November plus 83 in 'homelands')
1983	? (238, unofficial)	1983	238 (plus 215 in 'homelands')
1984	? (595, unofficial)	1984	595 (plus 554 in 'homelands')
1985	?(1684, unofficial)	1985	1684 (plus 1953 in 'homelands')
Total	7988 (includes unofficial figures for 1983–1985)	Total	6197 (9229 if 'homeland' detentions are included)

Plus 7996 emergency detentions during state of emergency 1985-1986.

Official figures from Minister of Police, or Commissioner of Prisons, or Minister of Law and Order (from 1980).

Unofficial figures from H. Kleinschmidt, *Detention and Detente* (Christian Institute, 1976); South African Institute of Race Relations as given in the *Annual Survey of Race Relations in South Africa;* and Detainees' Parents Support Committee, *Review of 1984* and *Review of 1985*.

APPENDIX M

1. Deaths in detention

Mampe, B.	September 1963
Ngudle, Looksmart Solwandle	5 September 1963
Tyitya, James	24 January 1964
Saloojee, Suliman	9 September 1964
Gaga, Negeni	9 May 1965
Hoye, Pongoloshe	9 May 1965
Hamakwayo, James	August 1966
Shonyeka, Hangula	9 October 1966
Pin, Leong Yun	19 November 1966
Yan, Ah	5 January 1967
Madiba, Alpheus F.	9 September 1967
Tubakwa, J. B.	11 September 1968
Unnamed	1968
Kgoathe, Nicodemus	5 February 1969
Modipane, Solomon	28 February 1969
Lencoe, James	10 March 1969
Mayekiso, Caleb	1 June 1969
Shivute, Michael	17 June 1969
Monnakgotla, Jacob	10 September 1969
Haron, Imam Abdullah	27 September 1969
Cuthsela, Mthayeni	21 January 1971
Timol, Ahmed Essop	27 October 1971
Mdluli, Joseph	19 March 1976
Tshwane, William N.	26 July 1976
Mohapi, Mapetla Frank	5 August 1976
Mazwembe, Luke	2 September 1976
Mbatha, Dumisani	25 September 1976
Mogatusi, Fenuel	28 September 1976
Mashabane, Zungwane Jacob	5 October 1976
Unnamed	6 October 1976
Mzolo, Edward	9 October 1976
Mamashila, Ernest	18 November 1976
Mosala, Thalo	26 November 1976
Tshazibane, Wellington	11 December 1976
Botha, George	15 December 1976
Ntshuntsha, Dr Nanaoth	8 January 1977
Ndzanga, Lawrence	8 January 1977
Malele, Elmon	20 January 1976
Mabelane, Matthews	15 February 1976
Joyi, Tswafifeni	15 February 1976
Malinga, Samuel	22 February 1977
Khoza, Aaron	26 March 1977
Mabija, Phakamile	1977
Loza, Elijah	1 August 1977
Haffejee, Dr Hoosen Mia	3 August 1977
Mzizi, Byempin	13 August 1977
Biko, Steve Bantu	12 September 1977

James, Mbulelo Rocky	9 November 1977
Malaza, Bonaventure Sipho	16 November 1977
Nobhadula, Mzukisi	20 December 1977
Tabalaza, Lungile	10 July 1978
Ndzumo, Saul	10 September 1980
Matalazi, Sifundile	20 December 1980
Mgqweto, Manana	17 September 1981
Muofhe, Tshifiwa Isaac	12 November 1981
Aggett, Dr Neil Hudson	5 February 1982
Dipale, Ernest Moabi	8 August 1982
Dlodlo, Linda	23 September 1982
Mndawe, Simon Tembuyise	8 March 1983
Malatji, Paris Molefe	5 July 1983
Tshikudo, Samuel	20 January 1984
Mthethwa, Ephraim	25 August 1984
Sipele, Mxolisi	June 1984
Raditsela, Andries	6 May 1985

2. Deaths in police custody to the end of 1985 (people arrested not formally under detention provisions but under circumstances appearing to be politically related).

Johannes Ngalo	25 July 1984	Parys
Jacob Moleleke	September 1984	Sebokeng
Anthony Mazunyane	November 1984	Germiston
Samson Maseko	November 1984	Katlehong
Abel Ngwenya	22 November 1984	Benoni
Tatlheho Korotsoane	early 1985	Katlehong
Bheki Mvulani	28 March 1985	Katlehong
Sipho Mutsi	5 May 1985	Odendaalsrus
Mzwandile Muggels	3 July 1985	Steytlerville
Johannes Spogter	5 July 1985	Steytlerville
Sonnyboy Mokoena	16 Aguust 1985	Pilgrim's Rest
Thembalake George	16 August 1985	Ginsberg
Loyiso Ndzandze	18 August 1985	Ginsberg
Mbuyiselo Mbotya	21 September 1985	Ginsberg
Batandwa Ndondo	24 September 1985	Cala, Transkei
Ngoako Ramalepe	12 October 1985	Lebowa
Meshack Mogale	17 November 1985	Mamelodi East

Sources

Catholic Institute for International Relations, *Torture in South Africa: Recent Documents* (London: Catholic Institute, 1982).

Detainees' Parents Support Committee, *Report of May 1985* and *Review of 1985* (Bramley: DPSC).

Dugard, C. J. R. *et al.* (eds.), *Report on the Rabie Report* (Johannesburg: Centre for Applied Legal Studies, University of the Witwatersrand, 1982).

Lawyers' Committee for Civil Rights under Law, *Deaths in Detention and South Africa's Security* Laws (Washington, D.C.: LCCRL, 1983).

Moultrie, C., 'A survey of twenty years of deaths under security legislation in South Africa 1963–1983'. Unpublished B.A. Honours thesis, University of Cape Town, 1983.

Weekly Mail, 14 June 1985.

References

1. Detention and torture in South Africa

1. Public Safety Act 3 of 1953.
2. C. J. R. Dugard, 'A triumph for executive power – an examination of the Rabie Report and the Internal Security Act 74 of 1982', *South African Law Journal*, 99 (1982), 589–604.
3. C. J. R. Dugard, *Human Rights and the South African Legal Order* (Princeton, 1978); C. J. R. Dugard, 'Human rights in South Africa – retrospect and prospect', in C. Forsyth and J. Schiller (eds.), *Human Rights: The Cape Town Conference* (Cape Town, 1979), pp. 263–285; D. Fine 'Re-examining the validity of the detainee evidence: a psycho-legal approach', *South African Journal of Criminal Law and Criminology*, 8 (1984), 156–194; A. S. Mathews, *Law, Order and Liberty in South Africa* (Cape Town, 1971).
4. Medical Association of South Africa (MASA), Report on Medical Care of Prisoners and Detainees, Supplement to the *South African Medical Journal* (21 May 1983); S. A. Strauss, 'The legal rights of prisoners and detainees to medical treatment', *South African Journal of Criminal Law and Criminology*, 7 (1983), 20–32; J. Frankish, 'The medical care of prisoners and detainees', *South African Medical Journal*, 64 (1983), 117.
5. D. Davis, 'Confessions and security legislation', *South African Law Journal*, 99 (1982), 516–524; Fine 'Re-examining validity'; C. R. Nicholson, 'Admissibility and reliability of detainee evidence', *South African Journal of Criminal Law and Criminology*, 5 (1981), 122–136; J. G. Riekert, 'Police assaults and the admissibility of "voluntary" confessions', *South African Law Journal*, 99 (1982), 175–183.
6. G. Marcus, 'Assaults in detention: time running out', *Reality*, 16 (1984), 9–10.
7. Some examples are to be found in the following: Amnesty International, *Report on Torture* (New York, 1975); Amnesty International, *Torture in the Eighties* (London, 1984); H. Bernstein, *South Africa: The Terrorism of Torture* (London, 1972); Catholic Institute for International Relations, *Torture in South Africa* (London, 1982); Christian Institute, *Torture in South Africa?* (Braamfontein, 1977); S. Cronje, *Witness in the Dark: Police Torture and Brutality in South Africa* (London, 1964); Detainees' Parents Support Committee, *Memorandum on Security Police Abuses of Political Detainees* (Johannesburg, 1982); N. Haysom, *Ruling with the Whip* (Johannesburg, 1983); Lawyers' Committee for Civil Rights Under Law, *Torture in South Africa* (Washington, D.C., 1985); M. Pheto, *And Night Fell* (London, 1983); A. Sachs, *Stephanie on Trial* (London, 1968); United Nations, *Maltreatment and Torture of Prisoners in South Africa* (New York, 1973); G. Winter, *Inside Boss* (Harmondsworth, 1981).
8. The most definitive published account claimed 60 deaths under security legislation by September 1983. See Lawyers' Committee for Civil Rights Under Law, *Deaths in Detention and South Africa's Security Laws* (Washington, D.C., 1983). Since then a further 4 deaths have occurred under security laws, while a further 8 persons died while arrested on political but not necessarily security-related charges. See Weekly Mail, 14 June 1985. Appendix M provides a full list of names and dates of death of those who have died. By this count, the total number of deaths in detention by the end of 1985 was 64. The inquest into Andries Raditsela who died on 6 May 1985 is still being heard. See also C. Moultrie, 'A survey of twenty years of deaths under security legislation in South Africa 1963–1983', unpublished B.A. Honours thesis, University of Cape Town, 1983.

References

9. Lawyers for Human Rights, 'Any hope for detainees? The Aggett inquest and Rabie Report compared', *Bulletin No. 2* (June 1983), 3.
10. *Report of the Commission of Inquiry into Security Legislation* (RP 90/1981), hereafter referred to as the 'Rabie Report'.
11. C. J. R. Dugard et al. (eds.), *Report on the Rabie Report. An Examination of Security Legislation in South Africa* (Centre for Applied Legal Studies, University of the Witwatersrand, 1982).
12. Dugard, *Report on the Rabie Report*, pp. 16–17.
13. At that time particularly Section 6 of the Terrorism Act 63 of 1967.
14. Dugard, *Report on the Rabie Report*, pp. 25–26.
15. Rabie Report, paras. 10.35–10.44.
16. Dugard, *Report on the Rabie Report*, p. 11.
17. A. S. Roux, 'Sensory and perceptual deprivation', *South African Psychologist*, monograph no. 69 (October 1967).
18. A. S. Mathews and R. C. Albino, 'The permanence of the temporary – an examination of the 90-day and 180-day detention laws', *South African Law Journal*, 83 (1966), 16.
19. Roux, 'Sensory deprivation', p. 8.
20. Medical Association of South Africa, 'Report on Medical Care'.
21. A. D. Biderman, 'Social psychological needs and "involuntary" behaviour as illustrated by compliance in interrogation', *Sociometry*, 23 (1960), 120–147; M. Brenton, 'Solitary confinement: a review of the literature', unpublished paper, Metropolitan Toronto Forensic Service (Toronto, 1981); I. E. Farber, H. F. Harlow and L. J. West, 'Brainwashing, conditioning and DDD', *Sociometry*, (1957), 271–285; L. E. Hinkle and H. G. Wolff, 'Communist interrogation and indoctrination of "enemies of the state"', *Archives of Neurology and Psychiatry*, 76 (1956), 115–174; T. Shallice, 'The Ulster depth interrogation techniques and their relation to sensory deprivation research', *Cognition*, 1 (1972), 385–405.
22. Gratitude is expressed to Derek Fine and Clifford Luyt for some of the information used in this section.
23. Rabie Report, para. 14.2.
24. See D. Davis, 'Political trials in South Africa', in D. Davis and M. Slabbert (eds.), *Crime and Power in South Africa* (Cape Town, 1985), pp. 34–47.
25. Dugard, *Human Rights*, p. 212.
26. R. Suttner, 'Political trials and the legal process', in *South African Review Two* (Johannesburg, 1984).
27. Fine, 'Re-examining validity', p. 159.
28. Intimidation Act 72 of 1982.
29. Act 84 of 1982.
30. Suttner, 'Political trials', p. 72.
31. On 29 June 1984 a 'consolidated list' of 200 people who may not be quoted in terms of Section 56(1) of the Internal Security Act was published, replacing the earlier consolidated list of almost 450 people. In terms of Section 56(2), no 'utterance, speech and statement' of a listed person may be published and disseminated without the permission of the Minister of Law and Order. Contravention carries a prison sentence of up to three years. Of the total of 200 people, 25 were in South African prisons, 33 resident in South Africa, 123 living in exile abroad, and 19 deceased.
32. For example, the recent deportation in 1984 of a number of academics from the Transkei.
33. It has been argued that security police have in the past used systematic forms of psychological terrorism to intimidate political opponents. See P. Lambley, *The Psychology of Apartheid* (London, 1980).
34. Haysom, *Ruling with the Whip*.
35. For example, in 1983 some 189 policemen were convicted of common assault, 40 of assault with intent to grievous bodily harm, 14 of culpable homicide, and 3 of murder. The late Mr Harry Pitman described these figures as 'disgraceful'. *Survey of Race Relations*

in South Africa (1983), p. 534.

36. The as yet unsolved murder of Dr Richard Turner on 8 January 1978 may be recalled in this respect. During late June 1985 four Eastern Cape community leaders and UDF members from Cradock, Matthew Goniwe, Fort Calata, Sparrow Mkhonto and Sicelo Mhlawuli, were found murdered after disappearing. Since 1981 more than ten activists in the Eastern Cape have either disappeared or been murdered but no one has been charged. See *Cape Times*, 4 July 1985.

37. During 1984 a total of 1 149 people were detained, 617 of them in South Africa (excluding the homelands). Only 1,4 per cent of these had been convicted of offences by February 1985. Of those still in detention in February 1985, 35 had been held without trial for 7 months or more. Students and scholars accounted for the largest single grouping of detainees: 51 per cent. See *Cape Times*, 6 February 1985; Detainees' Parents Support Committee, *Review of 1984* (Bramley, 31 January 1985).

38. Detainees' Parents Support Committee, *Review of 1985* (Bramley, 31 January 1986).

39. In February 1986, the Detainees' Parents Support Committee became the first recipient of the prestigious new *Liberté, Egalité, Fraternité* Human Rights Award from the French government. See *Weekly Mail*, 27 February 1986.

40. One may note in this respect the establishment of a new journal, the *South African Journal on Human Rights*, which carries an up-to-date human rights index.

41. Between 21 and 26 August 1984, during elections for the tricameral parliament, 18 leaders of those protesting against the elections (mainly UDF leaders) were detained under Section 28. On 7 September the Pietermaritzburg Supreme Court ruled that detention notices to Natal detainees were invalid since reasons had not been given. New orders were immediately issued but could not be given, since the released detainees had gone into hiding.

On 13 September 1984 Archie Gumede, Paul David, Mewa Ramgobin, Billy Nair, M. J. Naidoo and George Sewpersadh moved from hiding into the British Consulate in Durban, requesting the British government to intervene on their behalf. Although the British did not evict the men, they said they could not be involved in a matter involving foreign nationals and their own government. A good deal of international attention was given to the plight of the six.

On 6 October Ramgobin, Sewpersadh and Naidoo left the Consulate and were rearrested in terms of Section 28. On 10 December, all Section 28 notices were withdrawn. Two days later, 90 days after having entered, Nair, Gumede and David left the Consulate, and the latter two were immediately arrested. All but one of the six were charged with treason, but charges were withdrawn in late 1985 after the collapse of the state's case.

42. *Cape Times*, 27 December 1984. See also the December 1984 edition of *De Rebus*.

43. *Cape Times*, 15 November 1984.

44. See *Cape Times*, 30 November 1984.

45. Amnesty International, *Torture in the Eighties*.

46. For further details of various documents pertaining to human rights in relation to torture see Amnesty International, *Torture in the Eighties*; and United Nations, *Human Rights International Instruments* (New York, 1984).

47. On 13 May 1977 the Council approved the addition of rule 95 to the Standard Minimum Rules. In essence the new rule provides that persons arrested or imprisoned without charge are to be accorded the same protection as persons under arrest, awaiting trial and under sentence. In 1984 the procedures for implementing the rules were completed and approved. See United Nations, *Standard Minimum Rules for the Treatment of Prisoners and Procedures for the Effective Implementation of the Rules* (New York, 1984).

48. Amnesty International, *Report on Torture*.

49. See E. Stover and E. Nightingale, *The Breaking of Bodies and Minds* (New York, 1985), for a listing of international organisations concerned with the abolition of torture.

50. B. Vischer, 'Christians against torture', *South African Outlook*, 114 (July 1984), 105–106.

222 References

51. J. Rex (ed.), *Apartheid and Social Research* (Paris, 1981).

2. Historical considerations

1. A. S. Mathews, *Law, Order and Liberty in South Africa* (Cape Town, 1971), p. 285.
2. S. Hall et al., *Policing the Crisis* (London, 1978), p. 217.
3. Act 38 of 1927.
4. Section 29(5).
5. Section 5(1)(b).
6. E. H. Brookes and J. B. Macaulay, *Civil Liberty in South Africa* (Cape Town, 1958), p. 158.
7. The original Act was Act 27 of 1914.
8. Section 1(7) of Act 19 of 1930 which amended Act 27 of 1914.
9. Section 1(4).
10. See in particular C. J. R. Dugard, 'Human rights in South Africa – retrospect and prospect', *Acta Juridica*, 263 (1979), 267 and, more generally, H. Corder, *Judges at Work* (Cape Town, 1984).
11. R. F. A. Hoernlé, *South African Native Policy and the Liberal Spirit* (Johannesburg, 1945), p. 55.
12. Mathews, *Law, Order and Liberty*, p. 235.
13. Ibid.
14. Dugard, 'Human rights', p. 269; Mathews, *Law, Order and Liberty*, pp. 234–235.
15. This section is gleaned in the main from the following: M. Legassick, 'Legislation, ideology and economy in post-1948 South Africa', *Journal of Southern African Studies*, 1 (1974), 5–35; S. Greenberg, *Race and State in Capitalist Development* (Johannesburg, 1980); S. Greenberg, 'The political economy of change: problems of hegemony in contemporary South Africa', in F. van Zyl Slabbert and J. Opland (eds.), *Dilemmas of Evolutionary Change* (Grahamstown, 1980); R. H. Davies, *Capital, State and White Labour in South Africa 1900–1960* (Brighton, 1979).
16. Legassick, 'Legislation', p. 6.
17. See in particular Greenberg, *Race and State in Capitalist Development*, and M. Morris, 'The development of capitalism in South African agriculture', *Economy and Society*, 5 (1976), 292–343.
18. Greenberg, 'Political economy', pp. 101–103.
19. D. O'Meara, 'The 1946 African mineworkers' strike', *Journal of Commonwealth and Comparative Politics*, 13 (1975), 146–173.
20. O'Meara, '1946 strike'.
21. Report of the Native Laws Commission 1946–48 (UG 28/48).
22. M. Morris, 'Apartheid, agriculture and the state: the farm labour question', Southern Africa Labour and Development Research Unit, Working paper no. 8 (1977).
23. Legassick, 'Legislation', p. 13 quotes from the parliamentary debate in 1947 to illustrate this particular point.
24. Act 44 of 1950.
25. House of Assembly Debates (1950), col. 9340.
26. See Mathews, *Law, Order and Liberty*, pp. 116ff for a detailed analysis of these Acts
27 J. McCarthy, as quoted by H. Zinn, *Postwar America: 1954–1971* (Indianapolis, 1973), p. 151.
28. R. Griffith, as quoted by H. Zinn, *Postwar America*, p. 154.
29. Robert Menzies, as quoted by D. Marr, *Barwick* (London, 1980), p. 80.
30. See the comments of the Minister of Justice in House of Assembly Debates (1950), col. 8910. See also D. Kemp 'The Nationalists and apartheid', *Contemporary Issues* (1949), p. 10 where the author points to collaboration between the Nationalist government and the MI5 in respect of the 'Communist threat in Africa'.
31. House of Assembly Debates (1950), col. 9378.
32. House of Assembly Debates (1956), cols. 180–183.
33. J. A. Grey Coetzee, *Industrial Relations in South Africa* (Cape Town, 1976), p. 43.
34. Coetzee, *Industrial Relations*, pp. 42–44.

35. *Ibid.*
36. Act 3 of 1953.
37. Act 8 of 1953.
38. T. G. Karis and G. M. Carter (eds.), *From Protest to Challenge: A Documentary History of African Politics in South Africa 1882–1964*, vol. III, (Stanford, 1977), p. 418.
39. Moses Kotane, J. B. Marks, J. N. Negwela, D. W. Bopape and Y. Dadoo.
40. Senate Debates (February 1953), col. 752.
41. Karis and Carter, *From Protest to Challenge*, p. 67.
42. *Ibid.*, p. 348.
43. Interview with Sheridan Johns, 29 January 1959, in *ibid.*, p. 275.
44. Act 68 of 1951.
45. Act 46 of 1959.
46. The best-known account is by Govan Mbeki, *The Peasants' Revolt* (Harmondsworth, 1963).
47. A useful analysis of the Mpondo revolt has been written by John Copelyn, 'The Mpondo revolt', unpublished B.A. Honours thesis, University of the Witwatersrand (1974).
48. Proclamation R400, Government Gazette No. 6852 of 30 November 1960.
49. Regulation 16 of Proclamation 400.
50. *Sunday Express*, 4 December 1960.
51. C. Hooper, *Brief Authority* (London, 1960), p. 209.
52. Proclamation 413, Government Gazette No. 6594.
53. *Rand Daily Mail*, 16 December 1960.
54. House of Assembly Debates (1961), col. 226.
55. Karis and Carter, *From Protest to Challenge*, p. 352.
56. T. Lodge, 'The rural struggle: Poqo and Transkei resistance', paper delivered at the Conference on the History of Opposition in South Africa, University of the Witwatersrand (January 1978).
57. Proclamation 90 of 30 March 1960.
58. Government Notice 551 of 11 April 1960.
59. E. Feit, *Urban Revolt in South Africa 1960–1964* (Evanston, 1971), p. 49.
60. House of Assembly Debates (1960), col. 4302.
61. Karis and Carter, *From Protest to Challenge*, Document 56: Resolution of the All-In African Conference, March 1961.
62. *Ibid.*, Document 75: Statement during Rivonia Trial by Nelson Mandela.
63. More fully, the General Law Amendment Act 76 of 1962.
64. *Survey of Race Relations in South Africa* (1962), p. 46.
65. Section 17 of the General Law Amendment Act 37 of 1963.
66. House of Assembly Debates (1963), col. 7634.
67. *Ibid.*, col. 4688.
68. 1964(2) SA 545(A).
69. House of Assembly Debates (1965), cols. 252, 256–257, 265 and 267.
70. Feit, *Urban Revolt*, pp. 316ff.
71. Act 56 of 1955, which was amended by Act 96 of 1965.
72. Dugard, 'Human rights', p. 113.
73. Act 56 of 1955.
74. Act 62 of 1966.
75. Act 83 of 1967.
76. House of Assembly Debates (1967), cols. 7023–7026.
77. *Ibid.*, cols. 7100–7120.
78. Dugard, 'Human rights', p. 119.
79. Section 6(7).
80. H. Rudolph, *Security, Terrorism and Torture: Detainees' Rights in South Africa and Israel* (Cape Town, 1984), p. 15.
81. Dugard, 'Human rights', p. 119.
82. *Survey of Race Relations in South Africa* (1973), p. 78.

83. Dugard, 'Human rights', p. 120.
84. *Administration of Security Legislation in South Africa* (South African Institute of Race Relations, 1976).
85. *Rand Daily Mail*, 2 September 1977.
86. *Survey of Race Relations in South Africa* (1983), p. 547.
87. *S. v Tuhadeleni and Others* 1969(1) SA 153(A).
88. The Pietermaritzburg trial of 1969 appears to be the first in this regard. See *Survey of Race Relations* (1969), pp. 64–65. Interestingly P. Hillyard, 'From Belfast to Britain', in *Politics and Power*, 4 (1981), 83, shows how legislation initially justified on the basis of its being necessary for Northern Ireland has been used increasingly on the mainland even in cases unrelated to the Irish problem. See also J. Sim and P. A. Thomas, 'The Prevention of Terrorism Act: normalising the politics of repression', *Journal of Law and Society*, 10 (1983), 71–84.
89. C. S. Mennel, 'The changing character of South African finance houses in the post-war period', unpublished MBA thesis, University of Pennsylvania (1961).
90. D. H. Houghton, *The South African Economy*, 4th edition (Cape Town, 1976), pp. 212–213.
91. *Ibid.*, pp. 212–213.
92. Unreported judgment of TPD, 29 October 1971.
93. *Survey of Race Relations in South Africa* (1973), p. 27.
94. House of Assembly Debates (1973), col. 1490 (B. J. Vorster).
95. *Survey of Race Relations in South Africa* (1973), p. 284.
96. As quoted by R. W. Johnson, *How Long Will South Africa Survive?* (Johannesburg, 1977), p. 195.
97. Act 79 of 1976.
98. Rudolph, *Security*, pp. 15–16.
99. House of Assembly Debates (1976), col. 6306.
100. *Ibid.*
101. Proclamation 133, Government Gazette No. 5229 of 16 July 1976, and Proclamation 159, Government Gazette No. 5253 of 11 August 1976.
102. *Administration of Security Legislation in South Africa* (1976).
103. House of Assembly Debates (1982), col. 368.

3. Legal considerations

1. Report of the Commission of Inquiry into Security Legislation, RP 90/1981 (hereafter referred to as the Rabie Report).
2. General Magnus Malan, in a speech to the Institute of Town Clerks, as reported in *Pretoria Daily News*, 13 June 1979.
3. Commission of Inquiry into the Mass Media, RP 89/81 (hereafter cited as the Steyn Commission).
4. Steyn Commission, p. 715.
5. *Ibid.*, p. 945.
6. As quoted by the Rabie Report, para 3.2.
7. *Ibid.*, para 10.34.
8. *Ibid.*
9. C. J. R. Dugard *et al.*, *Report on the Rabie Report. An Examination of Security Legislation in South Africa* (Centre for Applied Legal Studies, University of the Witwatersrand, 1982).
10. *Survey of Race Relations in South Africa* (1982), p. 255.
11. Lawyers for Human Rights, 'Any hope for detainees? The Aggett inquest and the Rabie Report compared', *Bulletin No. 2*, special issue (June 1983).
12. Act 74 of 1982.
13. Internal Security Act 74 of 1982; Protection of Information Act 84 of 1982; Intimidation Act 72 of 1982; Demonstrations in or near Court Buildings Prohibition Act 71 of 1982.
14. Section 31 of the Internal Security Act of 1982.

15. Section 50 of *ibid*.
16. Act 62 of 1966.
17. Section 29 of the Internal Security Act of 1982.
18. Defined in Section 54(1) of the Internal Security Act of 1982.
19. Section 29(1).
20. For more detailed discussion of these matters see C. J. R. Dugard, 'A triumph for executive power – an examination of the Rabie Report and the Internal Security Act 74 of 1982', *South African Law Journal*, 99 (1982), 589–604; and Rudolph, *Security*, pp. 24–27.
21. Section 45(1) of the Internal Security Act of 1982.
22. Lawyers for Human Rights, 'Any hope for detainees?', pp. 82–83.
23. *Survey of Race Relations in South Africa* (1983), p. 548.
24. *Ibid*.
25. Detainees' Parents Support Committee, *Review of 1984* (Bramley, January 1985).
26. Detainees' Parents Support Committee, *Review of 1985* (Bramley, January 1986).
27. Section 28 of the Internal Security Act of 1982.
28. Section 29(1) of *ibid*.
29. In terms of schedule 2 of *ibid*.
30. Section 38 of *ibid*. specifies the nature of the review procedure.
31. Dugard, 'A triumph for executive power', p. 604; Rudolph, *Security*, p. 35.
32. Rudolph, *Security*, pp. 26–27.
33. Rabie Report, para 10.44.
34. Lawyers for Human Rights, 'Any hope for detainees?', p. 7.
35. *Ibid*., p. 29.
36. *Cape Times*, 5 November 1982. See Notice 877 in the Government Gazette No. 8467 of 3 December 1982 for full details of the Directions.
37. A. S. Mathews, *Freedom, State Security and the Rule of Law* (Cape Town, 1986), p. 86.
38. *Cape Times*, 21 February and 15 March 1984.
39. Report of the Committee of Inquiry into Police Interrogation Procedures in Northern Ireland, Cmnd. 7497 (1979).
40. *Cape Times*, 3 May 1983.
41. See *Argus*, 3 May 1983; *Cape Times*, 4 May 1983.
42. *Cape Times*, 5 May 1983.
43. N. Haysom, 'Closed circuit television for detainees', *Lawyers for Human Rights Bulletin* (August 1984), 101–102.
44. Medical Association of South Africa, 'Report on Medical Care of Prisoners and Detainees', Supplement to the *South African Medical Journal* (21 May 1983).
45. For example, the South African Medical and Dental Council (SAMDC) and the Medical Association of South Africa (MASA) consistently refused to conduct a full investigation into the alleged involvement of certain doctors in the death of Steve Biko. However, a decision of the Transvaal Supreme Court early in 1985 ordered the SAMDC to hold an inquiry into the conduct of the doctors concerned. See also M. Bennun, 'Doctors, torture and the law – a South African case study', *Radical Community Medicine*, 20 (1984–5), 30–40; L. Baxter, 'Doctors on trial', *South African Journal on Human Rights*, 1 (1985), 137–151.
46. For a fuller discussion of the limitations of the recommendations, see D. H. Foster, 'Implications for the Psychological Association of South Africa of the MASA Report on Detainees', paper delivered at the National Psychology Congress, Pietermaritzburg, September 1983; G. Hayes, 'MASA and the politics of detention', *Work in Progress*, 30 (1984), 40–45.
47. Rudolph, *Security*, p. 51.
48. MASA Report, para 6.2.
49. *Ibid*., paras 7.1 and 7.2.
50. World Medical Association, *Guidelines for Medical Doctors Concerning Torture and Other Cruel, Inhuman or Degrading Treatment or Punishment in Relation to Detention and Imprisonment* (Tokyo, 1975).

51. MASA Report, para 6.1.
52. Ibid., para 5.4.
53. Ibid., para 7.5.
54. *Cape Times*, 27 May 1983.
55. Ibid., 23 November 1985.
56. A. S. Mathews, 'Public safety', in W. Joubert (ed.), *Laws of South Africa*, vol. 21 (Durban, 1984), para 364.
57. Act 51 of 1977. There has been some uncertainty as to whether the word 'voluntarily' in Section 219A should be given its common law meaning. Such a view has now been confirmed in *S. v Yolelo* 1981(1) SA 1002(A) and *S. v Mpetha and Others* 1983(1) SA 576(C).
58. 1976(3) SA 745(D).
59. A. S. Mathews and R. C. Albino, 'The permanence of the temporary – an examination of the 90-day and 180-day detention laws', *South African Law Journal*, 83 (1966), 23.
60. *S. v Mpetha* 1983(2) SA 406 (C) at 414.
61. L. H. Hoffman and D. Zeffert, *The South African Law of Evidence* (Durban, 1981), p. 190.
62. AD June 1981 (unreported). See J. G. Riekert, 'Police assaults and the admissibility of "voluntary" confessions', *South African Law Journal*, 99 (1982), 175.
63. Rabie Report, para 10.72.
64. Ibid., para 10.74.
65. Ibid., para 10.76.
66. 384 US 436 (1966). Since the *Miranda* decision the American Supreme Court has attempted to restrict the applicability of the ruling. See J. Gruhl, 'State supreme courts and the US supreme courts: post *Miranda* rulings', *Journal of Criminal Law and Criminology*, 73 (1982), 886.
67. *R. v Stewart* (1972) 56 CR APP R 272; *R. v Kilner* (1976) Crim LR 740; *R. v Powell* (1980) Crim LR 39.
68. *R. v Isequilla* (1974), 60 LR APP R 52 at 54.
69. Mathews, *Law, Order and Liberty*; Mathews and Albino, 'The permanence of the temporary'. See also M. Inman, 'The admissibility of confessions', *Criminal Law Review* (1981); E. D. Driver, 'Confessions and the social psychology of coercion', *Harvard Law Review*, 82 (1968), 42; K. Danziger, 'How solitary confinement affects prisoners', *Cape Times*, 12 November 1963; J. Riekert, 'The silent scream', *South African Journal on Human Rights*, 1 (1985), 245–250.
70. Royal Commission on Criminal Procedure, Cmnd. 8092 (1981), para 4.75.
71. Affidavit of R. C. Albino in *S. v Hassim* 1973(3) SA 443(A).
72. D. Davis, 'Confessions and security legislation', *South African Law Journal*, 99 (1982), 516–524; D. Fine, 'Re-examining the validity of detainee evidence: a psycho-legal approach', *South African Journal of Criminal Law and Criminology*, 8 (1984), 156–194; C. Murray, 'The right of the accused to his own earlier statements', *South African Journal of Criminal Law and Criminology*, 6 (1982), 290–294; C. R. Nicholson, 'Admissibility and reliability of detainee evidence', *South African Journal of Criminal Law and Criminology*, 6 (1982), 250–261; A. P. Paizes, 'Undue influence and involuntary admissions and confessions', *South African Journal of Criminal Law and Criminology*, 5 (1981), 122–136; S. K. Parmanand and C. Vorster, 'South Africa's state security legislation: exit Section 6', *Journal of Contemporary Roman Dutch Law*, 147 (1984), 180–199; Riekert, 'Police assaults'; R. C. Williams, 'The admissibility of confessions elicited during detention under the security law: a bold initiative from the Cape Provincial Division', *South African Law Journal*, 101 (1984), 7–17.
73. See particularly Parmanand and Vorster, 'State security legislation'; C. Vorster, 'The mind in solitary', *Rand Daily Mail*, 11 February 1982; S. J. Saunders, 'Solitary is torture', *Rand Daily Mail*, 20 May 1982.
74. O. Kirchheimer, *Political Justice* (Princeton, 1961), p. 52.
75. M. L. Norton, 'The political trial in South Africa – the quest for legitimacy', *Natal*

University Law Review, 3 (1982–83), 76.

76. S. Kentridge, 'Apartheid, law and justice', *The Listener*, 30 November 1978, p. 708.
77. Y. Kamisar, 'Equal justice in American criminal procedure', in his *Police Interrogation and Confessions: Essays in Law and Policy* (Ann Arbor, Mich., 1980), p. 27.
78. *Ibid.*, pp. 32–33.
79. Fine, 'Re-examining validity', p. 161.
80. *Ibid.*, p. 157.
81. See *ibid.*; Paizes, 'Undue influence'; D. S. Greer, 'The admissibility of confessions under the Northern Ireland Emergency Act', *Northern Ireland Law Quarterly*, 3 (1980), 233.
82. MASA Report, para 3.8.
83. Fine, 'Re-examining validity', p. 187; Paizes, 'Undue influence'.
84. 1964(2) SA 551(A).
85. At 561D–E.
86. At 564F.
87. At 564E.
88. 1965(1) SA 446 (N).
89. At 448C.
90. At 449B.
91. 1964(4) SA 429(E).
92. At 435H–436A.
93. At 436A.
94. 1965(2) SA 796(A).
95. 1965(4) SA 606(AD).
96. At 619H.
97. 1973(3) SA 443(A).
98. At 454E.
99. At 454F.
100. Fine, 'Re-examining validity', p. 167.
101. Norton, 'The political trial', pp. 77–78.
102. Mathews, 'Public safety', para 364.
103. 1973(3) SA 109(T).
104. At 117A–B.
105. 1976 CPD (unreported).
106. *S.* v *Gwala* 1977 NPD (unreported) at 523–5.
107. Fine, 'Re-examining validity', p. 172; Parmanand and Vorster, 'State security legislation', p. 195.
108. *S.* v *Gwala* 1980 AD (unreported). For further discussion of this case see J. G. Riekert, 'The DDD syndrome: solitary confinement and a South African security trial', in A. D. Bell and R. D. A. Mackie (eds.), *Detention and Security Legislation in South Africa* (Durban, 1985), pp. 121–147.
109. As quoted by Fine, 'Re-examining validity', p. 172.
110. *Ibid.*, pp. 172–173.
111. 1982(1) SA 464 (A).
112. *Miranda* v *Arizona* 384 US 436 (1966) at 458.
113. Act 76 of 1962.
114. At 478C.
115. At 479B–C.
116. Quoted by the court at 480H.
117. At 480H.
118. At 482B–C.
119. At 483F–G.
120. At 483H.
121. At 479H.
122. 1960(4) SA 712(A) at 720.

123. At 479C.
124. Davis, 'Confessions', p. 522; J. van der Berg, 'Treason: evaluating the evidence of political detainees', unpublished paper, University of the Western Cape, 1985, p. 13. For a completely different approach see *R. v McCool*, 1977 (unreported judgment of the Northern Ireland Court of Appeal). On similar facts to those of *Christie*'s case, the court held that although there were no allegations of impropriety at an interview, the statement made at that interview was excluded on the ground that the Crown had not satisfied the court that the effect of any possible ill-treatment on the previous day had effectively been dissipated by the time the statement was made. See Greer, 'The admissibility of confessions', p. 216.
125. 1983(1) SA 576 (C).
126. At 584H.
127. At 587H–588A.
128. At 588D.
129. At 588E.
130. At 588H.
131. At 589G.
132. At 598C–E. See also the comment by Williams, 'The admissibility of confessions', pp. 7–17.
133. 1984(4) SA 59 (SWA).
134. 1974(1) SA 14(A) at 40.
135. At 248H.
136. At 249–250.
137. 1985(4) SA 147 (N).
138. At 151E.
139. 1977(2) SA 209 (T).
140. At 151J–152C.
141. At 152E.
142. 1985(4) SA 709 (D).
143. At 721C–D.
144. 1985(4) 211 (SWA).
145. At 221I.
146. At 222D–E.
147. See for example, Mathews, *Law, Order and Liberty*, pp. 147–149; G. M. Nienaber, 'Discretions, ouster clauses and the Internal Security Act', *Tydskrif*, 46 (1983) pp. 211–222.
148. Levy J., 1985(4) SA 211 pp. 220–221.
149. 1986(3) SA 568(A) at 579.
150. Dr Louis West giving evidence in *S. v Gwala* NPD (unreported) at p. 3997 of the record. See also Riekert, 'The silent scream'.
151. *Gwala* 1978 AD.
152. For example, although the major expert witness called in security cases, American psychiatrist Dr Louis West, has done extensive work on the subject, in the main it relates to American prisoners during the Korean War. See I. E. Farber, H. F. Harlow and L. J. West, 'Brainwashing, conditioning, and DDD (debility, dependency and dread)', *Sociometry*, 20 (1957), 271–285. Wessels, J.A. alluded to the difference between prisoners of war and detainees under the protection of the Commissioner of Police in *S. v Gwala*.
153. Davis, 'Confessions'; Fine 'Re-examining validity'; Mathews and Albino, 'The permanence of the temporary'; Nicholson, 'Admissibility and reliability'; Parmanand and Vorster, 'State security legislation'; Van der Berg, 'Treason'.

4. Psychological investigations

1. Detention as used in this chapter refers almost exclusively to detention for purposes of interrogation, as specified by Section 6 of Act 83 of 1967 or Section 29 of Act 74 of 1982.
2. Examples of papers using this analogy are: M. Brenton, 'Solitary confinement: a review of the literature', unpublished paper, Metropolitan Toronto Forensic Service,

Toronto (1981); W. E. Lucas, 'Solitary confinement: isolation as coercion to conform', *Australian and New Zealand Journal of Criminology*, 9 (1976), 153–167; A. S. Mathews and R. C. Albino, 'The permanence of the temporary – an examination of the 90-day and 180-day detention laws', *South African Law Journal*, 83 (1966); S. K. Parmanand and C. Vorster, 'South Africa's state security legislation: exit Section 6', *Journal of Contemporary Roman Dutch Law*, 147 (1984), 180–199; T. Shallice, 'The Ulster depth interrogation techniques and their relation to sensory deprivation research', *Cognition*, 1 (1972), 385–405; T. Shallice, 'Solitary confinement – a torture revisited', *New Scientist* (28 November 1974), 666–667; S. Saunders, 'Solitary is torture', *Rand Daily Mail*, 20 May 1982.

3. P. Suedfeld, 'Solitary confinement as a rehabilitative technique: reply to Lucas', *Australian and New Zealand Journal of Criminology*, 11 (1978), 106–112; P. Suedfeld, *Restricted Environmental Stimulation* (New York, 1980).

4. Suedfeld, *Restricted Environmental Stimulation*.

5. Results from the first phase of research are reviewed variously in A. D. Biderman and H. Zimmer, *The Manipulation of Human Behaviour* (New York, 1961); J. A. C. Brown, *Techniques of Persuasion* (Harmondsworth, 1963); D. P. Schultz, *Sensory Restriction* (New York, 1965); M. D. Solomon (ed.), *Sensory Deprivation* (Cambridge, Mass., 1961); J. A. Vernon, *Inside the Black Box* (New York, 1963).

6. M. T. Orne and K. E. Scheibe, 'The contribution of non-deprivation factors in the production of sensory deprivation effects', *Journal of Abnormal and Social Psychology*, 68 (1964), 3–12.

7. Extensive reviews of this research were provided by J. P. Zubek, *Sensory Deprivation: Fifteen Years of Research* (New York, 1969) and J. P. Zubek, 'Behavioral and physiological effects of prolonged sensory and perceptual deprivation', in J. Rasmussen (ed.), *Man in Isolation and Confinement* (Chicago, 1973). See also P. Watson, *War on the Mind* (Harmondsworth, 1977).

8. P. Suedfeld, 'Social isolation: a case for interdisciplinary research', *Canadian Psychologist*, 15 (1974), 1–15; P. Suedfeld, 'The clinical relevance of reduced sensory stimulation', *Canadian Psychological Review*, 16 (1975), 88–103; Suedfeld, *Restricted Environmental Stimulation*.

9. P. Suedfeld, 'Solitary confinement in the correctional setting', *Corrective and Social Psychiatry*, 20 (1974), 10–20; P. Suedfeld, C. Ramirez, J. Deaton and G. Baker–Brown, 'Reactions and attributes of prisoners in solitary confinement', *Criminal Justice and Behaviour*, 9 (1982), 302–340.

10. C. A. Schulman, M. Richlin and S. Weinstein, 'Hallucinations and disturbances of affect cognition and physical state as a function of sensory deprivation', *Perceptual and Motor Skills*, 25 (1967), 1001–1024.

11. J. P. Zubek and M. MacNeil, 'Perceptual deprivation phenomena', *Journal of Abnormal Psychology*, 72 (1967), 147–150.

12. But less vivid and persistent than drug-induced images. See Suedfeld, *Restricted Environmental Stimulation*, p. 30.

13. Zubek, 'Behavioral and physiological effects', p. 20.

14. Suedfeld, *Restricted Environmental Stimulation*.

15. *Ibid*.

16. Zubek, 'Behavioral and physiological effects'.

17. A. Jones, 'Stimulus-seeking behaviour', in Zubek (ed.), *Sensory Deprivation*.

18. Suedfeld, *Restricted Environmental Stimulation*, p. 55.

19. D. W. Harper and M. Bross, 'The effect of unimodal sensory deprivation on sensory processes', *Canadian Psychological Review*, 19 (1979), 128–144.

20. Zubek, 'Behavioral and physiological effects'.

21. Zubek, *Sensory Deprivation* and 'Behavioral and physiological effects'.

22. Suedfeld, *Restricted Environmental Stimulation*, p. 51.

23. T. I. Myers, 'Tolerance for sensory and perceptual isolation', in Zubek, *Sensory Deprivation*.

24. Zubek, 'Behavioral and physiological effects'.

25. Schultz, *Sensory Restriction*.
26. M. Goldfried, 'A psychoanalytic interpretation of sensory deprivation', *Psychological Record*, 10 (1960), 211–214; S. C. Miller, 'Ego-autonomy in sensory deprivation, isolation and stress', *International Journal of Psycho-Analysis*, 43 (1962), 1–20.
27. Lucas, 'Solitary'; Suedfeld, 'Solitary'; Suedfeld, *Restricted Environmental Stimulation*.
28. C. Vorster, 'The mind in solitary', *Rand Daily Mail*, 11 February 1982; Shallice, 'Solitary confinement'.
29. Suedfeld, 'Solitary', p. 111.
30. W. W. Haythorn, 'The miniworld of isolation', in J. Rasmussen (ed.), *Man in Isolation and Confinement* (Chicago, 1977).
31. For reference to these accounts see Miller, 'Ego-autonomy'; Rasmussen, *Man in Isolation*; Suedfeld, 'Social isolation'.
32. P. Suedfeld, D. S. Rank and A. D. Rank, 'Incentive value of social and non-social stimuli after social and sensory restriction', *Australian Journal of Psychology*, 32 (1980), 209–215.
33. J. P. Zubek, L. Bayer and J. M. Shepherd, 'Relative effects of prolonged social isolation and confinement', *Journal of Abnormal Psychology*, 74 (1969), 625–631.
34. Haythorn, 'Miniworld of isolation', p. 225.
35. L. H. Bukstel and P. R. Kilman, 'Psychological effects of imprisonment on confined individuals', *Psychological Bulletin*, 88 (1980), 469–493.
36. P. Gendreau, N. L. Freedman, G. Wilde and G. D. Scott, 'Changes in EEG alpha frequency and evoked response latency during solitary confinement', *Journal of Abnormal Psychology*, 79 (1972), 54–59.
37. C. Ecclestone, P. Gendreau and C. Knox, 'Solitary confinement of prisoners', *Canadian Journal of Behavioural Science*, 6 (1974), 178–191.
38. Suedfeld *et al.*, 'Reactions', p. 330.
39. Data recalculated from the original and expressed as percentages. See Suedfeld *et al.*, 'Reactions'.
40. S. Grassian, 'Psychopathological effects of solitary confinement', *American Journal of Psychiatry*, 140 (1983), 1450–1454.
41. M. Zuckerman, H. Persky, K. E. Link and G. K. Basu, 'Experimental and subject factors determining responses to sensory deprivation, social isolation, and solitary confinement', *Journal of Abnormal Psychology*, 73 (1968), 183–194.
42. Zubek *et al.*, 'Relative effects'.
43. Haythorn, 'Miniworld of isolation'.
44. Zubek, 'Behavioral and physiological effects', p. 70.
45. Suedfeld, 'Solitary'.
46. Articles 1 and 2 of the Declaration on the Protection of All Persons from Being Subjected to Torture and Other Cruel, Inhuman or Degrading Treatment or Punishment (United Nations General Assembly resolution 3452, annex). See in addition Amnesty International, *Torture in the Eighties* (London, 1984); and E. Stover and E. O. Nightingale (eds.), *The Breaking of Bodies and Minds* (New York, 1985).
47. Standard Minimum Rules for the Treatment of Prisoners, approved by the United Nations Economic and Social Council on 31 July 1957. Articles 31 to 33 prohibit corporal punishment, use of dark cells, chains or irons, and all cruel, inhuman and degrading punishments. Severe limitations are placed on the use of diet restriction or close confinement.
48. *Danish Medical Bulletin*, 27, 5 (1980) and *American Journal of Forensic Medicine and Pathology*, 5, 4 (1984).
49. See T. Karlsmark *et al.*, 'Tracing the use of electrical torture', *American Journal of Forensic Medicine and Pathology*, 5 (1984), 333–337.
50. F. Allodi and G. Cowgill, 'Ethical and psychiatric aspects of torture: a Canadian study', *Canadian Journal of Psychiatry*, 27 (1982), 98–102; F. Allodi and G. R. Randall, 'Physical and psychiatric effects of torture: two medical studies', in Stover and Nightingale, *Breaking of Bodies and Minds*, pp. 58–78; O. V. Rasmussen and I. Lunde, 'Evaluation

of investigation of 200 torture victims', *Danish Medical Bulletin*, 27 (1980), 241–243; C. Warmhoven *et al.*, 'The medical after-effects of torture: an investigation among refugees in the Netherlands', *Nederlands Tijdschrift voor Geneeskunde*, 125 (1981), 104–108.

51. Shallice, 'Ulster depth interrogation'.

52. O. V. Rasmussen and H. Marcussen, 'The somatic sequelae to torture', *Manedsskrift for Praktisk Laegegerning* (March 1982).

53. L. M. Cathcart, P. Berger and B. Knazan, 'Medical examination of torture victims applying for refugee status', *Canadian Medical Association Journal*, 121 (1979), 179–184; Warmhoven *et al.*, 'The medical after-effects'.

54. I. Lunde, 'Mental sequelae to torture', *Manedsskrift for Praktisk Laegegerning* (August, 1982).

55. I. Lunde, O. V. Rasmussen, J. Lindholm and G. Wagner, 'Gonadal and sexual functions in tortured Greek men', *Danish Medical Journal*, 27 (1980), 243–245.

56. F. Allodi, 'Psychiatric sequelae of torture and implications for treatment', *World Medical Journal*, 29 (1982), 71–76; F. Allodi and A. Rojas, 'The health and adaptation of victims of political violence in Latin America', *Proceedings of the 7th World Congress of Psychiatry*, Vienna (July 1983).

57. See below for a discussion of the DSM-III classification of post-traumatic stress disorder; see also notes 73 and 74.

58. Refer to notes 52, 53 and 59.

59. Similar patterns have also been found by the following studies: A. Fossum, E. Hauff, U. Malt and L. Eitinger, 'Psykiske og sociale folger av tortur' *Tidskrift for den Norke Laegeforening*, 102 (1982), 613–616; G. Randall, E. Lutz, J. Quiroga *et al.*, 'Long-term physical and psychological sequelae of torture on 44 victims examined in the United States', unpublished paper, Symposium of the American Association for the Advancement of Science, Washington, D.C., 1983.

60. F. Allodi, 'The psychiatric effects in children and families of victims of political persecution and torture', *Danish Medical Journal*, 27 (1980), 229–232.

61. J. Cohn, K. Holtzer, L. Koch and B. Severin, 'Children and torture; an investigation of Chilean immigrant children in Denmark', *Danish Medical Journal*, 27 (1980), 238–239.

62. B. Weile and L. B. Wingender, 'Children of tortured immigrant Chileans in Denmark', paper presented at the Seminar on Examination of and Aid to Torture Victims and Their Families, Copenhagen, October 1983.

63. F. Askevold, 'The war sailor syndrome', *Danish Medical Journal*, 27 (1980), 220–223; E. de Wind, 'Persecution, aggression and therapy', *International Journal of Psycho-Analysis*, 53 (1972), 173–177; L. Eitinger, *Concentration Camp Survivors in Norway and Israel* (London, 1964); K. D. Hoppe, 'Re-somatization of affects in survivors of persecution', *International Journal of Psycho-Analysis*, 49 (1968), 324–326; E. Simenauer, 'Late psychic sequelae of man-made disasters', *International Journal of Psycho-Analysis*, 49 (1968), 306–309; A. Strom (ed.), *Norwegian Concentration Camp Survivors* (New York, 1968); P. Thygesen, 'The concentration camp syndrome', *Danish Medical Bulletin*, 27 (1980), 224–228.

64. P. Matussek, *Internment in Concentration Camps and Its Consequences* (New York, 1975); Strom, *Norwegian Concentration Camp Survivors*.

65. L. Eitinger and A. Strom, 'New investigations on the mortality and morbidity of Norwegian ex-concentration camp prisoners', *Israeli Journal of Psychiatry and Related Sciences*, 18 (1981), 173–195.

66. H. O. Bluhm, 'How did they survive? Mechanisms of defence in a Nazi concentration camp', *American Journal of Psychotherapy*, 2 (1948), 3–22; E. de Wind, 'The confrontation with death', *International Journal of Psycho-Analysis*, 49 (1968), 302–305; H. F. Fink, 'Developmental arrest as a result of Nazi persecution during adolescence', *International Journal of Psycho-Analysis*, 49 (1968), 327–329; R. Jaffe, 'Dissociative phenomena in former concentration camp inmates', *International Journal of Psycho-Analysis*, 49 (1968), 310–312.

67. Hoppe, 'Re-somatization'.

68. Matussek, *Internment*.
69. O. Fenichel, 'The concept of trauma in contemporary psycho-analytic theory', *International Journal of Psycho-Analysis*, 26 (1945), 34.
70. Bluhm, 'How did they survive?'
71. Askevold, 'The war sailor syndrome'.
72. W. Stofsel, 'Psychological sequelae in hostages and the aftercare', *Danish Medical Bulletin*, 27 (1980), 239–241.
73. N. C. Andreasen, 'Post-traumatic stress disorder', in H. Kaplan, A. Freedman and B. Sadock (eds.), *Comprehensive Textbook of Psychiatry*, 3rd ed. (Baltimore, 1980), pp. 1517–1525; M. R. Trimble, 'Post-traumatic stress disorder: the history of a concept', *Psychotherapeia*, 34 (1984), 37–39; G. A. Tyson, 'Stress and detention', *South African Medical Journal*, 64 (1983), 858–859.
74. American Psychiatric Association, *Diagnostic and Statistical Manual of Mental Disorders*, 3rd ed. (Washington, 1980).
75. Matussek, *Internment*.
76. See Trimble, 'Post-traumatic stress disorder'.
77. I. L. Janis, *Stress and Frustration* (New York, 1969).
78. Amnesty International, *Report on Torture* (New York, 1975); Biderman and Zimmer, *Manipulation of Human Behavior*; Brown, *Techniques of Persuasion*; L. E. Hinkle and H. G. Wolff, 'Communist interrogation and indoctrination of "enemies of the state"', *Archives of Neurology and Psychiatry*, 76 (1956), 115–174; R. J. Lipton, *Thought Reform and the Psychology of Totalism* (New York, 1961); W. Sargant, *Battle for the Mind* (New York, 1957); E. H. Schein, *Coercive Persuasion* (New York, 1961).
79. A. D. Biderman 'Social psychological needs and "involuntary" behavior as illustrated by compliance in interrogation', *Sociometry*, 23 (1960), 120–147.
80. The following paper formed the basis for some of these ideas: F. Somnier, 'Psychological aspects of torture', paper presented at the Seminar on Examination of and Aid to Torture Victims and Their Families, Copenhagen, October 1983. See also F. Somnier and J. K. Genefke, 'Psychotherapy for victims of torture', *British Journal of Psychiatry* (in press, 1986).
81. J. E. Farber, H. F. Harlow and L. J. West, 'Brainwashing, conditioning and DDD', *Sociometry*, 20 (1957), 271–285; L. J. West, 'Effects of isolation on the evidence of detainees', in A. D. Bell and R. D. A. Mackie (eds.), *Detention and Security Legislation in South Africa* (Durban, 1985), pp. 69–80.
82. M. E. P. Seligman, *Helplessness* (San Francisco, 1975), p. 17.
83. D. C. Glass and J. E. Singer, *Urban Stress* (New York, 1972).
84. D. S. Hiroto, 'Locus of control and learned helplessness', *Journal of Experimental Psychology*, 102 (1974), 187–193.
85. J. H. Weiss, 'Somatic effects of predictable and unpredictable shock', *Psychosomatic Medicine*, 32 (1970), 397–409.
86. J. W. Pennebaker, M. A. Burnham, M. A. Schaeffer and D. Harper, 'Lack of control as a determinant of perceived physical symptoms', *Journal of Personality and Social Psychology*, 35 (1977), 167–174.
87. J. W. A. Brehm, *A Theory of Psychological Reactance* (New York, 1966); C. B. Wortman and J. W. Brehm, 'Responses to uncontrollable behavior', in L. Berkowitz (ed.), *Advances in Experimental Social Psychology*, vol. 8 (New York, 1975), pp. 227–336.
88. Wortman and Brehm, 'Responses'.
89. G. Katz, 'The attitudes and feelings of South African former detainees during their detention', unpublished B.A. Honours thesis, University of the Witwatersrand, 1982.
90. Refer to note 7 in Chapter 1 for a list of some publications alleging physical torture.
91. Detainees' Parents Support Committee, *Memorandum on Security Police Abuses of Political Detainees* (Johannesburg, 1982).
92. See *Survey of Race Relations in South Africa* (1982), p. 253.
93. O. Geldenhuys, 'A study of South African security legislation, with the emphasis on detention laws – examining the historical circumstances of its formulation, and a study of torture within this system', unpublished B.Soc.Sc. Honours thesis, University of

Cape Town, 1983.
94. United Nations, Report of the Special Committee on Apartheid, *Maltreatment and Torture of Prisoners in South Africa* (New York, 1973).
95. S. D. Bluen and E. R. Goodman, 'The stigmatization of ex-political detainees in employment practices', *South African Journal of Psychology*, 14 (1984), 137–139.

5. The empirical study

1. Commissioner for Prisons and Director General of Justice, as reported in *Survey of Race Relations in South Africa* (1979), pp. 142–143, (1980), p. 264 and (1982), p. 206.
2. *Survey of Race Relations in South Africa* (1982), p. 244.
3. P. Kallaway (ed.), *Apartheid and Education* (Johannesburg, 1984); F. Molteno, 'The uprisings of 16th June: a review of the literature', *Social Dynamics*, 5 (1979), 54–76; F. Molteno, 'The schooling of black South Africans and the 1980 Cape Town students' boycotts', unpublished M.Soc.Sc. thesis, University of Cape Town, 1983.
4. For example see *Cape Times*, 30 November 1984; P. Lambley, *The Psychology of Apartheid* (London, 1980).
5. A. Sachs, *Jail Diary* (London, 1966); A. Sachs, *Stephanie on Trial* (London, 1968).
6. Y. Kamisar, 'Equal justice in American criminal procedure', in his *Police Interrogation and Confessions* (Ann Arbor, 1980).
7. B. Breytenbach, *The True Confessions of an Albino Terrorist* (Emmarentia, 1984); M. Dlamini, *Hell-Hole Robben Island* (Nottingham, 1984); R. First, *117 Days* (Harmondsworth, 1965); Q. Jacobsen, *Solitary in Johannesburg* (London, 1973); H. Lewin, *Bandiet* (London, 1974); I. Naidoo, *Island in Chains* (Harmondsworth, 1982); M. Pheto, *And Night Fell* (London, 1983). See also note 5 of this chapter.
8. Notice 877 of 1982, in Government Gazette No. 8467 of 3 December 1982.
9. See Lawyers for Human Rights, 'Any hope for detainees?', pp. 7 and 60–62.
10. S. A. Strauss, 'The legal rights of prisoners and detainees to medical treatment', *South African Journal of Criminal Law and Criminology*, 7 (1983), 20–32, and J. G. Frankish, 'The medical care of prisoners and detainees', *South African Medical Journal*, 64 (1983), 117.
11. Notice 877 of 1982, para. 31.
12. 1964(2) SA 545 (A).
13. Appellate Division in *Rossouw* v *Sachs* 1964(2) SA 551 (A) at 565. See also Rudolph, *Security*, pp. 8–10, for discussion of this matter.
14. Lawyers for Human Rights, 'Any hope for detainees?'.
15. *Van Heerden* v *Cronwright*, TPD September 1984, Case No. 2/83, unreported.
16. In 1980 the Minister of Police said that 32 actions were brought by persons detained under Section 6 of the Terrorism Act and that all were pending (*Survey of Race Relations* (1980), p. 271). Between July 1981 and December 1982, 12 actions for damages were brought against the police by Section 6 detainees, and all actions were pending as of December 1983 (*Survey of Race Relations* (1983), p. 550).
17. Examples of such settlements are, for 1970: Ms S. Kemp (R1 000), Mr A. de Oliviera (R1 100), Mr F. Gordinho (R1 100); for 1971: family of Imam A. Haron (R5 000); for 1976: widow of J. Mdluli (R15 000); for 1978: Mrs S. Biko (R65 000 and costs); for 1980: Mrs C. Montwedi (unspecified); for 1983: family of Mr Isaac Muofhe (R150 000 paid by Venda government). See *Survey of Race Relations* (1970) and (1980), and Lawyers' Committee for Civil Rights under Law, *Deaths in Detention and South Africa's Security Laws* (Washington, 1983), p. 12.
18. P. Suedfeld, 'Solitary confinement as a rehabilitative technique', *Australian and New Zealand Journal of Criminology*, 11 (1978), 106–112; P. Suedfeld, *Restricted Environmental Stimulation* (New York, 1980).
19. G. Randall *et al.*, 'Long-term physical and psychological sequelae of torture on 44 victims examined in the United States', unpublished paper given at the Symposium of the American Association for the Advancement of Science (1983).
20. Differences in obtained percentages between African and white sub-samples, where Africans show higher frequencies, are given in parentheses.

21. For example see L. S. Gillis, R. Elk, O. Ben–Arie and A. Teggin, 'The present state examination: experiences with Xhosa-speaking psychiatric patients', *British Journal of Psychiatry*, 141 (1982), 143–147.

22. Criticism of the use of cultural factors as explanations of psychiatric disorders and symptomatology may be found in L. Swartz and D. H. Foster, 'Images of culture and mental illness: South African psychiatric approaches', *Social Dynamics*, 10 (1984), 17–25.

23. In particular see F. Allodi, 'Psychiatric sequelae of torture and implications for treatment', *World Medical Journal*, 29 (1982), 71–76; F. Allodi and G. Cowgill, 'Ethical and psychiatric aspects of torture', *Canadian Journal of Psychiatry*, 27 (1982), 98–102; L. M. Cathcart *et al.*, 'Medical examination of torture victims applying for refugee status', *Canadian Medical Association Journal*, 121 (1979), 179–184.

24. P. Matussek, *Internment in Concentration Camps and Its Consequences* (New York, 1975).

25. S. D. Bluen and E. R. Goodman, 'The stigmatization of ex-political detainees in employment practices', *South African Journal of Psychology*, 14 (1984), 137–139.

6. The process of detention: detainees' descriptions

1. Some important insights regarding psychological processes have emerged through personal accounts of detention experiences, such as the following: R. First, *117 Days* (Harmondsworth, 1965); Q. Jacobsen, *Solitary in Johannesburg* (London, 1983); M. Pheto, *And Night Fell* (London, 1983); A. Sachs, *Jail Diary* (London, 1966); A. Sachs, *Stephanie on Trial* (London, 1968).
2. 'Yes, this fucking kaffir, come out.'
3. *Klapping*, hitting.
4. A local name for a specific method of physical torture.
5. Colloquial term for a specific torture method.
6. Colloquial term for a specific method of torture
7. 'Let him fly.'
8. 'Oh, he is not only a student leader, he is also an acrobat.'
9. This is a reference to the Imam Abdullah Haron who died in detention at Maitland police cells on 27 September 1969. It was claimed that he had fallen down stairs.
10. Inkatha refers to the Zulu-dominated cultural and political organisation led by Chief Buthelezi. It is a moderate political movement, and in the context of this quotation would be regarded favourably by the white South African authorities.
11. See E. Goffman, *Interaction Ritual* (Harmondsworth, 1967), pp. 5–45.

7. Conclusions, interpretations and recommendations

1. Detainees' Parents Support Committee, *Monthly Report*, April 1986; House of Assembly Debates (1986), Questions and Replies, col. 634.
2. G. Gordon and D. Davis, 'The courts, justice and the emergency', *Cape Times*, 4 February 1986.
3. C. J. R. Dugard, 'The judiciary and national security', in A. D. Bell and R. D. A. Mackie (eds.), *Detention and Security Legislation in South Africa* (Durban, 1985), pp 43–5.
4. D. Basson, *Die Regbank en 'n Mensregtehandves* (University of Pretoria, 1986).
5. 1986(2) SA 264 (WLD). There were also some exceptions to the pro-executive approach during the emergency. See for example *Marajee v Minister of Law and Order*, unreported decision of the Durban Supreme Court, and *Nkwinti v Minister of Law and Order*, 1986(2) SA 421 (E).
6. Government Gazette No. 9878 of 21 July 1985. See also *Omar v Minister of Law and Order*, 1986(3) SA 306 (C), which adopted a similar approach.
7. 1986 (2) 756 (A); at 772 I–J.
8. 1986(3) SA 568 (A).
9. Detainees' Support Committee, *Hidden Repression* (Johannesburg, 1984); Detainees' Support Committee and Detainees' Parents Support Committee, *Democratic Movement under Attack* (Bramley, 1985).

10. See also the findings of the Law Society's Le Roux Commission on Detention in *De Rebus* (1985), pp. 452ff.
11. United Nations, *Convention Against Torture and Other Cruel, Inhuman or Degrading Treatment or Punishment* (New York, 1984).
12. American Psychiatric Association, *Diagnostic and Statistical Manual of Mental Disorders*, 3rd ed. (Washington, D.C., 1980), pp. 236–239.
13. Refer to Chapter 4 for discussion of these varying positions.
14. American Psychiatric Association, *DSM-III*, p. 236.
15. Refer to Chapter 4, in the section on concentration camp studies, for details of Matussek's work.
16. The 1984 civil trial of Auret van Heerden against ten South African security policemen is a typical case in point. Dr Louis West argued that Van Heerden displayed symptoms of a post-traumatic stress disorder.
17. For a strong argument in favour of viewing post-traumatic stress as the most appropriate description of the outcome of detention in South Africa, see G. A. Tyson, 'Stress and detention', *South African Medical Journal*, 64 (1983), 858–859.
18. For discussion of some of these issues see J. Busfield, 'Gender and mental illness', *International Journal of Mental Health*, 11 (1982), 46–66.
19. For example, J. Suls, 'Social support, interpersonal relations and health', in G. Sanders and J. Suls (eds.), *Social Psychology of Health and Illness* (Hillsdale, 1982), pp. 255–277.
20. See S. C. Kobasa, 'The hardy personality', in *ibid.*, pp. 3–32.
21. A. Antonovsky, *Health, Stress and Coping* (San Francisco, 1979).
22. E. D. Driver, 'Confessions and the social psychology of coercion', *Harvard Law Review*, 82 (1968), 42–61.
23. B. Irving and E. L. Hilgendorf, *Police Interrogation* (London, 1980). Also E. L. Hilgendorf and B. Irving, 'A decision-making model of confessions', in S. Lloyd-Bostock (ed.), *Psychology in Legal Contexts* (London, 1981), pp. 67–84.
24. See for example *S. v L. M. Mogale*, unreported Appellate division decision, June 1981.
25. Driver, 'Confessions'.
26. Amnesty International, *Report on Torture*, rev. ed. (London, 1975).
27. S. Milgram, *Obedience to Authority* (New York, 1974).
28. Amnesty International, *Report on Torture*, p. 32.
29. The 'victims' in this case were of course experimental 'stooges', that is, they were instructed to simulate the behaviour of a victim receiving serious electrical shocks, up to 450 volts, while in fact they were not. All subjects however believed the situation to be real. The experimental procedure itself raised numerous ethical issues. For discussion of these, see Milgram, *Obedience to Authority*.
30. P. G. Zimbardo, C. Haney, W. C. Banks and D. Jaffe, 'A Pirandellian prison', *New York Times Sunday Magazine*, 8 April 1973, pp. 38–60.
31. M. Haritos–Fatouros, 'The official torturer: learning mechanisms involved in the process', unpublished paper, University of Thessaloniki, Greece, 1984.
32. *Ibid.*, p. 14.
33. F. Allodi, 'The making of a torturer: a heuristic model', paper read at the World Psychiatric Association Regional Symposium, Rome, Italy, 9–13 October 1984.
34. Amnesty International, *Report on Torture*, p. 66.
35. F. Fanon, *The Wretched of the Earth* (Harmondsworth, 1967), p. 213.
36. M. J. Lerner, *The Belief in a Just World* (New York, 1980), p. 73.
37. *Ibid.*, p. 149.
38. Police Act 7 of 1958.
39. Amnesty International, *Report on Torture*, p. 131.
40. Some of the international conventions and declarations effectively prohibiting torture are: United Nations (UN) Universal Declaration of Human Rights (1948); the four Geneva Conventions of the International Red Cross (1949); UN International Covenant on Civil and Political Rights (1966); European Convention for the Protection

of Human Rights and Fundamental Freedoms (1963); American Convention on Human Rights (1969); UN Declaration on Torture (1975); African Charter on Human Rights and Peoples' Rights (1981); Universal Islamic Declaration of Human Rights (1981).

41. Amnesty International's annual reports, and *Torture in the Eighties*.
42. Ruthven, *Torture*, p. 292.
43. *Ibid.*, pp. 297–298.
44. For further discussion of conspiracy theory see M. Billig, *Fascists* (London, 1978), pp. 296–343.
45. Ruthven, *Torture*, p. 296.
46. Rudolph, *Security*, especially pp. 218–222.
47. *Ibid.*, p. 221 (emphasis in the original).
48. *Ibid.*, pp. 221–222.
49. While Rudolph is careful not to use the term 'innocent people' within his scenario, he does so further on in the same paragraph, p. 218.
50. H. Shue, 'Torture', *Philosophy and Public Affairs*, 7 (1978), pp. 141–142. It is worthy of note that Rudolph, who actually based his imaginary situation on that used by Shue, failed to remark on Shue's scathing criticism of the use of such artificial situations. Rudolph also failed to note Shue's conclusion, which was totally opposed to any legal sanctioning of torture.
51. See W. L. and P. E. Twining, 'Bentham on torture', *Northern Ireland Legal Quarterly*, 24 (1973), 305–356. Also Ruthven, *Torture*, pp. 17–22.
52. Bentham, cited in Twining, 'Bentham on torture', p. 334.
53. *Ibid.*, p. 338.
54. Ruthven, *Torture*, p. 31.
55. Recommendations offered here are by no means the only ones. In 1982 the Detainees' Parents Support Committee *Memorandum* offered safeguard recommendations. In 1983 the Medical Association of South Africa presented recommendations, but these were largely inadequate (see Chapter 3). More recently the Le Roux report of the Association of Law Societies gave recommendations. See F. Bosman and D. H. van Wyk, 'Die prokureursberoep en veiligheidswetgewing', *De Rebus*, 213 (September 1985), 452–455.

Over the past four years or so the DPSC and other detainee support groups have made repeated but unheeded demands for abolition of the system as well as for safeguards against torture. Demands have also come from other groups such as academics, churches, student organisations and the press.

On an international level, Amnesty International has produced a 12-point Programme for the Prevention of Torture. Our recommendations are offered in keeping with the spirit of this Programme. See Amnesty International, *Torture in the Eighties*. Since the declaration of a state of emergency in 1985 Amnesty has provided a specific set of recommendations for South Africa. See Amnesty International, *South Africa: Briefing* (London, 1986), p. 17.

56. House of Assembly Debates, 30 April 1986.
57. Report of the Committee of Inquiry into Police Interrogation Procedures in Northern Ireland, Cmnd. 7497.
58. Royal Commission on Criminal Procedure, Cmnd. 8092.
59. See, for example, Sections 7, 12, 13, 21, 22, 23 and 25 of the Directions.
60. For a devastating critique of the ministerial directions see Marcus and Dugard, 'The inadequacies of the Minister's Directions', *Lawyers for Human Rights Bulletin*, 2 (June 1983), 77–87. They argue that the Directions do not have the force of law, but as mentioned in Chapter 3, the better view is that they do have legally binding effect.

Postscript

1. As a result of the effect of the judgment by the Appellate division in *Nkondo and Others v Minister of Law and Order* in 1986, the state was forced to lift the restriction on most of those who had been banned. See 1986(2) SA 756(A).
2. *De Rebus* (1984), 452.

3. *Ibid.*, p. 562.
4. Act 3 of 1953.
5. House of Assembly Debates (12 June 1986), cols. 840–8112.
6. Anton Harber, unpublished paper delivered at a Conference on Professionalism, University of the Witwatersrand, August 1986.
7. *Weekly Mail*, 5 September 1986.
8. See for example *Mawu and Another* v *State President and Others* (unreported NPD decision of 16 July 1986) which cut down on the definition of 'subversive statement'; and *Demsey* v *Minister of Law and Order* (unreported CPD decision of 9 July 1986) and *Radebe* v *Minister of Law and Order* (unreported WCD decision of 7 July 1986) in which a measure of judicial control was imposed over the decision to detain. The Appellate division has delivered one judgment concerning emergency regulations. Although it adopted a disappointingly cautious approach, the court left open the possibility of future legal attacks on the emergency regulations. See *Minister of Law and Order* v *Tsenoli* (unreported Appellate division judgment, September 1986).
9. *Weekly Mail*, 15 August 1986.

Bibliography

Albino, R. C. 1973. Affidavit in the case of *S. v Hassim*, 1973
Allodi, F. 1980. The psychiatric effects in children and families of victims of political persecution and torture. *Danish Medical Bulletin*, 27, 229–232
Allodi, F. 1982. Psychiatric sequelae of torture and implications for treatment. *World Medical Journal*, 29, 71–76
Allodi, F. and Cowgill, G. 1982. Ethical and psychiatric aspects of torture: a Canadian study. *Canadian Journal of Psychiatry*, 27, 98–102
Allodi, F. and Rojas, A. 1983. The health and adaptation of victims of political violence in Latin America. Proceedings of the 7th World Congress of Psychiatry, July 1983, Vienna
Allodi, F. 1984. The making of a torturer: a heuristic model. Paper delivered at the World Psychiatric Association Regional Symposium, Rome, 9–13 October
Allodi, F. and Randall, G. R. 1985. Physical and psychiatric effects of torture: two medical studies: In E. Stover and E. Nightingale (eds.), *The Breaking of Bodies and Minds*. New York: Freeman
American Psychiatric Association. 1980. *Diagnostic and Statistical Manual of Mental Disorders*, third edition. Washington
Ames, F. 1985. Brain dysfunctions in detainees. In A. N. Bell and R. D. A. Mackie (eds.), *Detention and Security Legislation in South Africa*. Durban: University of Natal
Amnesty International. 1975. *Report on Torture*. New York: Farrar, Strauss and Giroux
Amnesty International's Work on Prison Conditions of Persons Suspected or Convicted of Politically Motivated Crimes in the Federal Republic of Germany: Isolation and Solitary Confinement. 1980. London: Amnesty International
Amnesty International. 1984. *Torture in the Eighties*. London: Martin Robertson and Amnesty International
Andreasen, N. C. 1980. Post-traumatic stress disorder. In H. Kaplan, A. Freedman and B. Sadock (eds.), *Comprehensive Textbook of Psychiatry*, vol. 2, third edition. Baltimore: Williams and Wilkins
Antonovsky, A. 1979. *Health, Stress and Coping*. San Francisco: Jossey–Bass
Askevold, F. 1980. The war sailor syndrome. *Danish Medical Bulletin*, 27, 220–223
Basson, D. 1986. *Die Regbank en 'n Mensregtehandves*. University of Pretoria
Baxter, L. 1985. Doctors on trial: Steven Biko, medical ethics, and the courts. *South African Journal on Human Rights*, 1, 137–151
Bell, A. N. and Mackie, R. D. A. (eds.). 1985. *Detention and Security Legislation in South Africa*. Durban: Centre for Adult Education, University of Natal
Bennun, M. 1984–5. Doctors, torture and the law – a South African case study. *Radical Community Medicine*, 20, 30–40
Bernstein, H. 1972. *South Africa: The Terrorism of Torture*. London: Christian Action Publications
Bettelheim, B. 1943. Individual and mass behaviour in extreme situations. *Journal of Abnormal and Social Psychology*, 38, 417–452
Biderman, A. D. 1960. Social psychological needs and 'involuntary' behaviour as illustrated by compliance in interrogation. *Sociometry*, 23, 120–147
Biderman, A. D. and Zimmer, H. 1961. *The Manipulation of Human Behaviour*. New

York: Wiley

Billig, M. 1978. *Fascists*. London: Academic Press

Bluen, S. D. and Goodman, E. R. 1984. The stigmatization of ex-political detainees in employment practices. *South African Journal of Psychology*, 14, 137–139

Bluhm, H. O. 1948. How did they survive? Mechanisms of defence in a Nazi concentration camp. *American Journal of Psychotherapy*, 2, 3–32

Bosman, F. and Van Wyk, D. H. 1985. Die prokureursberoep en veiligheidswetgewing. *De Rebus*, 213, 452–455

Brehm, J. W. A. 1966. *A Theory of Psychological Reactance*. New York: Academic

Brenton, M. 1981. Solitary confinement: a review of the literature. Unpublished paper, Metropolitan Toronto Forensic Service, Toronto

Breytenbach, B. 1984. *The True Confessions of an Albino Terrorist*. Emmarentia: Taurus

Brookes, E. H. and Macaulay, J. B. 1958. *Civil Liberty in South Africa*. Cape Town: Oxford University Press

Brown, J. A. C. 1963. *Techniques of Persuasion*. Harmondsworth: Penguin

Brownfield, C. A. 1965. *Isolation: Clinical and Experimental Approaches*. New York: Random House

Bukstel, L. H. and Kilman, P. R. 1980. Psychological effects of imprisonment on confined individuals. *Psychological Bulletin*, 88, 469–493

Busfield, J. 1982. Gender and mental illness. *International Journal of Mental Health*, 11, 46–66

Cathcart, L. M., Berger, P. and Knazan, B. 1979. Medical examination of torture victims applying for refugee status. *Canadian Medical Association Journal*, 121, 179–184

Catholic Institute for International Relations. 1982. *Torture in South Africa: Recent Documents*. London: Catholic Institute

Christian Institute of Southern Africa. 1975. *Fourth Report on Detention and Trial under the Terrorism Act, South Africa*. Braamfontein: Christian Institute

Christian Institute of Southern Africa. 1977. *Torture in South Africa?* Braamfontein: Christian Institute

Coetzee, J. A. Grey. 1976. *Industrial Relations in South Africa*. Cape Town: Juta

Cohn, J., Holtzer, K., Koch, L. and Severin, B. 1980. Children and torture: an investigation of Chilean immigrant children in Denmark. *Danish Medical Journal*, 27, 238–239

Copelyn, J. 1974. The Mpondo revolt. Unpublished B.A. Honours thesis, University of the Witwatersrand

Corder, H. 1984. *Judges at Work*. Cape Town: Juta

Cronje, S. 1964. *Witness in the Dark: Police Torture and Brutality in South Africa*. London: Christian Action

Davies, R. H. 1979. *Capital, State and White Labour in South Africa 1900–1960*. Brighton: Harvester

Davis, D. 1982. Confessions and security legislation. *South African Law Journal*, 99, 516–524

Davis, D. 1985. Political trials in South Africa. In D. Davis and M. Slabbert (eds.), *Crime and Power in South Africa*. Cape Town: David Philip

Detainees' Parents Support Committee. 1982. *Memorandum on Security Police Abuses of Political Detainees*. Johannesburg: DPSC

Detainees' Parents Support Committee. 1985. *Review of 1984*. Bramley: DPSC

Detainees' Support Committee. 1984. *Hidden Repression: Report of Result of a Survey of 37 Transvaal Organisations, September 1983–July 1984*. Johannesburg: DESCOM

Detainees' Support Committee and Detainees' Parents Support Committee. 1985. *Democratic Movement Under Attack: A Report on the State of Emergency, July–September 1985*. Bramley: DESCOM and DPSC

De Wind, E. 1968. The confrontation with death. *International Journal of Psycho-Analysis*, 49, 302–305

De Wind, E. 1972. Persecution, aggression and therapy. *International Journal of Psycho-Analysis*, 53, 173–177

Dlamini, M. 1984. *Hell-Hole Robben Island: Reminiscences of a Political Prisoner*. Nottingham: Spokesman

Driver, E. D. 1968. Confessions and the social psychology of coercion. *Harvard Law Review*, 82, 42–61

Dugard, J. 1979. Human rights in South Africa – retrospect and prospect. In C. F. Forsyth and J. E. Schiller (eds.), *Human Rights: The Cape Town Conference*. Cape Town: Juta

Dugard, J. 1982. A triumph for executive power – an examination of the Rabie Report and the Internal Security Act 74 of 1982. *South African Law Journal*, 99, 589–604

Dugard, J. et al. (eds.). 1982. *Report on the Rabie Report. An Examination of Security Legislation in South Africa*. Centre for Applied Legal Studies, University of the Witwatersrand

Dugard, C. J. R. 1985. The judiciary and national security. In A. N. Bell and R. D. A. Mackie (eds.), *Detention and Security Legislation in South Africa*. Durban: University of Natal

Ecclestone, C., Gendreau, P. and Knox, C. 1974. Solitary confinement of prisoners: an assessment of its effects on inmates' personal constructs and adrenocortical activity. *Canadian Journal of Behavioural Science*, 6, 178–191

Eitinger, L. 1964. *Concentration Camp Survivors in Norway and Israel*. London: Allen and Unwin

Eitinger, L. and Strom, A. 1981. New investigations on the mortality and morbidity of Norwegian ex-concentration camp prisoners. *Israeli Journal of Psychiatry and Related Sciences*, 18, 173–195

Fanon, F. 1967. *The Wretched of the Earth*. Harmondsworth: Penguin

Farber, I. E., Harlow, H. F. and West, L. J. 1957. Brainwashing, conditioning and DDD (debility, dependency and dread). *Sociometry*, 20, 271–285

Feit, E. 1971. *Urban Revolt in South Africa 1960–1964*. Evanston, Ill.: Northwestern University Press

Fenichel, O. 1945. The concept of trauma in contemporary psycho-analytic theory. *International Journal of Psycho-Analysis*, 26, 33–44

Fine, D. 1984. Re-examining the validity of detainee evidence: a psycho-legal approach. *South African Journal of Criminal Law and Criminology*, 8, 156–194

Fink, H. F. 1968. Developmental arrest as a result of Nazi persecution during adolescence. *International Journal of Psycho-Analysis*, 49, 327–329

First, R. 1965. *117 Days: An Account of Confinement and Interrogation under the South African Ninety-Day Detention Law*. Harmondsworth: Penguin

Forsyth, C. F. and Schiller, J. E. 1979. *Human Rights: The Cape Town Conference*. Cape Town: Juta

Fossum, A., Hauff, E., Matt, U. and Eitinger, L. 1982 Psykiske og sosiale folger av tortur. *Tidskrift for den Norke Lar ;eforening*, 102, 613–616

Foster, D. H. 1983. Implications for the Psychological Association of South Africa of the Medical Association of South Africa's Report on Detainees. Unpublished paper read at the National Psychology Congress, Pietermaritzburg

Foster, D. and Sandler, D. 1985. *A Study of Detention and Torture in South Africa: Preliminary Report*. Institute of Criminology, University of Cape Town

Frankish, J. G. 1983. The medical care of prisoners and detainees. *South African Medical Journal*, 64, 117–120

Geldenhuys, O. 1983. A study of South African security legislation with the emphasis on detention laws. Unpublished B.Soc.Sc. Honours thesis, University of Cape Town

Gendreau, P., Freedman, N. L., Wilde, G. J. S. and Scott, G. D. 1972. Changes in EEG alpha frequency and evoked response latency during solitary confinement. *Journal of Abnormal Psychology*, 79, 54–59

Gillis, L. S., Elk, R., Ben–Arie, O. and Teggin, A. 1982. The present state examination: experiences with Xhosa-speaking psychiatric patients. *British Journal of Psychiatry*, 141, 143–147

Glass, D. C. and Singer, J. E. 1972. *Urban Stress*. New York: Academic

Goffman, E. 1967. *Interaction Ritual*. Harmondsworth: Penguin

Goldfried, M. R. 1960. A psychoanalytic interpretation of sensory deprivation. *Psychological Record*, 10, 211–214
Gramsci, A. 1971. *Selections from the Prison Notebooks*. Edited and translated by Q. Hoare and G. N. Smith. London : Lawrence and Wishart
Grassian, S. 1983. Psychopathological effects of solitary confinement. *American Journal of Psychiatry*, 140, 1450–1454
Greenberg, S. 1980. *Race and State in Capitalist Development*. Johannesburg: Ravan
Greenberg, S. 1980. The political economy of change: problems of hegemony in contemporary South Africa. In F. van Zyl Slabbert and J. Opland (eds.), *Dilemmas of Evolutionary Change*. Grahamstown: Institute of Social and Economic Research, Rhodes University
Greer, D. S. 1980. The admissibility of confessions under the Northern Ireland Emergency Act. *Northern Ireland Law Quarterly*, 3, 205–238
Gruhl, J. 1982. State supreme courts and the U.S. supreme courts: post *Miranda* rulings. *Journal of Criminal Law and Criminology*, 73, 886–934
Hall, S., Critcher, C., Jefferson, T., Clarke, J. and Roberts, B. 1978. *Policing the Crisis*. London: Macmillan
Haritos–Fatouros, M. 1984. The official torturer: learning mechanisms involved in the process. Unpublished paper, University of Thessaloniki
Harper, D. W. and Bross, M. 1979. The effect of unimodal sensory deprivation on sensory processes: a decade of research from the University of Manitoba. *Canadian Psychological Review*, 19, 128–144
Hayes, G. 1984. MASA and the politics of detention. *Work in Progress*, 20, 40–45
Haysom, N. 1983. Ruling with the whip: a report on the violation of human rights in the Ciskei. Johannesburg: Development Studies Group and Southern African Research Service
Haysom, N. 1984. Closed circuit television for detainees. *Lawyers for Human Rights Bulletin*, 100–104
Haythorn, W. W. 1973. The miniworld of isolation: laboratory studies. In J. E. Rasmussen (ed.), *Man in Isolation and Confinement*. Chicago: Aldine
Hellmann, E. (ed.). 1949. *Handbook on Race Relations in South Africa*. Cape Town: Oxford University Press
Hilgendorf, E. L. and Irving, B. 1981. A decision-making model of confessions. In S. Lloyd–Bostock (ed.), *Psychology in Legal Contexts*. London: Macmillan
Hillyard, P. 1981. From Belfast to Britain, in *Politics and Power*, 4. London: Routledge and Kegan Paul
Hinkle, L. E. and Wolff, H. G. 1956. Communist interrogation and indoctrination of 'enemies of the state'. *Archives of Neurology and Psychiatry*, 76, 115–174
Hiroto, D. S. 1974. Locus of control and learned helplessness. *Journal of Experimental Psychology*, 102, 187–193
Hoernlé, R. F. A. 1945. *South African Native Policy and the Liberal Spirit*. Johannesburg: Witwatersrand University Press
Hoffman, L. H. and Zeffert, D. 1981. *The South African Law of Evidence*. Durban: Butterworth
Hooper, C. 1960. *Brief Authority*. London: Collins
Hoppe, K. D. 1968. Re-somatization of affects in survivors of persecution. *International Journal of Psycho-Analysis*, 49, 324–326
Houghton, D. H. 1976. *The South African Economy*, 4th ed. Cape Town: Oxford University Press
Inman, M. 1981. The admissibility of confessions. *Criminal Law Review*, 469–482
Irving, B. and Hilgendorf, E. L. 1980. *Police Interrogation: The Psychological Approach*. London: Her Majesty's Stationery Office
Jacobsen, Q. 1973. *Solitary in Johannesburg*. London: M. Joseph
Jaffe, R. 1968. Dissociative phenomena in former concentration camp inmates. *International Journal of Psycho-Analysis*, 49, 310–312
Janis, J. L. 1969. *Stress and Frustration*. New York: Harcourt Brace Jovanovich

Johnson, R. W. 1977. *How Long Will South Africa Survive?* Johannesburg: Macmillan
Jones, A. 1969. Stimulus-seeking behavior. In J. P. Zubek (ed.), *Sensory Deprivation*. New York: Appleton–Century–Croft
Kallaway, P. (ed.). 1984. *Apartheid and Education: The Education of Black South Africans*. Johannesburg: Ravan Press
Kamisar, Y. 1980. Equal justice in American criminal procedure. In *Police Interrogation and Confessions: Essays in Law and Policy*. Ann Arbor: University of Michigan Press
Karis, T. G. and Carter, G. M. (eds.). 1977. *From Protest to Challenge: A Documentary History of African Politics in South Africa 1882–1964*, vol. 3. Stanford: Hoover Institution Press
Karlsmark, T., Thomsen, H. K., Danielsen, L., Aalund, O., Nielsen, O., Nielsen, K. G. and Genefke, I. K. 1984. Tracing the use of electrical torture. *American Journal of Forensic Medicine and Pathology*, 5, 333–337
Katz, G. 1982. The attitudes and feelings of South African former detainees during their detention. Unpublished B.A. Hons. thesis, University of the Witwatersrand
Kemp, D. 1949. The Nationalists and apartheid. *Contemporary Issues*, 1, 5–12
Kirchheimer, O. 1961. *Political Justice: The Use of Legal Procedure for Political Ends*. Princeton University Press
Kleinschmidt, H. 1976. *Detention and Detente in Southern Africa*. Braamfontein: Christian Institute
Kobasa, S. C. 1982. The hardy personality. In G. Saunders and J. Suls (ed.), *Social Psychology of Health and Illness*. Hillsdale, N. J.: Erlbaum
Lambley, P. 1980. *The Psychology of Apartheid*. London: Secker and Warburg
Lawyers' Committee for Civil Rights Under Law. 1983. *Deaths in Detention and South Africa's Security Laws*. Washington, D.C.
Lawyers for Human Rights. 1983. Any hope for detainees? The Aggett inquest and the Rabie Report compared. *Bulletin No. 2*, special issue
Legassick, M. 1974. Legislation, ideology and economy in post-1948 South Africa. *Journal of Southern African Studies*, 1, 5–35
Lerner, M. J. 1980. *The Belief in a Just World*. New York: Plenum Press
Lewin, H. 1974. *Bandiet: Seven Years in a South African Prison*. London: Barrie and Jenkins
Lifton, R. J. 1961. *Thought Reform and the Psychology of Totalism*. New York: Norton
Lodge, T. 1978. The rural struggle: Poqo and Transkei resistance. Paper delivered at the Conference on the History of Opposition in South Africa, University of the Witwatersrand
Lodge, T. 1983. *Black Politics in South Africa since 1945*. Johannesburg: Ravan Press
London, P. 1977. *Behavior Control*, rev. ed. New York: New American Library
Lucas, W. E. 1976. Solitary confinement: isolation as coercion to conform. *Australian and New Zealand Journal of Criminology*, 9, 153–167
Lunde, I. 1982. Mental sequelae to torture. *Manedsskrift for Praktisk Laegegerning*
Lunde, I. Rasmussen, O. V., Lindholm, J. and Wagner, G. 1980. Gonadal and sexual functions in tortured Greek men. *Danish Medical Journal*, 27, 243–245
Marcus, G. and Dugard, J. 1983. The inadequacies of the Minister's Directions. *Lawyers for Human Rights Bulletin*, 2, 77–89
Marcus, G. 1984. Assaults in detention: time running out. *Reality*, 16, 9–10
Marr, D. 1980. *Barwick*. London: Allen and Unwin
Mathews, A. S. 1971. *Law, Order and Liberty in South Africa*. Cape Town: Juta
Mathews, A. S. 1984. Public safety. In W. Joubert (ed.), *Laws of South Africa*, vol. 21. Durban: Butterworth
Mathews, A. S. 1986. *Freedom, State Security and the Rule of Law*. Cape Town: Juta
Mathews, A. S. and Albino, R. C. 1966. The permanence of the temporary – an examination of the 90-day and 180-day detention laws. *South African Law Journal*, 83, 16–43
Matussek, P. 1975. *Internment in Concentration Camps and Its Consequences*. New York: Springer–Verlag
Mbeki, G. 1963. *The Peasants' Revolt*. Harmondsworth: Penguin

Medical Association of South Africa. 1983. Report on Medical Care of Prisoners and Detainees. Supplement to the *South African Medical Journal*

Milgram, S. 1974. *Obedience to Authority*. New York: Harper and Row

Miller, S. C. 1962. Ego-autonomy in sensory deprivation, isolation and stress. *International Journal of Psycho-Analysis*, 43, 1–20

Molteno, F. 1979. The uprisings of 16th June: a review of the literature. *Social Dynamics*, 5, 54–76

Molteno, F. 1983. The schooling of black South Africans and the 1980 Cape Town students' boycotts: a sociological interpretation. Unpublished M.Soc.Sci. thesis, University of Cape Town

Morris, M. 1976. The development of capitalism in South African agriculture. *Economy and Society*, 5, 292–343

Morris, M. 1977. Apartheid, agriculture and the state: the farm labour question. Southern African Labour and Development Research Unit, Working paper no. 8

Moultrie, C. 1983. A survey of twenty years of deaths under security legislation in South Africa 1963–1983. Unpublished B.A. Honours thesis, University of Cape Town

Murray, C. 1982. The right of the accused to his own earlier statements. *South African Journal of Criminal Law and Criminology*, 6, 290–294

Myers, T. I. 1969. Tolerance for sensory and perceptual isolation. In J. P. Zubek (ed.), *Sensory Deprivation*. New York: Appleton–Century–Croft

Naidoo, I. 1982. *Island in Chains*. Harmondsworth: Penguin

Nicholson, C. R. 1982. Admissibility and reliability of detainee evidence. *South African Journal of Criminal Law and Criminology*, 6, 250–261

Nienaber, G. M. 1983. Discretions, ouster clauses and the Internal Security Act. *Tydskrif*, 46, 211–222

Norton, M. L. 1982–83. The political trial in South Africa – the quest for legitimacy. *Natal University Law Review*, 3, 75–97

O'Meara, D. 1975. The 1946 African mineworkers' strike. *Journal of Commonwealth and Comparative Politics*, 13, 146–173

Orne, M. T. and Scheibe, K. E. 1964. The contribution of non-deprivation factors in the production of sensory deprivation effects: the psychology of the panic button. *Journal of Abnormal and Social Psychology*, 68, 3–12

Paizes, A. P. 1981. Undue influence and involuntary admissions and confessions. *South African Journal of Criminal Law and Criminology*, 5, 122–136

Parmanand, S. K. and Vorster, C. 1984. South Africa's state security legislation: exit Section 6. *Journal of Contemporary Roman Dutch Law*, 147, 180–199

Pennebaker, J. W., Burnham, M. A., Schaeffer, M. A. and Harper, D. 1977. Lack of control as a determinant of perceived physical symptoms. *Journal of Personality and Social Psychology*, 35, 167–174

Pheto, M. 1983. *And Night Fell: Memoirs of a Political Prisoner in South Africa*. London: Allison and Busby

Randall, G., Lutz, E., Quiroga, J., Zunzunegui, V., Kolff, C. A., Deutsch, A., and Doan, R. 1983. Long term physical and psychological sequelae of torture on 44 victims examined in the United States. Unpublished papers at the Symposium of the American Association for the Advancement of Science

Rasmussen, O. V. and Lunde, I. 1980. Evaluation of investigation of 200 torture victims. *Danish Medical Bulletin*, 27, 241–243

Rasmussen, O. V. and Marcussen, H. 1982. The somatic sequelae to torture. *Manedskrift for Praktisk Laegegerning*

Rex, J. (ed.). 1981. *Apartheid and Social Research*. Paris: Unesco Press

Riekert, J. G. 1982. Police assaults and the admissibility of 'voluntary' confessions. *South African Law Journal*, 99, 175–183

Riekert, J. 1985. The silent scream: detention without trial, solitary confinement and evidence in South African 'security trials'. *South African Journal on Human Rights*, 1, 245–250

Riekert, J. G. 1985. The DDD syndrome: solitary confinement and a South African security law trial. In A. N. Bell and R. D. A. Mackie (eds.), *Detention and Security Legislation in South Africa*. Durban: University of Natal

Ristow, W. and Shallice, T. 1976. Taking the hood off British torture. *New Scientist*, 272–274

Roux, A. S. 1967. Sensory and perceptual deprivation. *The South African Psychologist*, monograph no. 69

Rudolph, H. 1984. *Security, Terrorism and Torture: Detainees' Rights in South Africa and Israel*. Cape Town: Juta

Ruthven, M. 1978. *Torture: The Grand Conspiracy*. London: Weidenfeld and Nicholson

Sachs, A. 1966. *Jail Diary*. London: Harvill Press

Sachs, A. 1968. *Stephanie on Trial*. London: Harvill Press

Sampson, A. 1958. *The Treason Cage*. London: Heinemann

Sargant, W. 1957. *Battle for the Mind*. New York: Doubleday

Schein, E. H. 1961. *Coercive Persuasion*. New York: Norton

Schulman, C. A., Richlin, M. and Weinstein, S. 1967. Hallucinations and disturbances of affect cognition and physical state as a function of sensory deprivation. *Perceptual and Motor Skills*, 25, 1001–1024

Schultz, D. P. 1965. *Sensory Restriction: Effects on Behavior*. New York: Academic Press

Schwitzgebel, R. 1962. A comparative study of Zulu and English reactions to sensory deprivation. *International Journal of Social Psychiatry*, 8, 220–225

Seligman, M. E. P. 1975. *Helplessness*. San Francisco: W. H. Freeman

Sells, S. B. 1973. The taxonomy of man in enclosed space. In F. Rasmussen (ed.), *Man in Isolation and Confinement*. Chicago: Aldine

Shallice, T. 1972. The Ulster depth interrogation techniques and their relation to sensory deprivation research. *Cognition*, 1, 385–405

Shallice, T. 1974. Solitary confinement – a torture revisited. *New Scientist*, 666–667

Shue, H. 1978. Torture. *Philosophy and Public Affairs*, 7

Sim, J. and Thomas, P. A. 1983. The Prevention of Terrorism Act: normalising the politics of repression. *Journal of Law and Society*, 10, 71–84

Simenauer, E. 1968. Late psychic sequelae of man-made disasters. *International Journal of Psycho-Analysis*, 49, 306–309

Slabbert, F. van Zyl and Opland, J. (eds.). 1980. *Dilemmas of Evolutionary Change*. Grahamstown: Institute of Social and Economic Research, Rhodes University

Solomon, M. D. (ed.). 1961. *Sensory Deprivation*. Cambridge, Mass.: Harvard University Press

Somnier, F. 1983. Psychological aspects of torture. Paper presented at the Seminar on the Examination of and Aid to Torture Victims and their Families, Copenhagen

Somnier, F. and Genefke, J. K. 1986. Psychotherapy for victims of torture. *British Journal of Psychiatry* (in press)

Stofsel, W. 1980. Psychological sequelae in hostages and the aftercare. *Danish Medical Bulletin*, 27, 239–241

Stover, E. and Nightingale, E. O. (eds.). 1985. *The Breaking of Bodies and Minds: Torture, Psychiatric Abuse and the Health Professions*. New York: W. H. Freeman

Strauss, S. A. 1983. The legal rights of prisoners and detainees to medical treatment. *South African Journal of Criminal Law and Criminology*, 7, 20–32

Strom, A. (ed.). 1968. *Norwegian Concentration Camp Survivors*. New York: Humanities Press

Suedfeld, P. 1974. Social isolation: a case for interdisciplinary research. *Canadian Psychologist*, 15, 1–15

Suedfeld, P. 1974. Solitary confinement in the correctional setting: goals, problems and suggestions. *Corrective and Social Psychiatry*, 20, 10–20

Suedfeld, P. 1975. The clinical relevance of reduced sensory stimulation. *Canadian Psychological Review*, 16, 88–103

Suedfeld, P. 1978. Solitary confinement as a rehabilitative technique: reply to Lucas. *Australian and New Zealand Journal of Criminology*, 11, 106–112

Suedfeld, P. 1980. *Restricted Environmental Stimulation: Research and Clinical Applications*.

New York: Wiley

Suedfeld, P., Ramirez, C., Deaton, J. and Baker–Brown, G. 1982. Reactions and attributes of prisoners in solitary confinement. *Criminal Justice and Behaviour*, 9, 302–340

Suedfeld, P., Rank, D. S. and Rank, A. D. 1980. Incentive value of social and non-social visual stimuli after social and sensory restriction. *Australian Journal of Psychology*, 32, 209–215

Suls, J. 1982. Social support, interpersonal relations and health. In G. Saunders and J. Suls (eds.), *Social Psychology of Health and Illness*. Hillsdale, N. J.: Erlbaum

Survey of Race Relations in South Africa, 1979–1985. Johannesburg: South African Institute of Race Relations

Suttner, R. 1984. Political trials and the legal process. In *South African Review Two*. Johannesburg: Ravan Press

Swartz, L. and Foster, D. 1984. Images of culture and mental illness: South African psychiatric approaches. *Social Dynamics*, 10, 17–25

Thygesen, P. 1980. The concentration camp syndrome. *Danish Medical Bulletin*, 27, 224–228

Trimble, M. R. 1984. Post–traumatic stress disorder: the history of a concept. *Psychotherapeia*, 34, 37–39

Twining, W. L. and P. E. 1973. Bentham on torture. *Northern Ireland Legal Quarterly*, 24, 305–356

Tyson, G. A. 1982. The psychological effects of detention. Unpublished paper read at the Detention and Security Legislation Conference, University of Natal, Durban

Tyson, G. A. 1983. Stress and detention. *South African Medical Journal*, 64, 858–859

United Nations. Report of the Special Committee on Apartheid. 1973. *Maltreatment and Torture of Prisoners in South Africa*. New York: United Nations

United Nations. 1975. *Declaration on the Protection of All Persons from being Subjected to Torture and Other Cruel, Inhuman or Degrading Treatment or Punishment*. New York: United Nations

United Nations. 1980. *Code of Conduct for Law Enforcement Officials*. New York: UN Department of Public Information

United Nations. 1984. *Human Rights: International Instruments*. New York: United Nations

United Nations. 1984. *Standard Minimum Rules for the Treatment of Prisoners*. New York: UN Department of Public Information

Van der Berg, J. 1985. Treason: evaluating the evidence of political detainees. Unpublished paper, University of the Western Cape

Vernon, J. A. 1963. *Inside the Black Box*. New York: Clarkson Potter

Vischer, B. 1984. Christians against torture. *South African Outlook*, 114, 105–106

Warmhoven, C., Van Slooten, H., Lachinsky, N., de Hoog, M. I. and Smeulers, J. 1981. The medical after-effects of torture: an investigation among refugees in the Netherlands. *Nederlands Tijdschrift voor Geneeskunde*, 125, 104–108

Watson, P. 1977. *War on the Mind*. Harmondsworth: Penguin

Weile, B. and Wingender, L. B. 1983. Children of tortured immigrant Chileans in Denmark. Paper presented at the Seminar on the Examination of and Aid to Torture Victims and their Families, Copenhagen

Weiss, J. H. 1970. Somatic effects of predictable and unpredictable shock. *Psychosomatic Medicine*, 32, 397–409

West, L. J. 1985. Effects of isolation on the evidence of detainees. In A. D. Bell and R. D. A. Mackie (eds.), *Detention and Security Legislation in South Africa*. Durban: University of Natal

Williams, R. C. 1984. The admissibility of confessions elicited during detention under the security law: a bold initiative from the Cape Provincial Division. *South African Law Journal*, 101, 7–17

Winter, G. 1981. *Inside Boss: South Africa's Secret Police*. Harmondsworth: Penguin

World Medical Association. 1975. *Guidelines for Medical Doctors Concerning Torture and*

Other Cruel, Inhuman or Degrading Treatment or Punishment, in Relation to Detention and Imprisonment. Tokyo

Wortman, C. B. and Brehm, J. W. 1975. Responses to uncontrollable behavior. In L. Berkowitz (ed.), *Advances in Experimental Social Psychology*, vol. 8. New York: Academic

Zimbardo, P. G., Haney, C., Banks, W. C. and Jaffe, D. 1973. The mind is a formidable jailer: a Pirandellian prison. *New York Times,* 8 April

Zinn, H. 1973. *Postwar America: 1945–1971.* Indianapolis: Bobbs–Merrill

Zubek, J. P. 1969. *Sensory Deprivation: Fifteen Years of Research.* New York: Appleton–Century–Croft

Zubek, J. P. 1973. Behavioral and physiological effects of prolonged sensory and perceptual deprivation. In J. Rasmussen (ed.), *Man in Isolation and Confinement.* Chicago: Aldine

Zubek, J. P., Bayer, L. and Shepherd, J. M. 1969. Relative effects of prolonged social isolation and confinement: behavioral and EEG changes. *Journal of Abnormal Psychology,* 74, 625–631

Zubek, J. P. and MacNeil, M. 1967. Perceptual deprivation phenomena: role of the recumbent position. *Journal of Abnormal Psychology,* 72, 147–150

Zuckerman, M., Persky, H., Link, K. E. and Basu, G. K. 1968. Experimental and subject factors determining responses to sensory deprivation, social isolation, and solitary confinement. *Journal of Abnormal Psychology,* 73, 183–194

Index

Acts of Parliament: Bantu Authorities (1951), 19; Criminal Law Amendment (1983), 17, 18; Criminal Procedure (1955), 24, 41; Demonstrations in or near Court Buildings Prohibition (1982), 224; General Law Amendment (1962), 5, 22, 24, 49, 51, 89; Group Areas (1950), 17; Internal Security (1982), 5, 24, 28–9, 33–9, 89, 95, 97, 98, 177, 189–90; Intimidation (1982), 220; Native Administration (1927), 12; Police (1958), 172; Population Registration (1950), 17; Prisons (1959), 172; Promotion of Bantu Self-Government (1959), 19; Protection of Information (1982), 5; Public Safety (1953), 1, 17, 18, 23, 181, 193; Riotous Assemblies Amendment (1930), 12; 'Sabotage', see General Law Amendment; Suppression of Communism (1950), 15–17, 23; Terrorism (1967), 5, 25–7, 48, 51, 89; Unlawful Organizations (1960), 22, 23

African National Congress (ANC), 17–19, 21, 22, 23, 24
Aggett, Neil, 7, 33
Aggett inquest, 33, 34, 36, 97, 99, 156, 189
Albino, R. C., 3, 43
Algoa Park police station, 122, 145
All-In Conference (1961), 22
Allodi, F., 70, 170
American Psychiatric Association, 159
Amnesty International, 9, 69, 104, 157, 170, 172
ANC, see African National Congress
apartheid, see segregation
Association of Law Societies (SA), 7, 189, 192
Association of South African Chambers of Commerce, 7
Attenborough, Richard, 188
Banks, B. F. J., 46
bannings: meetings, 181; organisations, 23, 183; people, 6, 12, 23, 27, 183; publications, 12, 23
Bantustans, see homelands
Basson, D., 155
Beccaria, Cesare de, 176
Becker, H. J., 52
Bennett Committee Report, 38, 177, 190
Bentham, Jeremy, 176
Biderman, A. D., 77

Biko, Steve, 1, 30, 31, 36, 100, 130, 147, 188
Biko inquest, 3, 30, 97, 99, 143
Boshoff, W. G., 48
Brehm, J. W. A., 81
Brookes, E. H., 12
Die Burger, 186–8
Caledon Square police station, 123
Cathcart, L. M., 70
Christian Institute, 27
Christians Against Torture, 9
Ciskei, 6, 10
Code of Conduct for Law Enforcement Officials, 8
Coetzee, Grey, 17
Cohn, J., 71
communicative devices, 78, 106
Communist Party (SA), 27, 174
concentration camp survivor studies, 71–4
concentration camp syndrome, 2, 72–4, 75, 160
confessions, 41, 49; see also detainees, evidence of
confinement, 67; see also solitary confinement
Congress of South African Students (COSAS), 183
conspiracy theory, 173–4
Corbett, M. M., 52
court cases, see judicial decisions; *for specific cases see appended list*
Declaration Against Torture, 8, 9, 68
Defiance Campaign, 17–18
deprivation: food, 58, 69, 104; sensory, 2, 58–63; social isolation, 64–8
detainees: arrest of, 20, 120–3, 94–5; contact with state officials, 34–7, 100–1, 142–6, 156, see also district surgeons, inspectors of detainees, magistrates; coping with detention, 93–4, 146–9, 163; evidence of, 41–56, 165–6; harassment of, 92–3; health of, 108–11, 116–17, 159, 160, 191; interrogation of, see interrogation techniques; post-detention problems of, 84–5, 112–15, 149–52, 159, 160; regulations for treatment of, international, 8–9; regulations for treatment of, South African, 36–8, 97, 98, 177, 189–90
Detainees Parents Support Committee, 7, 83, 184, 191, 193
detention: children, 183; criticism of, 1–2, 7,

248 Index

186–92; deaths in, 2, 124, 185; period of, 95–6; physical conditions, 140–2, 156, 96–7; physical effects of, 108–10, 159; process of, 3–4, 57, 120–4, 156; psychological effects of, 3–4, 45, 48, 82–4, 123–4, 137–40; purpose of, 5, 173–4, 192; state witnesses, 33, 89; statistics, (1960) 22, (1965) 24, (1967) 24, (1976) 27, 28, (1977–81) 91, (1981) 29, (1982) 26, (1984) 184, (1985–6) 154, 183, (1986) 193; types of, 23–5, 28, 33–4, 41, 46, 89, 182
Diagnostic and Statistical Manual of Mental Disorders (DSM-III), 75, 159–62, 164
Didcott, J. M., 41, 53
Diemont, M. A., 49–50
district surgeons, 41, 97–8, 100–1, 143–5
DPSC, see Detainees' Parents Support Committee
Driver, E. D., 164, 166
DSM-III, see Diagnostic and Statistical Manual of Mental Disorders
Dugard, C. J. R., 154
empirical study, 86; procedure for, 86–7; recommendations, 176–80; results, 91–117, 156–9; sample, 87–91
Essop, Mohammed, 27
evidence, admissibility of, see detainees, evidence of
European Convention for the Protection of Human Rights and Fundamental Freedoms, 189
Fagan Commission, 14
Fanon, Frantz, 171
Farber, I. E., 79
Federation of South African Trade Unions (FOSATU), 185
Fenichel, D., 74
Fine, D., 44
Foster, Don, 188, see also 'Torture Report'
Franchise Action Council (FRAC), 17
funerals, 181, 183
Geldenhuys, O., 83–4
Glass, D. C., 80
Goldstone, R. J., 155
Grassian, S., 66
Hall, Stuart, 11
Haritos-Fatouros, M., 169
Harlow, H. F., 79
Haron, Imam Abdullah, 141
Haythorn, W. W., 67
Health and Welfare, Minister of, 40
hegemony, crisis of, 11
helplessness, 2, 80–2, 164
Hilgendorf, E. L., 164
Hiroto, D. S., 80
Hoernlé, R. F. A., 12
homelands, 6, 10, 13, 14, 19
Hooper, Charles, 20
Hoppe, K. D., 72
inspector of detainees, 36, 100, 144, 187, 189
International Rehabilitation and Research Centre for Torture Victims, Copenhagen, 9, 69

interrogation, 77, 82, 124; techniques 79–80, 82–3, 98–9, 124–7, 172
Irving, B., 164
Janis, I. L., 77
John Vorster Square police station, 38, 121 125, 142, 146
Jones, A., 61
judicial decisions concerning: banning o people, 155, 236; effects of detention o detainees, 45–9, 52, 98; flow of informa tion, 237; redetention, 23; rightful deten tion, 155–6, 237; terrorism, 224 treatment of detainees, 52–5, 235
Justice, Minister of, 18, 22, 23, 25, 28, 31
Kamisar, Y., 44
Kannemeyer Commission (1985), 182
Katz, G., 82–3
Kentridge, Sydney, 32, 44
Labour, Minister of, 15
Law and Order, Minister of, 32, 40, 83, 177 187–8
laws, see Acts of Parliament
learned helplessness, see helplessness
legislation: race, 1, 17; security, 12, 15, 17 33–9, 153–4, 177; see also Acts of Parliament
Leon, R. N., 53–4
Lerner, M. J., 171
Le Roux Commission (1984), 189
Levy, H., 54
Lodge, Tom, 19
Lucas, W. E., 64
McCarthyism, 15
Macaulay, J. B., 12
magistrates, 24, 52, 100–1
Maitland police station, 141
Malan, Magnus, 31
Malatji, Paris, 38
Mandela, Nelson, 18, 22
MASA, 8; Report, 3, 39–41, 86, 191
Mathews, A. S., 3, 37
Matussek, P., 72–3, 76, 114, 161
Medical Association of South Africa, se« MASA
Milgram, S., 167-8
Miller, S. C., 63
Milne, A. J., 46
Ministers of state, see under specific portfolios
Moroka, J. S., 17, 18
Mpondo Revolt, 19–20
National Detainees' Day, 7
National Party, 5, 12, 14, 27; and reform, 7. 30–1, 153–4, 177
National Union of South African Students, (NUSAS), 6, 27
Ogilvie Thompson, N., 46
Orr, Wendy, 184, 186, 191
Pan-Africanist Congress (PAC), 22, 23, 24
Pennebaker, J. W., 81
Pirow, Oswald, 19
police stations, see under specific names
Pondoland revolt, see Mpondo Revolt
Poqo, 23, 24

post-traumatic stress disorder, 2, 75–7, 83, 159–62
Pretoria Prison, 141
'Principles of Medical Ethics', 8
prisoners, *see* detainees
Rabie, P. J., 30, 55, 155
Rabie Commission, 2–3, 30–3, 42, 177
Raditsela, Andries, 185
Randall, G., 70
Rasmussen, O. V., 70
reactance, 2, 81–2
reform, *see under* National Party
Rehabilitation Centre for Torture Victims, *see* International Rehabilitation and Research Centre for Torture Victims
restricted environmental stimulation techniques (REST), 58–63, 65, 82; *see also* deprivation, sensory
Roux, A. S., 3
Royal Commission on Criminal Procedure, 43, 177
Rudolph, H., 174–6
Ruthven, M., 173
Sachs, Albie, 94
Sachs, Solly, 17
Sandler, Diane, *see* 'Torture Report'
Saunders, Stuart, 188
Schlebusch Commission, 27
Schreiner, O. D., 50
security legislation, *see* legislation, security
segregation, 12, 14, 19
Seligman, M. E. P., 80–1
sensory deprivation, *see* deprivation, sensory
Sharpeville, 21
Shue, H., 175
Singer, J. E., 80
Sisulu, Walter, 18
solitary confinement: as a feature of security legislation, 24, 41, 106; psychological effects of, 58, 64–8, 79, 106, 136–40; *see also under* deprivation
South African Indian Congress, 17
South African Institute of Race Relations, 6, 27
Soweto unrest (1976), 28
Standard Minimum Rules for the Treatment of Prisoners, 8, 68
state of emergency, (1960) 6, 21–2, (1985) 6, 154, 174, 181–4, (1986) 6, 174, 193
state witnesses, 33, 89
Steyn Commission into the Mass Media, 31
stress, 164–5; *see also* detention, psychological effects; post-traumatic stress syndrome; torture, effects of
strikes, 15, 27; African mineworkers' (1946), 14, 17
Suedfeld, P., 58–9, 60, 64, 65
Swart, Freek, 188
symptoms, psychological, *see* torture, effects of
syndromes, *see* post-traumatic stress syndrome; torture syndrome

Timol, Ahmed, 27
Tokyo Declaration, 8, 143
torture, 172–3; definition of, 68, 104–5, 158; effects of, 68–71, 84, 159; international, 69–71, 104, 169–70, 171; opposition to, 8–9, 174–6; physical, 69, 79, 83–4, 102–4, 124–36, 157–8; psychological, 69–71, 84, 104–7, 127, 157–8; recommendations regarding, 176–80; syndrome, 70, 75, 160
'Torture Report', 185–92
torturers, 167–72
Transkei, 10, 19
Trengrove, J. J., 53
trials: political, 5, 43–5, 185; treason, 18–19, 185, 192
Tsenoli, L., 193
UDF, *see* United Democratic Front
Umkonto we Sizwe, 23, 24
Unilateral Declarations Against Torture and Other Cruel, Inhuman or Degrading Treatment or Punishment, 9
United Democratic Front, 6, 174, 182, 183, 185
United Nations, 1, 8, 9, 104, 157, 191; *UN statements, codes, rules, etc. are to be found as well under their specific titles*
United Party, 14
Universal Declaration of Human Rights, 8
University Christian Movement (UCM), 27
Van As, J. H., 38
Van der Walt Commission (1985), 182
Van Winsen, L. de V., 46
Warmhoven, C., 70
Wessels, P. J., 48
West, Dr Louis, 48, 55, 79, 235
Williamson, D. M., 47, 50
Wilson, A. B. M., 52
World Medical Association, 8
Zimbardo, P. G., 168–9
Zubek, J. P., 62, 65, 67
Zuckerman, M., 67

Court cases
Cooper and Others v *Minister of Police and Others*, 53
Demsey v *Minister of Law and Order*, 237
Goldberg and Others v *Minister of Police and Others*, 52
Hurley and Another v *Minister of Law and Order and Others*, 53, 54, 55, 155–6
Katofa v *Administrator-General for South West Africa and Another*, 54
Loza v *Police Station Commander, Durbanville*, 23
Marajee v *Minister of Law and Order*, 234
MAWU and Another v *State President and Others*, 237
Minister of Law and Order v *Hurley and Another*, 55
Minister of Law and Order v *Tsenoli*, 237
Miranda v *Arizona*, 42, 166

Mkhize v Minister of Law and Order and Another, 52
Momoniat and Naidoo v Minister of Law and Order, 155
Nestor and Others v Minister of Police and Others, 51
Nkondo and Other v Minister of Law and Order and Another 155, 236
Nkwitini v Minister of Law and Order, 234
Nxasana v Minister of Justice, 41, 53
R. v Isequilla, 42
R. v Kilner, 226
R. v Nhleko, 50
R. v Powell, 226
R. v Stewart, 226
Radebe v Minister of Law and Order, 237

Rossouw v Sachs, 45, 46, 52, 98
S. v Alexander, 47
S. v Christie, 49
S. v Gwala, 42, 48, 49, 55
S. v Hassim, 43, 47
S. v Hlekani, 46, 47
S. v Hoffman, 48
S. v Ismail and Others, 46
S. v L. M. Mogale, 41
S. v Moumbaris, 48
S. v Mpetha and Others, 50, 226
S. v Tuhadeleni and Others, 224
S. v Yolelo, 226
Schermbrucker v Klindt, 47
Van Heerden v Cronwright, 99, 235